A Dangerous Engagement

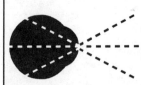

This Large Print Book carries the
Seal of Approval of N.A.V.H.

A DANGEROUS ENGAGEMENT

ASHLEY WEAVER

THORNDIKE PRESS
A part of Gale, a Cengage Company

Copyright © 2019 by Ashley Weaver.
An Amory Ames Mystery.
Thorndike Press, a part of Gale, a Cengage Company.

Thorndike Press® Large Print Mystery.
The text of this Large Print edition is unabridged.
Other aspects of the book may vary from the original edition.
Set in 16 pt. Plantin.

LIBRARY OF CONGRESS CIP DATA ON FILE.
CATALOGUING IN PUBLICATION FOR THIS BOOK
IS AVAILABLE FROM THE LIBRARY OF CONGRESS

ISBN-13: 978-1-4328-7288-5 (hardcover alk. paper)

Published in 2020 by arrangement with Macmillan Publishing Group, LLC/St. Martin's Publishing Group

Printed in the United States of America
1 2 3 4 5 6 7 24 23 22 21 20

For Ann Collette,
the best agent a writer could ever ask for

1

Chelsea Piers, New York City
October 1933

I came to New York for a wedding; I never imagined I would bear witness to two deaths. Strange the turns life takes when one least expects it.

A cool breeze ruffled my hair as I stood on the deck of our cruise liner, watching the city grow closer. Before us lay Chelsea Piers, and, behind them, the buildings of Manhattan rising proudly against the cloudless blue sky. It gave me a thrill to look at that skyline. It was almost as though I could feel the energy increasing with every passing moment. Already the soft silence of the sea was fading as faint yet distinctly urban noises of the city began to be carried out across the water on the wind. Gulls soared and dipped above, calling raucously as if welcoming us to their lively domain.

"It presents a pretty picture, doesn't it?"

my husband, Milo, said as he came to stand beside me at the rail. His normally smooth black hair was tousled by the wind, his eyes were far bluer than the water, and his complexion had been darkened by his time spent on deck during the voyage. He looked handsome, relaxed, and well-rested.

I felt none of those things. Though this was not my first trip to New York, it had been the least pleasant voyage thus far. The waters had been choppy, and I had spent most of the four days at sea in our stateroom feeling ill. I was immeasurably glad that land was in sight.

"I'm almost sad to see the voyage end," he said, in direct contradiction to my own thoughts, as he leaned against the rail. "Perhaps we should take a pleasure cruise when we return to England."

"Perhaps," I said, without any great enthusiasm. The water had been so unkind that, at the moment, I didn't want to think about taking a bath, let alone another voyage.

"But first things first," he went on, turning his back to the wind and cupping his hand around a cigarette to shield it from the damp gusts of sea air before flicking on his silver lighter. "We haven't been to New York in some time. When this dull business is over, we'll have some time to enjoy ourselves."

The "dull business" in question was the marriage of my old friend Tabitha Alden. It was this event which had drawn us to New York. While I was very much looking forward to seeing Tabitha and taking part in her wedding, Milo had accompanied me grudgingly, enticed more by the promise of riotous nightlife than by any desire to sit in a pew beside me on the special day.

"You needn't make it sound as though it's going to be a chore," I said. "Tabitha's wedding is going to be lovely."

"With alcohol illegal in this country, I don't see how it will even be tolerable."

I laughed. "Surely you don't mind weddings as much as all that."

"The only wedding I've ever wanted to attend was ours," he said, blowing a stream of smoke into the wind.

I turned to look at him, quirking a brow. "Indeed? No one had to drag you to the church? I've always wondered."

"I was there before you were," he replied. "I half expected you to change your mind, and it wasn't until you reached the altar and I looked into your eyes that I felt I could rest easy."

His tone was light, but he appeared perfectly serious and I was touched. Milo was rarely sentimental, and the unexpected moments when he revealed a hint of sincerity always caught me off guard.

"For that lovely sentiment," I said softly, "you needn't ever attend a wedding with me again."

His eyes met mine. "I'll follow you into as many ceremonies as your heart desires, my darling," he replied. Then he tossed his cigarette overboard and leaned in to kiss me.

For the next few moments, my seasickness was entirely forgotten.

Our romantic interlude concluded, I went back to the stateroom as we prepared to dock. I wanted to make sure that everything was in order. My mother would have been shocked that I had stood on the deck as long as I had; she disapproved of looking as though one were a vulgar tourist overanxious to reach New York. Not for the first time, I felt a traitorous sense of relief that a prior — and more prestigious — social obligation had prevented her from joining us on this trip.

The stateroom was paneled in dark wood, decorated in a tasteful, modern manner. If we hadn't been lurching from one side to

10

the other for several hours of each day, the furniture, mercifully, bolted to the floor, I might have almost believed that we were in a small hotel suite. I hoped the voyage home would find less tumultuous seas and I might enjoy it a bit more.

I walked through the sitting area with its geometric-print rug and dark blue sofa and chairs and into the well-appointed bedroom, avoiding, as I had done for the entirety of the voyage, the view of moving water visible through the glass doors that led onto a balcony.

Winnelda, my maid, looked up as I entered. "Oh, there you are, madam," she said, closing the suitcase that lay on the bed. "I'm nearly finished, I think. I've left your lighter coat, as well as your hat and gloves, in the wardrobe along with your handbag. Parks has gone to see about the trunks."

Milo's valet was sure to have everything well in hand. Between his rigid efficiency and Winnelda's rather more relaxed organizational style, we were quite well taken care of.

"Thank you, Winnelda. We'll be docking soon, but we've some time before we disembark. Go up on deck and get your first glimpse of the city, if you like."

"Thank you. I think I shall. I'm ever so

excited to see New York, madam," she said, her platinum curls bobbing in her enthusiasm. "I've only ever seen it at the cinema, and I can't wait to tell my friends what it's really like."

"I think you'll enjoy it," I said. "I don't expect I shall have much for you to do while I'm here, so you should have quite a good bit of free time."

"I'll look forward to exploring. It will be easier than Paris, I think, since we all speak the same language. Or nearly the same language, at least."

She turned to go but stopped in the doorway. "I didn't pack the things in the desk. I thought perhaps there would be documents and things you'd want to look after yourself."

"Yes, thank you, Winnelda."

She left then, and I crossed to the little wardrobe. Taking out my hat, a fetching thing of rust-colored straw bedecked with burgundy roses, I went to the mirror and put it on, adjusting it to a jaunty angle on my dark waves. My fair complexion looked even paler than normal, but at least the coloring of the hat gave the illusion of a bit of pinkness to my cheeks.

Gathering up my jacket, gloves, and handbag, I went back into the sitting room, moving to the little desk that sat in the corner. I hadn't had much need for writing letters on the voyage, and the rolling of the ship would have made it difficult, but I had placed a few documents there when unpacking.

I began sorting through the papers and my eyes fell on Tabitha's last letter to me, the one she had sent asking me to take part in her wedding.

I picked it up, pulling the pale pink stationery from the envelope, and glanced over the letter, feeling as I had the first time I read it, and all the times since, that there was more to it than met the eye.

Dearest Amory,

I can't tell you how excited I am to announce that I am to be married. I DO hope that you will be a bridesmaid (or is it brides-matron since you are married, I forget?). Tom is wonderful. I can't wait for you to meet him. It's been a bit of a whirlwind (almost strange the way we met and fell for one another so quickly) but we're madly in love, and I know we shall be very happy together. Even better, he is going to work with father. He's a genius at business things, and I know the two of them will be a smashing success. We've had our ups and downs, but

I believe with all my heart that things are going to be better than ever. It's as if all my dreams are coming true at once. Oh, DO say you'll be in the wedding. Then everything will be perfect.

Write back soon with your answer. I DO hope it will be yes!!

Yours fondly,
Tabitha

This letter was just as Tabitha's letters had always been: effusive, disorganized, and embellished with heavily underlined words for emphasis. I wasn't sure, then, why I had felt there was something different about this one, some undertone that made me a bit uneasy.

I supposed one aspect of this was the suddenness of her engagement. She and the young man in question had not known each other for long, and she had fallen madly in love and agreed to marry him in a short span of time. Of course, Tabitha had always been one to throw herself wholeheartedly into things, so there was no reason why love should be the exception. As I had done much the same thing myself when I met Milo, I had to acknowledge a hasty engagement in itself was not something to be concerned about.

However, I also knew that the Alden family had been in a somewhat difficult financial situation following the stock market crash of 1929. Tabitha's letters had spoken of it somewhat vaguely, though she had clearly not wished to elaborate upon the misfortune of her family.

The hint that her fiancé was going to contribute to the family's business dealings made me wonder if part of what she believed to be love was, in fact, a sense of duty she felt to her father. I did hope that Tabitha wasn't rushing into something to help her father's company in some way.

Then again, perhaps I was reading too much into things. Milo often said that, having been involved in several mysteries over the past year, I was constantly looking for trouble. On the contrary, I had a great abhorrence for anything of the sort. But once faced with a problem, my conscience wouldn't let me rest until I had come to some sort of conclusion.

Nevertheless, I reminded myself as I gathered up the rest of the letters and papers from the drawer and shuffled them into a stack, now was not the time for such things. Tabitha's wedding was a joyous occasion, and I did not intend to spoil the experience by worrying about things unnecessarily.

"Ready to disembark, darling?" Milo asked as he came into the stateroom.

I looked up, tucking the letters into my handbag. "Yes, please. I'm dying to set foot on dry land."

Free of the ship and customs at last, we found our way through the exuberant crowds of weary travelers and the friends and relations that awaited them to the car the Aldens had sent for us. Milo examined the sleek, low-roofed black automobile with a collector's eye, and apparently found it to his liking.

"He has good taste, for an American," he told me as we slid into the plush leather backseat.

"I trust you won't add that qualifier when talking to him," I said. Tabitha's father, Benjamin Alden, had met Tabitha's mother when traveling in London for business. The two had eventually wed and settled in England, not far from my family home. Mr. Alden had set about being as much of a country squire as it was possible for an American gentleman to be, and Tabitha and I had often found ourselves in each other's company, though she was a bit younger than I.

Then Mrs. Alden had died in an accident when Tabitha was fourteen, and she and a heartbroken Mr. Alden had returned to New York. We had kept up a correspondence since then and visited each other once or twice, and it seemed to me that she had acclimated well to life in the United States.

"Did you say Mr. Alden had experienced recent financial difficulties?" Milo inquired as the car pulled away from the curb.

"That was the impression I had from Tabitha. Why?"

"This car is a Duesenberg Model J Tourster, worth at least twelve thousand dollars," he observed, lighting a cigarette.

My brows rose. "Perhaps things have improved."

"It would seem so."

We drove along, enjoying the crowded, colorful streets of a city so like London, yet so different. There was something undeniably appealing about New York, a breathless vitality that seemed to pulse through it, making everything seem brighter and more alive every time I visited.

Eventually the crowded streets gave way to a neighborhood filled with stately houses and cheerful little parks, a quiet, unhurried haven in the middle of a bustling city. At last the car pulled to a stop before an imposing white edifice. I found myself a bit surprised at the grandeur of the building before me, especially given Tabitha's hints at her father's financial woes. Whatever Mr. Alden's difficulties had been, it seemed that they had, indeed, not been of a lasting nature.

We alighted from the car and made our way up the front steps to the grand front doors.

A butler pulled one open just as we reached it. "Welcome, Mr. and Mrs. Ames," he said, ushering us in and taking our jackets. "Miss Tabitha is expecting you in the drawing room, if you'll follow me."

He led us down a long hallway, decorated with an assortment of art in gold frames, to a large drawing room. Tabitha Alden was sitting at a desk along one wall writing something, but turned at our approach and jumped up from her seat and hurried toward us.

Then, in a display of what my mother would likely describe as an unfortunate by-product of her American upbringing, she threw herself into my arms with great enthusiasm.

"Hello, Amory! It's so good to see you." She pulled back from the embrace, her eyes moving over me. "You look wonderful, you've barely changed at all!"

"You look much the same yourself," I replied. Though the young lady she had been on my last visit, well before my marriage six years ago, had, of course, grown into an attractive young woman, she was still recognizable as the girl I had known. Her wavy hair was a bright golden hue that gleamed with hints of red when the sunlight shining through the window hit it, and her large blue eyes and the cheerful smile that flashed across her face were the same as they had always been. Indeed, I could still see in her features hints of the merry, energetic child with whom I had forsaken piano practice to parade before mirrors draped in our mothers' ball gowns.

"Of course, I've seen your pictures in the society columns from time to time, so I'm not entirely surprised at how you look. And this must be Mr. Ames," she said, turning to Milo.

"Yes, this is my husband, Milo," I said.

"How very nice to meet you," she said, extending her hand to him. "I've seen you in the society columns, too. You're even handsomer in person, though perhaps a bit less wicked-looking."

"Thank you. I think," Milo said dryly.

"Oh, you mustn't mind me. I'm always

19

saying improper things," she said without embarrassment. She really was just as I remembered her: lively and cheerfully forthright, with no hint of self-consciousness. In any case, she was right. Milo had begun to live down a good deal of his past infamy.

"Come sit down. We'll have tea." She led us to a cluster of very good furniture before the fireplace. "How was your voyage? I wanted so much to be there to meet you on your arrival, but the seamstress was just here for a fitting, and it's very difficult to put her off."

"I understand completely," I said. "The voyage was a bit rough; I'm glad to be on steady ground. How are the wedding preparations?"

"I never imagined there was so much to tend to, but it's all going well. I'm so glad that you could come. My wedding just wouldn't have been the same without you."

The maid brought a tea tray into the room just then and set it on the table near Tabitha.

"I suppose I ought to have asked you if you wanted to go to your room to freshen up," she said as she poured. "I sometimes get ahead of myself. It's just so nice to see you again."

"Tea sounds lovely," I told her truthfully.

"It's one of the things that remains with me from England," she said. "I'm fairly American now, but I must still have my tea." I had noticed that her accent had softened considerably. If one didn't know she had spent a good part of her life in England, one might not even notice it.

"Are you sure it's convenient for us to stay?" I asked as I accepted my cup and saucer. Though we had fully intended on going to a hotel, she had insisted that we stay at the Aldens' residence.

"Oh, yes," she said. "I'm very glad to have you here. Dad is gone a good deal of the time, so it's just me in this big house. Besides, we'll be able to catch up. Letters are a good way to stay in touch, but I'm looking forward to some long conversations. One can't always put what one wants to say in a letter."

She looked up at me as she said this, and I thought I caught something in her gaze, the hint that there was a deeper meaning beneath the words. I had the impression that there was something in particular she wanted to discuss, just as I had when I had first read her letter.

The moment passed, however, and she offered us sandwiches, biscuits, and little cakes, which I was eager to enjoy now that I had left the ship behind. I supposed now, with Milo sitting beside us, was not the time to press the matter.

Focus on the wedding details before you look for a mystery, Amory, I told myself. There would be plenty of time for that later.

2

We were shown to our rooms a short time later. Milo and I had adjoining bedrooms connected by a bathroom. Though Milo would no doubt be sleeping in my bed, the extra room meant extra wardrobe space, which was nice considering our mutually extensive luggage.

We went into my room together. Everything was beautifully decorated and spoke of wealth and taste, from the pale blue wallpaper and white satin bedspread, to the sleek, modern lines of the furniture, upholstered in gray-striped silk, arranged before the fireplace.

I put aside my hat and gloves, sitting on the bed with a relieved sigh. "I do believe this trip might prove rather exhausting," I said.

Milo glanced at me as he made his way to the window and pulled back the curtain. Over his shoulder I saw that this side of the house faced out onto a little park. "You do look a bit pale," he said. "Perhaps you should lie down for a while."

"Oh, I'm not really tired," I said. "I only meant that this whole affair is likely to prove less than restful. Tabitha is a bit of a whirlwind." I meant this fondly. It was good to see her again. I was glad that she appeared to have been happy in her life here in New York, and I was very much looking forward to helping her prepare for her wedding in whatever way I could.

I did wonder if there had been something behind her careful words in the drawing room. *One can't always put what one wants to say in a letter.* It seemed clear that there was something she wanted to discuss with me. Was there, despite her claims of perfect bliss, something wrong between her and her fiancé? I supposed she would confide in me when she saw fit.

"She does seem a very lively woman," Milo said. "I am curious to meet the groom."

"So am I," I admitted. I wondered what sort of man Tabitha would have chosen. I suspected her reckless nature would have made men of action appealing, but a calming influence might have been the best thing for her. I supposed we would see for ourselves what the gentleman was like soon enough.

Tabitha had invited the other members of the wedding party to dinner, so we would be able to meet them all this evening. Despite my travel weariness, I was looking forward to it.

As my thoughts drifted to what I might want to wear to dinner, there was a tap on the door.

"Come in," I called.

The door opened, and Winnelda looked into the room. "I just wanted to tell you that I've unpacked all your things while you were having tea. Will there be anything else, madam?"

"I'll need you to press my dress for dinner. There's no need to rush, though. I am trying to decide what I shall wear."

"The pale blue silk, I should think," she said with authority. "You look good in most colors, but best in blue."

"Very well. You've convinced me."

"And I think a bit of rouge might be in order," she added, studying my face.

"If you say so, Winnelda. Have you settled in?"

"Yes, they've given me a very nice room. It's a lovely house, isn't it, madam?"

"Very lovely, indeed."

"It's not like I expected. I thought it might be a flat overlooking all the tall buildings. I do like this house, though. And these American maids are different than I thought they would be."

"Oh? In what way?"

She considered this. "I'm not sure exactly. Very friendly, though. Parks isn't going to be happy, of course."

My brows rose. "Why not?"

Winnelda shook her head sadly. "He said he can already see that there is entirely too much informality about the place."

This was not surprising. Milo's valet was an incorrigible snob.

"I suppose he will have to make allowances," Milo said.

She looked sad at the thought. We all knew how Parks felt about making allowances.

"Mrs. Ames is going to lie down, Winnelda," Milo said. "Perhaps you might come back later to press her dress."

"Certainly, sir. Parks has told me to be especially careful with my duties. 'We must not set aside our rigid standards, no matter what poor examples we are met with,' " she said in a pitch-perfect imitation of his disapproving tones.

She went out at that and closed the door behind her, and I gave a laughing sigh and fell backward on the bed.

We met in the drawing room before dinner. I wore my pale blue silk dress and Winnelda had skillfully applied the rouge to my cheeks, so I felt quite presentable.

When we came downstairs, only Tabitha and her father were present. Benjamin Alden rose at once to greet us. He was much as I remembered him, tall and broad shouldered with thick orange hair, now flecked with silver, and a well-trimmed beard. He was a gregarious gentleman with sparkling blue eyes, a shade darker than Tabitha's, a ready smile, and the sort of crushing handshake that almost made one believe a hug would be preferable.

"It's good to see you again, Amory," he said when initial greetings were done and an introduction to Milo had been made. "You're looking more beautiful than ever."

"Thank you. I'm so pleased to be able to be here for Tabitha's wedding."

"Yes, we're all looking forward to it, though we'll certainly miss having her around the house. I've given them an apartment for a wedding gift, closer to the hustle and bustle young people enjoy, but I expect they'll visit me often enough. We're all very chummy. It helps when a father approves of his son-in-law. Tom's a good fellow, and I'm confident he'll make her happy."

"I'm very happy for Tabitha," I said, hoping Mr. Alden was right. He had always seemed to me to be an excellent judge of character. I was confident that, if he approved his daughter's choice of husband, the young man must be worthy of her. I took note, too, of the extravagant wedding gift, another sign of Mr. Alden's improved fortunes.

"How's the old neighborhood?" he asked, switching topics. "I keep meaning to come back to England for a visit, but there's always some matter of business to be tended to here."

"It's been a while since I visited my parents, but I imagine things are much the same. They seldom change in that part of the country," I said with a smile.

"True, true. Things seem to move more slowly in the country. I do miss it, though. It was a wonderful time in my life." He looked wistful for a moment and then shook off whatever nostalgic reverie had lodged in his mind. "And your parents are well?"

"They're very well, thank you."

"I do hope you'll send them my regards," he said warmly and then, abruptly, he turned to Milo and launched into a conversation about automobiles, pleased to find an appreciative admirer of his Duesenberg. The two of them were likely to get on well.

Tabitha pulled me aside, her face bright with enthusiasm. "I can't wait for you to meet Tom. I just know you're going to love him. He's so handsome and funny, and smart, too. The fact that he's going to help Dad with his business is just icing on the cake."

"I'm so glad for you, Tabitha," I said. "I look forward to meeting him."

I was glad that my earlier suspicions had been allayed. No matter how quickly their engagement had come about, it was very clear that she was not marrying him for her father's benefit; her face lit up when she spoke about him.

"Tell me about the other members of the wedding party," I said.

"It's going to be something of a small wedding party, all things considered. Just you and my good friend Jemma Petrie as bridesmaids. Tom only has two close friends in New York, so I didn't want to make him feel uncomfortable by choosing too many bridesmaids."

"I'm honored that you included me."

"Oh, you're one of my dearest friends, Amory. Even though we rarely see each other, your letters have always felt so warm and real. I feel closer to you than to a lot of my friends who live nearby. Oh, look. Here's Jemma now. Come and meet her."

She led me to her friend, who had just come into the drawing room, and introduced her as Miss Jemma Petrie. She was a tall, pretty girl with a head of dark curls and eyes so light brown they looked almost golden. Like Tabitha, she was possessed of an appealing boldness that made me feel instantly as though we were old acquaintances.

"Tabitha has talked of nothing but your visit," she told me. "I've been very excited to meet you."

"We're all going to be great friends," Tabitha said excitedly. "I've made plans for our dress fittings tomorrow, and we ought to have lunch together one day so we can discuss things properly. I know the men aren't going to want to hear talk of the wedding over dinner. Dad and Tom have listened to me talk about it endlessly, though I think both of them are just ready for the day to come and go."

Jemma smiled. "Don't pay any attention to them, Tab. You only get married once, after all. If you're lucky."

"Oh, yes," Tabitha said with a laugh. "Tom

will be my one and only."

"Did I hear my name?" came a voice from the doorway. I turned to see a gentleman standing there. This must be the groom.

He was tall and handsome, with boyish features, neatly parted dark blond hair, and warm brown eyes. His smile seemed one of true happiness, as though there was no other room he would rather be walking into. I felt that there was something very — for lack of a better term — *wholesome* about him, and I liked him at once. I could see why Tabitha had been smitten.

Tabitha hurried to the door and took the man's hand, dragging him across the room. He followed her good-naturedly until they stopped in front of me.

"This is my dear friend Amory Ames," Tabitha said. "Isn't she lovely? Amory, this is my darling fiancé, Mr. Thomas Smith."

"I'm pleased to meet you, Mrs. Ames," he said, shaking my hand warmly. "Tabitha has told me all about you."

"I was honored to be asked to take part in your wedding, Mr. Smith."

"Call me Tom, will you?"

"If you'll call me Amory."

"I think the wedding is going to be swell, Amory," he said. "A big event. Though I'd marry Tabitha tomorrow at City Hall if she'd let me."

She laughed. "Don't think I haven't considered it. Wedding planning is much more daunting than I thought it would be."

For just a moment, as she said the words, some unnamed emotion flickered in her eyes. It was too brief for me to interpret it, but I felt again that she was suppressing something beneath her exuberant happiness.

The impression was fleeting, however, for her eyes suddenly brightened.

"Oh, look," she said. "Here's Rudy."

Another gentleman had just come into the room.

"Good evening, everyone," he said.

Tabitha motioned him over to our little gathering and made introductions as he arrived at her side. "Amory, this is Mr. Rudolph Elliot. Rudy, this is Amory Ames."

He was a young man with thinning reddish-blond hair and sparkling green eyes. He reached out and shook my hand in his large, warm one. "Pleased to meet you, Mrs. Ames."

"And I you, Mr. Elliot."

"Oh, call me Rudy. Everyone does. I've been looking forward to dinner, Tab," he said, turning to Tabitha. "I haven't eaten since breakfast, and I'm half starved."

"Well, let's go into the dining room, then. I think everyone's here," Tabitha said, glancing around the room. Then her expression darkened. "Everyone except for Grant, that is."

"We needn't wait for him," Mr. Smith said quickly. I glanced at him. There was a certain uneasiness in his tone. Was it to do with the missing groomsman or with Tabitha's reaction to his tardiness?

"No, certainly not," Tabitha answered emphatically. "Let's go, shall we?"

As they led the way from the drawing room, I was curious about this errant groomsman. There had been some sort of unspoken tension between Tabitha and her young man at the mention of this Grant, whoever he was.

We were ushered into the dining room. It was a comfortable, brightly lit room, the long table laid with white linen and floral-printed china. The walls were papered in a lovely pale green-and-gold-diamond pattern, and a mahogany sideboard inlaid with mother-of-pearl sat along one wall. Everything was stylish, modern, and clearly expensive.

We sat down to dinner, and I found myself with Rudy Elliot on my right, the chair to my left remaining vacant.

Conversation was light and amusing as we began the first course. The group seemed to share the easy camaraderie of close friends. As I listened to the friendly and sometimes boisterous American chatter, I felt some of my unease melt away. Even my appetite had returned, and I ate with relish.

"This salad dressing is delicious," I commented as I took another bite of my salad.

Tabitha gave me a look from across the table. "Don't get Rudy started, Amory."

"I beg your pardon?"

She smiled. "It's Samson's Salad Dressing. Rudy tends to brag about it endlessly."

I looked at Mr. Elliot, who was smiling at Tabitha's teasing. "Are you involved with the company?"

"In a manner of speaking. I work in advertisement," Mr. Elliot said.

"Oh, newspaper?"

"No, radio. That's the way things are going these days. It's a modern world we're living in, Mrs. Ames."

"Yes, I suppose you're right."

"I've done some newspaper and magazine work in the past, but radio is really a fascinating challenge. You have to create your pictures with words." To Tabitha's chagrin, Mr. Elliot launched into a description of his work creating advertisements for

Samson's Salad Dressing during a popular radio show.

"You make it all sound so lively and interesting," I told him.

"If you'd ever like to stop by my office one day, I could show you a bit of how things work in the advertising field."

"I'd like that," I told him sincerely.

His enthusiastic anecdotes were interrupted not long after the salad plates had been cleared away.

"Late again. Will I never learn?" The voice came from the doorway as a young man in a black suit came into the room. He was tall and dark, with a handsome face that was marred in its symmetry only by a slightly crooked nose that looked as though it had once been broken.

This was no doubt the tardy groomsman. I looked at Tabitha. She made no effort to hide her annoyance. I glanced next at Tom Smith, wondering if he, too, was irritated by his friend's late arrival, but his expression gave nothing away. Indeed, he seemed determinedly focused on the plate in front of him, looking neither at Tabitha nor at the newly arrived guest.

"Won't you sit down, Grant?" Tabitha said coolly. "I'm afraid you've missed the first course."

"Thank you, Tabitha," he said with mock gravity. "I suppose I can live without the lettuce."

He dropped into the vacant seat beside me as conversation at the table resumed, and I couldn't help but catch the strong smell of alcohol about him. Whatever the country's laws on intoxicating beverages, it seemed that he had been in close proximity to them already this evening.

When he turned to me, however, his gaze was steady. "Grant Palmer," he said, extending his hand.

I shook it. "Amory Ames."

"Tabitha's English friend," he said.

"Yes."

"You're just as she described you. I'm surprised."

"How so?" I asked.

"It was a glowing description. I thought she must be exaggerating."

I gave him a small smile at this bit of flattery. "I'm afraid she didn't tell me much about you."

"I'm afraid there isn't much good to tell." Somehow I thought this was probably the truth. He seemed like the type of young man who did what he pleased, caring not at all what others thought of him.

He helped himself to a large serving of

the roast beef, then turned his attention back to me. "When did you arrive?"

"Only this afternoon."

"Your first time in New York?"

"No, I've been here before."

"I suppose it's nothing like London."

"They're similar in some ways," I said.

"I've always wanted to travel. I mean to do it someday. I think that's the best way a person can learn, seeing the world for themselves. I was never much of one for books, but if I see things I don't forget them."

"Are you from New York, Mr. Palmer?"

"Yes. Lived here all my life, though I didn't always move in these kinds of circles."

"Don't monopolize her, Grant," Rudy Elliot said from the other side of me.

"I do apologize, Mr. Elliot," I said, turning to him with a smile. "I didn't mean to neglect you."

"Oh, I'm used to it. But I have to say that it isn't fair that he comes in here with his good looks and nefarious reputation," Rudy said with a laugh. "Two things the ladies can't resist."

"I'm sorry, Rudy," Mr. Palmer said. "But if you want the lady's attention, you'll have to do a better job of making yourself interesting. No doubt you've been boring her

37

with your advertising stories."

Rudy Elliot took this jab with a smile, but I wondered if he'd found it as amusing as he pretended.

I glanced across the table at Milo. He was talking to Jemma Petrie, but he glanced at me and I could see that he was taking in the situation.

My gaze moved to Miss Petrie, and it was immediately apparent to me that she was making a concerted effort not to look in Mr. Palmer's direction. I suddenly had the distinct impression that there was something between them, or that there were some kind of suppressed feelings on Miss Petrie's part. She wanted him to observe her talking to Milo as though she hadn't a care in the world.

"Tom and I hope to go out dancing tomorrow night," Tabitha said. "We have so many places we want to show you, Amory and Milo. If you're feeling rested, perhaps we might all go to a nightclub."

"That sounds very nice," I said.

The conversation shifted then to what nightclubs we might go to, and the rest of dinner was spent discussing what highlights of the city Milo and I would need to see during our visit. I was relieved that the tension that had entered the room along with

Mr. Palmer seemed to have abated. By the time we finished eating and retired to the drawing room for coffee, everyone again seemed in the best of spirits.

I had been so tired earlier in the day that I had not taken much note of how elegant the drawing room was. The furniture was covered in silks the color of marigolds and cornflowers and sat atop a lovely Persian rug shot through with threads of the same hues. Some very good art hung on the walls and a small fire crackled in the fireplace, warding off the chilly evening air. It was a comfortable and welcoming room, made even more so as Tabitha turned on the wireless and the soft sounds of orchestra music floated in as a subtle backdrop to conversation.

I accepted a cup of coffee and took a seat on one of the sofas near the fireplace. A moment later Mr. Palmer wandered over, taking the seat beside me. He had a coffee cup in his hand, but I had seen him take a flask from his pocket and add something to it.

"I thought I would come and sit with you before Rudy came over and started shilling his salad dressing again."

"I enjoyed hearing about his work in radio," I said honestly. There was certainly nothing off-putting about the young man's enjoyment of his work.

Mr. Palmer smiled. "Then you've undoubtedly made a friend for life."

"You're not fond of Mr. Elliot, I take it?"

"Oh, Rudy's my best friend," he said with apparent sincerity, surprising me. "It's just that he can be so horribly boring at times. He's a good guy, though. A lot better friend than a lot of people ever dream of being."

There was something disarming about Grant Palmer. Though I had been prepared to dislike him for his inconsiderateness and the way he had waltzed late into dinner, as though he hadn't a care in the world, I couldn't help but feel the tug of his appeal. Perhaps it was that his breezy disregard for propriety reminded me a bit of Milo.

"It must be nice for you both to be in Tom's wedding," I said.

"Oh, I suppose. I'm kind of a black sheep around here. I think Tabitha would kick me out of the wedding if it wasn't for Tom."

"I don't expect that would hurt your feelings much."

He smiled, seeming to appreciate my plain speaking. "I don't care much about it one way or the other, but I suppose it'll be nice to see him marry the sort of girl he's always wanted to marry."

I glanced at him, wondering at his phrasing.

"Tabitha is a wonderful woman," I said. "I'm sure she'll make Tom very happy."

"She's a nice girl. She'll make Tom as happy as anyone, I suppose."

This less-than-glowing assessment of Tabitha made me bristle.

"I take it you're not a romantic, Mr. Palmer?"

He smiled, but I thought that it wasn't quite genuine. "You could say that. I don't believe there are matches made in Heaven, but I guess some of us occasionally stumble across someone worth going through life with."

I was not sure how to respond to this somewhat pessimistic view of love, so I changed the subject.

"How long have you and Mr. Smith been friends?"

It seemed to me that his gaze was searching. "Four or five years," he replied at last.

I was a bit surprised. From the way they talked, I thought that they had known each other for much longer.

"It's an honor, then, that he's asked you to stand up in his wedding."

"We've had a lot of laughs. I figured I should support him now that he's determined to stay on the straight and narrow."

Before I could ask him what he meant by this, another conversation caught my interest.

"How have things been at the warehouse, Mr. Alden? Any more trouble with the thieves?" Rudy Elliot asked.

I glanced at Tabitha and saw that her face had taken on a strained expression.

"Oh, no," Mr. Alden said easily. "We've been keeping a sharp eye on things, but there hasn't been any more trouble so far. I think it was just someone looking for an easy way to make money, or perhaps some young men with too much time on their hands."

"Yes, I'm sure that's what it was," Tom said. "The increased security should keep there from being any sort of reoccurrence."

"Tom's got things well under control," Mr. Alden said.

"Does anyone want to play cards?" Jemma Petrie asked, rising from her chair. I wondered if this was a sign of disinterest in the topic, or an attempt to change the subject for Tabitha's sake. Perhaps I hadn't been the only one to notice her worried countenance.

They let the matter drop then, and I couldn't very well press them on the subject, but I was curious to learn what sort of trouble had been occurring at Mr. Alden's warehouses. I would have to ask Tabitha later. Perhaps I could help set her mind at ease.

"I'll play with you, Jem," Rudy Elliot said.

"You can always count on good old Rudy. Anyone else?" She turned to look at Milo. "Mr. Ames?"

"I'm afraid I must decline," Milo said without making excuses.

"Mrs. Ames, then?" she asked me.

"No, thank you. In fact, it's been a rather long day. If you'll all excuse me, I think I shall retire."

3

A short while later found me enjoying the quiet solitude of my bedroom. The day had been a whirlwind, and I was looking forward to going to sleep. Milo had stayed with Mr. Alden in the drawing room, smoking and drinking from Mr. Alden's hidden store of illicit beverages, and I hoped that Milo would not be too late coming to bed. He had always seemed to require barely any rest, while I was feeling exceptionally weary.

After I had removed my jewelry and wiped away my makeup, I changed into the most comfortable of my night dresses and pulled a dressing gown over it. As I sat at the dressing table to brush out my hair, I thought over the events of the evening. Everyone in the wedding party seemed amiable and enthusiastic about the upcoming nuptials, with the exception, perhaps, of Mr. Palmer. I could see why Tabitha had reservations about his participation, but I didn't foresee his worldly cynicism causing too many difficulties. After all, he had only to show up and stand at the altar.

A tap on the door drew me from my thoughts.

"Come in," I called, setting the brush aside and turning toward the door.

It was Tabitha. She was still in her evening gown, and her lipstick was a bit smeared. The result of Tom's good-night kiss, I supposed.

"I wanted to come and say good night," she said.

"Oh, come in," I said.

"Are you sure? I don't want to disturb you."

"You're not. Come in and sit down. Milo is drinking with your father and may not be up for quite some time."

Tabitha came into the room and shut the door behind her, dropping onto the edge of the bed rather than one of the chairs. "Well, what did you think of him?"

I didn't have to ask whom she meant.

"He seems to be a very fine young man." I was glad that I could say this honestly. Mr. Smith seemed to me to be just the sort of man I might have chosen for Tabitha.

"He's perfectly wonderful," she said with a sigh.

"He certainly seems besotted with you. I'm sure you're going to be very happy."

"I know we are."

"How was it that you met?" I asked.

"It was at a dance. I had no intention of going that night, that's the funny thing about it. Just think what would have happened if I hadn't gone."

She didn't give me time to think about this, however, before she continued on. "As soon as I saw him I knew that I was going to marry him. That's how it happens in books, but I never really believed it would happen that way. But it did. I took one look at him and said to myself, 'Tabitha Alden, that's the man you're going to marry.' "

I could certainly see why Tabitha had been struck by Tom Smith. In addition to his golden good looks, he had an easy charm and a friendly, winning manner. I expected there must have been several girls who had had their sights set on him. Knowing Tabitha, however, I was sure those other women had never stood a chance.

"Are his people from New York?" I asked.

"Oh, no," she said with a wave of her hand. "He hasn't any family left, and he's only been in New York for a few years. So I feel like it was meant to be. As soon as I saw him, I went right up and asked him to dance with me. I'm sure you wouldn't have done anything like that, but what my father calls my 'American side' came out, and I couldn't seem to help myself. I knew I was going to marry him, and I didn't know how that could possibly come about unless I went up and introduced myself to him. Then I told the friends I had gone with to leave so I would need a ride home."

I couldn't help but admire this mixture of fate and American ingenuity.

"We started going steady almost right away, and it wasn't long before he asked me to marry him, just as I knew he would. Isn't it romantic?"

"Yes," I said. I thought it all a bit soon, but I certainly had no room to chastise Tabitha on the hazards of a whirlwind engagement. I had been months away from marrying another man when Milo had swept into my life and upset all the careful plans I had made for the future.

Besides, from what I had seen of her young man, he seemed perfectly pleasant and responsible. Despite her somewhat airy manner, Tabitha had a good head on her shoulders. What was more, I knew her father wouldn't have countenanced the match had he thought that Tom was anything less than what he seemed to be.

"Now that you're here," Tabitha continued, "we're all going to have such a grand time until the wedding."

"I was glad to have met the other members of the wedding party. Your friend Jemma seems very nice."

"Oh, Jemma's a lot of fun. We've always had good times together. I knew that she was going to make everything an adventure. She may seem a bit wild at times, but it's all harmless fun."

"Mr. Elliot also seems like an amusing gentleman."

"Yes, I feel like I've known Rudy for ages. He's just the sort of man that makes a woman feel at ease, don't you think? Tom says Rudy is a good egg. I admire him so much, especially given how he's overcome tragedy."

"What sort of tragedy?"

"Oh, of course you don't know," Tabitha said, a sudden sadness coming over her features. "Rudy's dad was in banking. He lost everything in the Crash, then jumped out a window ten stories up when he realized he wasn't going to be able to get it back."

"How dreadful." I found this news to be shocking. Looking at the cheerful Mr. Elliot, I hadn't imagined that his past held something so dark. I knew, however, that people were often very good about concealing their hurts.

"It hit Rudy hard," Tabitha went on. "Though he's always tried not to show it. He's been working a lot since then, trying to prove to his father that he's able to make a success of himself, I've always thought."

"Was he left destitute?"

"There was a little money, I think, but not much. Certainly not enough for him to maintain the lifestyle he had before. I don't think he really minds it, though. Rudy has always been a person who takes what comes to him and makes the most of it."

My already high opinion of Mr. Elliot was improved by this information, and I couldn't help but wonder what Tabitha might have to say about the other guest who had been there this evening. I had saved him for last.

"What about Mr. Palmer?"

Tabitha rolled her eyes in a good imitation of casual annoyance, but I could feel a shift in her at the mention of his name, something deeper than mere dislike. "Oh, Grant. He's such a nuisance. I've told Tom countless times that I wish he would have had someone else, but he insists that Grant is one of his closest friends and that he is good at heart, despite his behavior."

"What sort of behavior?" I asked.

"For one thing, he's a womanizer. I was going to warn you not to go anywhere alone with him."

My brows rose. "Is he as untrustworthy as all that?"

She looked a bit abashed. "Well, I don't really know. It's just that he's always after some woman or another, and I wouldn't like him to bother you."

"I think I can handle myself," I said lightly.

"I'm sure you can," she agreed. "But it isn't only that."

"Oh?"

She glanced around as though we might be overheard in the confines of my bedroom and then leaned closer. "He's involved with gangsters," she said.

"Really?" I asked. This had not been what I was expecting, but I found I was not entirely surprised. Grant Palmer had the air of a man who liked to involve himself in dangerous enterprises. I supposed that would also explain the scent of alcohol that had followed him into the dining room.

"Have you heard of Leon De Lora?"

"Yes," I said, my brows rising again. The name was familiar to me. Even in London, we were regaled with tales of gun battles in the street and the dramatic assassinations of underworld figures. It seemed to me that Mr. De Lora's name had been connected to several such occurrences, though he always made sure that they couldn't be traced back to him.

"Well, Grant has gotten involved with him. He started out drinking in a speakeasy with his friends and, somehow, he became involved in the bootlegging operation. I don't know all the details, of course. I don't want to know them. But I know enough to know he's up to no good. He's going to get himself killed one of these days if he isn't careful."

I considered this information. Considering that Grant Palmer was such a good friend of Tom, I hoped that there wasn't any connection between Tabitha's fiancé and criminal violence. The last thing Tabitha needed was to lose her husband in a bootleggers' dispute.

"Is Mr. Smith involved in that sort of thing?" I asked casually.

"Oh, no," Tabitha said with emphasis. "Tom doesn't approve of any of it."

I couldn't help but wonder. I didn't know Tom, of course, so Tabitha was likely to be a much better judge of his character than I was. Nevertheless, I hoped his association with Mr. Palmer wouldn't lead him into difficulties.

Granted, I was friends with people who did things of which I didn't approve. In fact, a good many of my friends had done things that had proved to be shocking, but that didn't mean I was treading the same path or had been tainted by their actions. Anyway, Tom Smith was a grown man, and I was sure he could take care of himself.

"He's not all bad, of course," Tabitha went on, appending this lukewarm praise to her list of Grant Palmer's sins. "He saved Tom's life, so I owe him a great deal."

"Oh, really?"

"Yes, Tom has always been a bit vague about it, but he always says that he wouldn't be here if it wasn't for Grant, so I suppose I have to put up with the man. Don't mention any of the more lurid stuff in front of my dad," she went on. "He obviously doesn't know, or I don't think he'd care to have Grant in the house."

I wondered if this could be true. Mr. Alden seemed a very astute gentleman; there was probably very little he didn't know.

"Well, I hope Mr. Palmer will behave himself, at least until the wedding is over," I said, by way of encouragement.

"So do I," she said. "I have enough on my

mind without worrying about what he might get up to."

"Oh?" I asked, feeling as though I was on the verge of discovering something at last.

"Yes, I . . . I wanted to talk to you . . ." She looked at me, a frown flickering across her brow. Her lips parted and she leaned toward me as though she were building up to telling me something, but just then the bedroom door opened and Milo came in. Tabitha sat up, the moment for confiding gone.

"Oh, hello," Milo said. "I didn't mean to disturb you. I'll come back, shall I?"

"No, no," Tabitha said, sliding from the bed and walking toward the door. "I'm just leaving. I know you must both be very tired."

I didn't contradict her, though I wanted to finish our discussion. I felt as though I had been awake for days, and no doubt the conversation would keep until morning.

"Good night," she said before departing. "I'm so glad you're here."

Milo closed the door behind her and came farther into the room. "You look all in, darling."

"I feel that way," I admitted.

"You didn't rest well on the ship. A good night's sleep on dry land will do wonders."

"Yes, I'm sure you're right." Milo went to his room to undress, and I got into bed and sighed with delight as I at last slid beneath the silky sheets.

As tired as I was, however, my mind didn't seem to want to rest. As Milo went to the bathroom to wash up, I turned over the events of the day. Though, on the surface, the atmosphere of the Alden household seemed to be one of joyous anticipation, there was something that was unsettling me, some undercurrent that I couldn't seem to put my finger on. But perhaps it was just the lingering suspense of waiting to hear whatever it was that Tabitha wanted to tell me. I supposed all would be clear soon enough.

"Tom seems like a very nice young man," I mused aloud to Milo through the open bathroom door.

"Yes, I suppose he does."

"You must be disappointed. I'm sure you would have liked someone a bit more wayward to show you the best unsavory places in New York to visit."

"I certainly don't need a tour guide to locate my vices," he said, coming out of the bathroom.

I shot him a look. "Well, if you're of a mind to find some dangerous company, Tabitha tells me Mr. Palmer is involved in some unsavory dealings with a gangster."

"Ah, yes, Mr. Palmer," he said, coming to the bed. "You like him, don't you?"

I looked up at him. "Why do you say that?"

"I can tell," Milo replied. "Anyway, he's the sort of man that women are drawn to. Absolute bounders with flashing eyes and sardonic smiles."

"He has a certain sort of charm," I admitted. "Besides, you of all people can't fault a man for being handsome and mischievous."

Milo could not deny it, for he knew perfectly well that a reputation for immorality had drawn a good deal of women to him in his day. There was something very exhilarating about that little dance one did with a man with bad intentions.

He pulled back the blankets and got into bed beside me.

"Mr. Alden interests me far more than Mr. Palmer."

"Oh?" I asked, moving closer to him for warmth and beginning to feel a soft haziness fall over my senses. It felt wonderful to be lying in a bed that didn't move to and fro as I tried to rest.

"Yes, we had quite a long talk over drinks. He was telling me about his business, which

I expected to be dull, but it's actually rather interesting."

"Really?" The question was practically all polite reflex, for I was having a very difficult time keeping my eyes open as I settled against him and his arm moved over me.

"Yes, he's in shipping, and has come up with some promising new ideas for expanding into other . . ."

I don't remember what he said next, for I had already drifted off to sleep.

4

The next morning dawned bright and sunny, and, though I awoke early, I felt much more rested than I had the day before. I was also rather looking forward to breakfast since, as excellent as last night's dinner had been, I was feeling quite hungry and eager to make up for the missed meals on our voyage.

Milo was still asleep and likely wouldn't rise for some time, so I slipped quietly from the bed and readied myself for the day. I chose a becoming dress in a pattern of dark blue flowers on a lighter blue background. A light blue hat with a navy-colored ribbon would complete the ensemble when we went out for the day.

I went down to breakfast and found that the only other occupant of the breakfast room was Mr. Alden. He set aside his newspaper when I came in and made a move to rise from his chair.

"Good morning, Amory."

"Please sit down, Mr. Alden," I said, waving him back into his seat before moving to the sideboard to fill a breakfast plate from the abundance of hot food laid before me. Everything looked and smelled delicious.

"Did you sleep well?" Mr. Alden asked.

"Oh, yes. Very well," I said as I scooped a helping of fruit onto my plate. "I must thank you again for allowing Mr. Ames and me to stay with you. I told Tabitha that I didn't wish to be an imposition."

"Not at all," he said. "I'm glad for her to have a friend here as the wedding approaches. It's been difficult for her without her mother, and I expect an old man isn't much help along these lines."

"I'm sorry Tabitha's mother isn't here to see her wedding," I said as I returned to the table and took my seat. "She would have loved it." I had pleasant memories of the late Mrs. Alden, and I knew that she had loved Tabitha dearly and would be very proud of the woman her daughter had become.

"Yes. She was a wonderful woman. Tabitha is a lot like her in many ways."

It seemed to me his eyes misted slightly, and he changed the subject.

"What do you girls have planned for to-day?"

"A fitting for the bridesmaid dresses, I think."

"I'm sure Tabitha will keep you busy, but I hope you have some time to see the city."

"I hope so, too. It's been some time since I've had the chance to explore it." We talked then for a while about New York and how it differed from London. As Mr. Alden had mentioned the previous evening, he hadn't been back to England in many years, due to the pressures of expanding his new business. His dedication was apparent, and I could see how he had made a success of it.

When we had finished eating, he pushed his plate away and stood.

"Will you come with me to my office for a moment? I'd like your opinion on something, and it's just as well I do it when Tabitha isn't around."

"Certainly," I said, curious.

We went from the dining room and down the long hallway, past the drawing room, and stopped before a solid oak door.

"Here we are," he said, pulling a key from his pocket.

I wondered fleetingly why he kept the door locked, but I supposed that there were business records and other items of a confidential nature.

The room was paneled in dark wood, with rows of bookshelves lined with leather-bound volumes. There was a large fireplace, above which rested a pair of polished hunting rifles, and a scattering of dark red leather chairs matched the heavy brocade drapes that hung over the windows. The paintings on the walls, depicting English hunting scenes, were of good quality, unless I was much mistaken.

It was very much a gentleman's room. And yet I would not have minded spending an evening there myself, drinking a cup of tea before a roaring fire and browsing one of the antiquarian volumes.

Mr. Alden had made his way behind his desk and reached into his waistcoat pocket to remove a smaller key than the one with which he had opened the office door. He fitted it into one of the drawers and pulled it open.

"I'm trying to choose a wedding gift for Tabitha," he said, leaning to reach into the drawer. "I had these sent over, but I'm trying to decide which she would like best. I thought that you, being a woman of excellent taste, might be able to give me your opinion on the matter."

"I should be happy to," I said, wondering

what it was that he was going to take out of the drawer.

He pulled out a velvet jewelry box, then another, then one more. He laid them out on the surface of his desk. He opened each one in turn, spinning it to face me on the polished wooden surface.

I drew in a breath. Each box contained a startlingly brilliant necklace, glittering with jewels. I could see now why he kept his office locked. The combined value of these pieces must have been a fortune.

"They're exquisite," I said.

"Yes, aren't they," he replied, though clearly he was not as awed as I was by the extravagance of the jewels displayed before us on the desk like so many costume baubles.

"I told the jeweler I wanted something a bit extravagant, and I narrowed it down to these three, but now I'm at a loss. What's your opinion?"

I stepped closer. The first box held a necklace awash in shimmering diamonds set in an intricate pattern of loops and swirls. The second was a necklace of sapphires, a thin line of them that would encircle the neck and then hang down the chest in a long strip of vibrant blue gems.

The third was a set of perfectly matched pearls.

"Pearls are always lovely for a wedding," I said.

"I was thinking along those lines," he said, the tips of his fingers on the box, turning it around to face him. "Though pearls aren't the most exciting of gems."

"They're less flashy, perhaps, but there's something quietly elegant about them."

He looked up at me then back down at the box, his expression growing soft. "I haven't thought of that phrase in a long time. 'Quietly elegant.' Someone said that about my wife once, and I thought it was the perfect phrase to describe her."

"I always remember how graceful she was," I said, recalling the image of Tabitha's mother from some long-ago dinner party. Tabitha and I had been young girls, watching the dinner over the bannister.

"I want Tabitha to have all the things that her mother would have wanted for her. I've made it my business to see that she has the life she deserves. I would do anything to make her happy."

"You've given her a wonderful life, Mr. Alden, and I'm sure she has been very happy, indeed."

He smiled. "I hope so."

He went about closing up the jewelry cases then and putting them back in the drawer of his desk. It seemed a very careless way to store such a large amount of expensive jewelry, but I supposed it was not so much of a risk if he could afford to replace them.

"The pearls it is, then," he said when they were carefully stored, the drawer locked.

"Tabitha is going to love them."

"Yes, I think you're right. Thank you for your help, Mrs. Ames."

I walked back toward the stairs, lost in thought. How was it that Mr. Alden could afford such jewelry? Not only that, the necklace was to be given to Tabitha in addition to the flat he had provided for the couple once they wed. I was not sure which gift might be more expensive. It was none of my concern, of course, but I couldn't help but wonder how, after having lost a great deal of money only a few years ago, he had suddenly come to be so extravagantly wealthy.

I supposed the shipping business had been good, but this answer didn't quite satisfy me. I did hope the family wasn't going into debt. I liked to think that Mr. Alden would be more responsible than that. I had always had the impression that he was a very shrewd gentleman, and I felt certain that, having faced financial difficulties once before, he wouldn't get himself into any more such trouble.

I had just reached the foyer when I came across Tabitha on the telephone. Her back was to me, but I couldn't help but overhear her words.

"You can't," she said in a hushed whisper. "I've told you not to press him on this. Do you hear me, Grant? He's not going to do it."

She paused for a moment, apparently listening to something he said, and then she shook her head vehemently, as though he could see her through the wires.

"You won't drag him into this. I won't let you. He's worked too hard for everything he has. If you push him, you'll have me to deal with!"

With that, she slammed the telephone down on the receiver.

I made a slight movement then, to alert her to my presence, and she turned. The lingering expression on her face was one of worry and something more — anger. It cleared quickly when she saw me, and she came over to me with a smile.

She was wearing a lovely marigold-colored

dress that would've looked ghastly on me but complemented her sunny complexion. She looked very young and pretty, but when her eyes met mine they were still troubled.

"Oh, Amory. Good morning."

"Good morning. Going to breakfast?"

"Yes, I think so. I . . . that is . . ." She stopped and stood there, as though debating something, and I waited for her to decide whether she wanted to confide in me.

"Is anything wrong?" I asked at last.

"Not exactly. But . . . As I said last night, there's something else I wanted to talk to you about." Her tone was casual, but I could sense that there was a weight behind the words.

"Of course," I said. "Do you want to talk now?"

"Yes, but . . ." She glanced down the hall, though it was perfectly clear that we were alone. "Is your room empty?"

"Milo's still sleeping, I'm afraid."

"Then let's go to my bedroom."

"All right." I followed her up the stairs and down the hallway to her room, wondering what it might be that she wanted to discuss. Was whatever she had been about to tell me last night connected in some way with the conversation she had just had with

Grant Palmer? From what I had heard, it sounded as though Mr. Palmer was trying to pull Tom into some kind of underhanded scheme. Did it have to do with the illegal activities and bootlegging connections Tabitha had mentioned? If so, I didn't know how exactly I would be able to help.

I found, however, the idea that she might want to discuss Grant Palmer's influence on Tom preferable to the idea that she and Tom might be having some sort of difficulty in their relationship about which she wanted to ask my advice. I felt better equipped to counsel her on criminal matters than on matrimonial ones, for I was still learning to navigate marriage myself, even after six years of it.

We reached her bedroom, and we went inside. It was a lovely room, done up in pastels and florals, with bright sunlight pouring in through white lace curtains. The configuration was much the same as in my room, with the window overlooking the park across the street and an arrangement of furniture before the fireplace, and Tabitha led me to a pair of pale pink chairs.

We sat, and she clutched her hands in her lap. Whatever this was, she viewed it as something serious. Tabitha was not the sort of woman who fretted about things. She was direct and forthcoming, so this pensiveness was unlike her.

"Now, what is it you want to discuss?" I asked.

She gave me a weak smile. "I've had something on my mind. I wanted to talk to you about it last night, but I lost my nerve. I suppose you're going to think I'm very silly."

"I'm sure I shan't think any such thing."

She opened her mouth as if to speak and then closed it again. I could tell she was weighing her words, deciding what she wanted to say.

"You may say anything you like to me, Tabitha," I encouraged. I knew it had been a while since we had spent any time together, but I had always felt that our friendship had remained strong through our letters and I hoped that she would feel able to confide in me.

The words came out in a rush. "I think Dad's in some sort of trouble."

This was not what I had expected her to say. Mr. Alden had seemed relaxed and genial since we had arrived. I was usually fairly adept at reading people, and I had seen no indication that there was anything troubling Tabitha's father, especially not this morning when he had eagerly showed me the jewelry he meant to give her. Of course, I realized that appearances could be deceiving, and the worries about the source of his newfound wealth still hovered in the back of my mind.

"What sort of trouble?"

"I don't really know how to explain it." She paused, and I waited, giving her a chance to collect her thoughts. "He's been different lately. There's something going on that he's not telling me. I don't know if it has to do with business or something else, but he's keeping things from me. I can tell."

I remembered suddenly that Milo had been saying something about Mr. Alden's business before I had fallen asleep. What had he said? I had been too delirious with sleepiness to pay attention. I would have to ask him about it.

"That may not be cause for alarm," I said carefully. Though I wasn't sure how to phrase it, I realized that this was not, in itself, anything unusual. I imagined a great many parents kept things from their children.

Tabitha seemed to realize this, for she went ahead. "What I mean is, he's been secretive in a way that he never used to be. It's been just the two of us since Mum died. We've always been partners in everything.

We've been closer than most fathers and daughters; we've been almost more like friends. But lately there's been something on his mind. He's been preoccupied, worried. Whenever I ask him about it, he smiles or pats my hand and tells me not to fret. That only makes me worry more."

"Perhaps it's the wedding that's preoccupying him," I suggested. "Things are going to be different for him when you marry Tom and move out of the house. He may be feeling melancholy but doesn't want to tell you and upset you."

"Yes, I considered that," she said. "I thought maybe he was just going to be lonely. But that was before these strange things started happening."

I looked over at her. " 'Strange things'? Is that the vandalism Mr. Elliot mentioned last night?"

"That's part of it. There have been some break-ins down at Dad's warehouses. It's not entirely out of the ordinary. These are difficult times, and a lot of people have been driven to desperate measures. But there have been other things."

"What sort of things?" I was becoming curious now.

"For one thing, he keeps having visitors late at night. At first I thought I was imagining it, but then I began to watch out my window. A car would pull up to the curb and a person — sometimes two — would get out and come up to the house."

"Did you recognize them?"

She shook her head. "The angle is wrong, and I could never see their faces. Once I went down the hallway and crept to the top of the stairs, but by the time I got there whoever it was had disappeared into Dad's study."

Suddenly everything seemed to click together in my mind.

"Tabitha," I said, trying to think of the best way to phrase it. "You don't think your father might be involved in bootlegging?"

She looked up in surprise then gave a laugh. "Oh, no. I'm sure he's not involved in anything like that."

I thought perhaps she was being naïve. It seemed to me that it was the best way to make sense of his mysterious behavior and the influx of wealth.

"But it would explain the things you've told me."

"Yes, but . . . You see, Grant's been trying to pull Dad in that direction." So now we had come around to the subject of her morning telephone conversation. It wasn't Tom she had been defending, but her father.

"What do you mean?"

"He's been trying to get Dad involved in some sort of shady business deal. He talked about it with Dad once in front of me, and he called this morning, insinuating that there was something he needed to talk to Dad about. It makes me so mad. Dad has refused so far, of course, but I worry about him getting drawn in by the promise of surefire success."

"Your father doesn't seem especially fond of Mr. Palmer."

"But Grant's persuasive." Her jaw set. "I won't allow it, though. I won't let him get Dad into trouble."

"I'm sure your father knows what he's doing, Tabitha," I said by way of reassurance. "He appears to be very successful."

"That's just it. I know we've been luckier than a lot of people, and I don't want him to risk it. We had our own tough times. He hasn't always been successful. You see, right before the Crash, Dad made a risky investment, a foolish one, you might even say. He lost a lot of money, and then, when the stock market failed, he lost more. For a while Dad was barely eating or sleeping. He had lost a lot of weight, and I was very worried about him. But he pulled himself back up and then business started picking up again, and he's been able to make a go of things."

Her eyes had taken on a glimmer of intensity as she spoke about her father, and I realized how much he meant to her. "He's a good businessman, but we've known a lot of good businessmen who lost everything, or very nearly everything. I don't think he could stand to go through it again. I think it would crush him. That's why I've got to protect him."

I tried to find the right words to reassure her. "Your concern is admirable, but try not to jump to conclusions. It may be nothing."

"But it is something," she insisted. "I can feel that something's wrong. That's why I wanted to talk to you about it. I saw that you had been involved in helping the police with some things in England, and I thought maybe you'd be able to find out what's going on with Dad."

"Good heavens," I said, horrified. "Has there been news about that here?"

"Oh, yes. You know how the press loves a good murder. That business with the murdered actress was in the news for days. And with you and Milo being beautiful people, it makes things all the more interesting."

I laughed. "I'm flattered, I suppose. But I don't much like the idea of being linked to such things."

"Well, you were pushed off the pages fast enough by another mob killing, but, anyway, it got me thinking."

I felt a warning sensation somewhere in the back of my mind. I was about to be pulled into something; I was sure of it.

"I know this isn't a murder mystery, but I thought perhaps you could help me keep an eye on Dad. See if you notice anything. Maybe Milo can talk to him. Dad might say things to another man that he wouldn't say to me."

"But, Tabitha, I don't even know your father well. How can I possibly tell if something is amiss?"

"You have a good instinct for things. I'm not asking you to do anything dramatic, like follow him around the city, but perhaps you'll notice something that I don't. Or perhaps he'll tell you something that he doesn't feel comfortable telling me."

"Oh, I doubt he'll find me a confidante," I protested.

"You're easy to talk to," Tabitha insisted. "And Dad's always liked you."

I highly doubted that if Mr. Alden was doing something such as involving himself with notorious bootleggers that he was likely to confide it in me. Perhaps he would do so to Milo, though, as Tabitha had suggested. They had, after all, apparently enjoyed each other's company last night. It was possible I could find a way to broach the subject with Milo, though I somehow doubted he would be very enthusiastic about meddling in Mr. Alden's affairs.

Tabitha reached out and caught my hand. "Please, Amory. You'll help me, won't you?"

I hesitated. While I didn't want to get involved in any sort of family troubles the Aldens might be having, I didn't see how I could possibly tell her no. She was worried about her father, and with the wedding looming, there was already a great deal on her mind. Besides, I doubted anything would come of it.

"Yes, Tabitha. I'll see what I can do."

It seems that I will never learn.

5

A short while later, Jemma Petrie arrived and the three of us left for the fitting of the bridesmaid dresses. Tabitha had hoped to have the gowns brought to the house, but as we were fitting en masse, it had been easier for us to go to the dressmaker's shop.

"I'm hoping, since you sent me your measurements, that there won't be many alterations," Tabitha said as we drove through the crowded streets, "but if there are, I'm sure they will have them done in time for the wedding. They're so obliging here."

The most expensive couturiers usually were.

We reached the dressmaker's, a little shop on Fifth Avenue, and went inside. The décor was chic and modern, everything in shades of cream and gold, and there was the subtle scent of roses in the air. We were ushered into the presence of a sleekly coiffured woman in black who set about our fitting with brisk efficiency.

The gown Tabitha had chosen for her bridesmaids was lovely, a confection of pale lilac-colored crepe. It had flounced sleeves and was fitted through the bodice with a long, flowing skirt. It was very elegant, and both Jemma and I were eager to model it for the bride.

Tabitha clasped her hands together in delight when I came out of the fitting room. "It's perfect!" she said. "I knew you wouldn't need many alterations done. You've got a figure like a model."

"You're sweet," I said, turning to study the effect of the dress in the mirror. "In fact, I feel as though I've gained a few pounds." I supposed I oughtn't to have indulged so heartily in breakfast before the fitting.

"Well, it looks swell on you," Jemma agreed. "Mine doesn't look half as good."

"I think you look marvelous," I contradicted her. She had a very nice figure, and the dress was flattering on her. Tabitha had done a marvelous job with her selection, and I was relieved that the gown would not require additional alterations.

"I love the color," I said as I examined our reflections once again.

"Yes, the color's divine," Jemma said. "I

feel like a goddess." She struck a dramatic pose, and we all laughed.

"I know the shade might be a bit unusual for autumn," Tabitha said, "but it's one of my favorite colors, and I thought it would look lovely on both you and Jemma."

I thought back to my wedding. I had chosen gowns of pale blue organza for my bridesmaids. My cousin Laurel had joked that I had chosen a color that would most flatter me, but I thought all the girls had looked lovely in it.

Jemma and I returned to our fitting rooms and took off our dresses, dressed again in our own clothes, and went to sit on the little ivory-colored sofa, where one of the salesgirls brought us tea as Tabitha went to try on her gown.

"It won't take long," she promised.

"Take all the time you need. Will we be able to see your gown?"

"Perhaps," she said with a smile. "Though I really want to wait until it's completely finished."

She disappeared then with the seamstress, and Jemma and I sipped our tea and chatted about the gowns and wedding plans.

"Have you known Tabitha long?" I asked.

"Several years," she replied. "We went to school together, in fact."

I was a bit surprised that I had never heard of her from Tabitha, but, then again, Tabitha's letters were very sporadic and also contained information on a great number of topics. Perhaps I just didn't remember.

"And what do you think of Tom?" I asked. "They seem made for each other, don't they?"

She looked at me, a bit sharply I thought at first, and then she gave a slight shrug. "Tom's all right, if you like that sort of man."

This was not the sort of answer I had been expecting. "What sort of man is that?" I asked lightly.

"Oh, I don't know. Tabitha always talked about wanting a knight in shining armor or a handsome prince like something out of a fairy tale. Tom doesn't exactly fit that bill."

"You don't think so?" I was growing more curious by the moment. It seemed surprising to me that Jemma should dislike Tom. He seemed to me to have the winning combination of good looks and an amiable disposition that would appeal to almost any woman.

She shrugged. "I've always thought him a bit of a milquetoast. But if Tabitha is happy, I'm happy for her. I like someone a bit more exciting myself."

I wondered if, perhaps, Jemma had also had her sights set on Tom. I couldn't help but notice that her manner seemed quite changed from the cheerful friendliness she had exhibited upon our first meeting, even from the camaraderie of our fitting a few moments ago. Were my comments about Tom the reason for it? I hadn't seen her pay any particular attention to him, but the way in which she spoke so carelessly of him made it seem as though she was hiding something beneath the surface.

I had no basis for assuming so, of course. As much as I hated to admit it, I did sometimes look too closely for signs of hidden conflict. Perhaps it was an unfortunate by-product of my involvement in several murder investigations, but I always felt as though I was trying to read between the lines, to catch the subtle undercurrents of conversation that might tell me something the person didn't want to reveal.

"Well, I think the wedding is going to be lovely," I said, forcing my mind away from its tendency to look for trouble where none might exist. Jemma's next words brought me back around to the idea that all might not be well, however.

"I hope so. I'm glad for Tabitha's sake that

things have been going as smoothly as they have."

"Is there some reason they shouldn't?"

"There's been some bad blood between Grant and Rudy the past few months. It made things a little awkward for a while."

"Oh, what sort of trouble?" I asked, remembering Grant Palmer had distinctly told me that Rudy Elliot was his best friend.

"I don't know exactly. They didn't discuss it in front of me, though you could feel them hating each other whenever they were in the same room. I wouldn't be surprised if it had something to do with a woman, because I heard them whispering heatedly one day. Rudy said something like, 'I'm going to have her,' or something like that, though I doubt he succeeded. Grant's always been fond of stealing women from Rudy."

"I see." I pictured Grant Palmer at the dinner table, with his dark good looks and the casually contemptuous way he had spoken of Rudy Elliot's career.

"I guess they've patched things up, though," Jemma went on. "They're always fighting, almost like brothers. Though they certainly don't come from the same sort of background."

"I understand Mr. Elliot's father was a banker."

She nodded. "It hit him hard when his dad died."

"And what about Mr. Palmer's background?"

"Oh, Grant's family has never had much money, as far as I know. I'm not really sure how he and Rudy ever came to be friends. To be honest, I always suspected Rudy got in with the wrong crowd of boys when he was young."

"Then Mr. Palmer has always been a troublemaker?"

"Well, I don't imagine he was ever a choirboy," she said with a laugh. "He's gotten into several scrapes with the police. He's always doing something underhanded."

"You sound as though you're not too fond of him."

"You're right. I don't care for Grant at all," she said easily. "Never have."

I had the sense it was more than just casual dislike.

"Have you known him long?" I asked, trying to draw her out.

"As long as I've known Rudy, I guess. A few years. The two of them are always together, usually with Rudy pulling Grant out of scrapes. Grant even worked with Rudy at Rudy's dad's banking business for a while before . . . before Mr. Elliot died.

The two of them have always been like oil and water. Of course, it doesn't help matters between them that Grant is so handsome, and Rudy, while very nice, isn't exactly the sort of man that women go crazy over."

I considered this. I could certainly see where Grant Palmer would be more appealing to women than Rudy Elliot. After all, I had married a tall, dark, and handsome rogue myself. Just the same, there was something undeniably appealing about Rudy Elliot. His easy confidence and friendly manner made him attractive in his own way.

"I think Mr. Elliot seems very nice."

"Oh, he is. Rudy can be a bore at times, but he's really sweet. I think he'd make an excellent husband someday."

"For you, perhaps?" I asked.

She laughed. "Goodness, no! I wouldn't be able to keep a straight face as we said our vows. But he's a nice guy, and I hope he finds the right woman."

"And what of Mr. Palmer?" I asked the question casually, and she answered it with apparent indifference.

"I don't think Grant has any interest in a wife. And I'd pity any woman who was married to him."

Tabitha came back out then. She was not wearing her wedding gown, and she looked a bit disappointed. "It isn't fitting quite right. I don't want you to see it yet."

"I'm sure it will be lovely," I said brightly.

"I hope so. I hope the fact that it's ill-fitting doesn't bode poorly for my marriage," she said lightly.

"Not a chance," I assured her. "Everything is going to be wonderful."

When Tom decided to spirit Tabitha away for a drive before dinner, I suggested to Milo that we might take a walk. It was the first time I had had an opportunity to be alone with him that day, and I was eager to discuss my morning conversation with Tabitha.

It was such a lovely afternoon, however, that I didn't want to broach the subject of Tabitha's suspicions immediately. We left the house and walked along the pavement parallel to the park for a while, admiring the large, stately houses that spoke of comfortable wealth. Many of the window boxes still held colorful flowers, though it was late in the season and a scattering of orange and brown leaves crunched beneath our feet. For a few moments I walked along, holding Milo's arm and enjoying the mild autumn breeze and the sunshine on our faces.

"What were you saying about Mr. Alden's business last night?" I eventually asked. "I'm afraid it was rather rude of me to fall asleep."

"Nonsense. I oughtn't to have been boring you with such things when you were clearly exhausted. He was relating to me some aspects of his recent business endeavors."

"Oh? Like what?"

"He's long been in shipping, as you know, but saw his profits fall sharply due to the depression. It's only as of late that he's begun to build up relationships with local businesses that are creating stores in other cities, housing items at his warehouses until they are ready for shipment to new locations."

I was a bit surprised that Milo had apparently taken an interest in the workings of Mr. Alden's business. Normally, such a topic would have been tedious to him.

"Are there many businesses expanding in this economy?" I asked.

"It seems so. He's beginning to have more business than he has trucks and space in his warehouse."

"I suppose the increased business has put

a great deal of pressure on him," I suggested, hoping to draw Milo out on the subject of any potential troubles Mr. Alden might have confided to him.

"I assume it's pressure he's happy to be experiencing. A great many people aren't faring so well at the moment."

"Of course. I only wondered . . . Did he seem at all concerned about anything in particular?" I asked casually, though apparently not casually enough, for Milo glanced at me, his gaze suddenly sharp.

"What is this about?"

I sighed. I ought to have known that I wouldn't be able to subtly bring up the topic without arousing his suspicions.

I briefly considered trying to recover, but I supposed now that Milo was aware that I was fishing for information, I might as well come out with it.

"Tabitha says that she thinks there's something strange going on with her father."

"Such as?"

As we crossed the street and walked into the park, I related what she had told me this morning. Though he listened carefully to my recitation of the facts, Milo appeared unmoved by the list of Mr. Alden's supposed strange behaviors.

"She's probably imagining things," he said

when I had finished.

"Imagining vandalism and strangers arriving in the night? I think not," I said, irritated at this casual dismissal. "She's not a simpleton, Milo."

"Of course not. That's not what I meant. I mean she's probably ascribing significance to these events that doesn't exist. She doesn't know the ins and outs of his business dealings. Those strangers could be anyone. And many businesses are forced to contend with attempted theft."

"But Tabitha is so adamant that he's been behaving strangely lately."

"Darling, Mr. Alden is a businessman. No doubt he has a great many things on his mind. Added to that, his only child is about to be married. I don't think a bit of changed behavior on his part is cause for alarm."

It was much the same argument I had made to Tabitha, but it was dissatisfying somehow to hear it from Milo.

"Do you suppose it has something to do with his sudden change in fortunes?" I asked, ignoring his skepticism. "I did wonder if he's taken up with bootleggers."

Milo seemed to consider this. "It doesn't seem likely, considering all he told me."

"You seem to know quite a lot about Mr. Alden's business dealings," I observed.

"We talked at length about them last night. You see, I've decided to invest in Alden Shipping."

I stopped walking and turned to face him. "You've what?"

"He is looking for investors, and it seems to me I could do worse than put my money into a thriving business belonging to a friend of the family."

I stared at him. I had not been expecting this. Milo had always made sound financial decisions, but I was concerned, given Tabitha's worries, whether this had been a wise thing to do. Of course, Milo had a good head for business; I wouldn't argue the point with him, especially if he had already committed himself.

"I'm glad for him, then," I said. "He could do much worse than to have someone like you on his side."

Milo smiled. "Thank you, darling. I hope this sets your mind at ease. Mr. Alden's company appears to be very successful and likely to continue to be."

"And you don't think there is something troubling him?"

"I suppose there could be. Any number of things. But what does Tabitha expect you to do about it?"

Milo was naturally inclined to be dismissive in cases such as these, the main problem being that he was not much interested in other people's problems. Lucky, then, that he now had a financial investment. It would give him something to care about.

"I didn't make her any promises," I said, as I took his arm again and we resumed walking. "I only told her that I would try to see if I could find anything amiss."

Milo sighed.

"You needn't be annoyed; there's not much I can do, really."

"You say that now, but one or two confirmed suspicions will find you rifling through his desk drawers in the dead of night."

"I certainly would do no such thing!"

He looked at me and smiled. "We're here for a wedding, Amory. Please try not to immerse us in another mystery."

"You used to enjoy the thrill of the chase," I challenged.

"Only when I'm chasing something worthwhile."

"Come now," I said, squeezing his arm. "You can't tell me that a little part of you doesn't enjoy these things, the hint that something might go wrong. I should think it's just the sort of thing that appeals to you in gambling and horse racing."

"All right," he said with a sigh. "I'll see if anything of interest happens to come up in my conversations with Mr. Alden."

I smiled. "Thank you."

We stopped walking then as we reached a little pond. The sun was shining on the water, and children were playing along its edges, two small boys pushing miniature boats into the shimmering surface. A soft breeze blew, and the birds were singing in the trees.

It was a lovely scene, and I suddenly felt a little rush of happiness to be standing there with the man I loved. Almost before I knew what I was doing, I had turned to him and, throwing my arms around his neck, kissed him.

He responded readily, and we stood there for a moment like a pair of young lovers who had met for a liaison in the park.

At last I pulled away, mindful of not making a scene in a public place.

"What was that for?" he asked, looking down at me.

"I don't know," I said. "Can't a woman kiss her husband if she feels so inclined?"

"You may kiss me anytime you like," he said. "In fact, the more often, the better."

I laughed. "Well, we'd better move along now. I'd hate for anyone to see us behaving scandalously. Shall we walk to the other end of the park?"

"I think we'd better go back instead," he said.

"Why?"

He flashed me a wicked smile. "Because we might just have time to sneak up to our room before the Aldens arrive home."

6

We went to a nightclub that evening with Tabitha, Tom, Jemma Petrie, and Rudy Elliot. Mr. Palmer did not accompany us, and I didn't ask Tabitha whether or not he had been invited.

I very much enjoyed the ride from the Aldens' quiet street into the heart of the city. There was something magical about New York at night. The streets glowed brightly with the lights of sleepless buildings and the advertisements for cigarettes and drugstores, Automats and all-night diners, and shows and cinemas. People and cars moved through the streets in what seemed to be a delicately timed dance, and there was the ever-present sound of calling voices, and music, and the beeping of automobile horns.

At our destination, we alighted from the car and made our way with a crowd of men in top hats and tailcoats and women in furs into the cool, marble interior of the Topaz

Club. It was a lovely place, with stylish, elegant décor. We were led to a silver-clothed table near the dance floor, which sat before a bandstand with an elaborate backdrop draped with yards of blue satin.

"Not much of a nightclub when there's nothing good to drink," Milo muttered to me as we settled into our seats, but Tom had assured us that the food was excellent enough to compensate for the lack of spirits, and Tabitha had said the band was one of the best in town.

"I love your dress, Amory," Jemma Petrie said to me from across the table. "I could never get away with wearing that color."

"Thank you. I purchased it only recently."

I had known Milo would want to take advantage of New York nightlife while we were here, and, to that end, I had brought an array of new evening gowns. For tonight I had chosen one of pale gray silk with a skirt of gauzy layers that seemed almost to float when I walked. I felt rather ethereal in it, and I supposed that my stubborn pallor, brought on by seasickness and travel weariness, only added to the effect.

"Are you all right, darling?" Milo leaned to ask me as our food arrived. I had looked down at the broiled chicken and potatoes and felt myself grow a shade paler.

"Yes," I said faintly. "I'm afraid I haven't quite shaken my sea legs."

"Do you want to leave?"

I shook my head, picking up my fork. "No, no. I'm having a lovely time."

We ate and enjoyed the floor show, a chorus line of dancers in bright and sparkling costumes and a comely soloist with a credible singing voice.

When the dancers and singer had departed, the band began to play and couples moved to the dance floor. It was just then that a waiter came to our table.

"There's a phone call for you, Mr. Elliot."

Rudy smiled, pulling his napkin from his lap and tossing it onto the table. "That might be the office. I've been waiting to hear about a new account. Excuse me, will you?"

He left the table then, and Tom turned to me. "Would you care to dance, Mrs. Ames?"

Though he did it out of duty, I suspected he was relieved when I told him to ask Tabitha instead. I had the impression that he wanted nothing more than to hold her in his arms. I had not missed the way they constantly touched, the way they seemed happier the closer they were to each other.

"Shall we, Miss Petrie?" Milo asked.

"I'd love to," she replied, taking his outstretched hand.

They all went off to the dance floor and I enjoyed watching the couples move about the room in time to beautifully played music. There was an aura of happiness and gaiety in the air, the sense of excitement and romance that seems to permeate the places where couples meet and hope and longing build.

My eyes fell again on Tom and Tabitha. He leaned to whisper something in her ear and she laughed, her arms tightening around his neck. They were clearly besotted with each other. I found myself hoping that all of Tabitha's worries about her father would amount to nothing and that she and Tom could get married and live happily ever after.

"Oh, hello, Mrs. Ames," said a voice at my side, drawing me from my reverie.

I looked up to see that Grant Palmer had arrived at the table. Though no one had mentioned his joining us, I found I was not entirely surprised that he had made an appearance.

"Good evening," I replied.

"I see I'm a bit late to the party, as usual. I was hoping to have a word with Tom about something, and I knew this is where he and Tabitha usually go when they want an evening out."

"Yes, they're dancing at the moment."

"So I see. And Jemma's got ahold of your husband. Not very nice for you, is it? Leaving you here all alone. Although, it's a wonder Rudy didn't try to drag you off to the dance floor."

"Oh, I don't need to be entertained," I said, hoping that he would take the hint and not ask me to dance. I felt perfectly happy being a spectator tonight.

To my relief, he didn't offer to escort me to the dance floor. Instead, he pulled out the chair beside me and dropped into it.

"You must find New York a bit wild compared to London," he said. "I suppose we must all seem a bit savage."

"Oh, I wouldn't say that," I said. "London has its share of excitements."

"Maybe you're just better at pretending to be civil than we are."

I looked up at him, wondering what he meant. My instinct was to be annoyed with him for his strange remarks, but I couldn't quite bring myself to reach that point.

"You said you've always lived in New York?" I asked, trying to steer the topic away from the unsteady ground upon which I had the sensation we were treading.

"Grew up in Brooklyn," he replied. "Not the sort of company you'd normally keep, I suppose. Or the Aldens, for that matter. But Tom and I met a few years ago and we got on all right. I'm learning to get around in their world."

"And do you find you've settled into 'their world,' as you call it?" I asked. I wasn't sure what had made me ask the question. I was curious somehow to know more about him. There was more to him than met the eye, depths that he didn't often reveal. I recognized this, for Milo had the same quality, that airy indifference that concealed whatever lay beneath.

"I find it more and more difficult to walk the tightrope."

"In what way?"

"In a lot of ways."

I wanted to press him further, but something in the way he said it made it clear he had brought this area of conversation to an end, so I switched topics.

"You said you met Tom four years ago? Where did you meet?"

He took a cigarette from a case in his pocket and put it in his mouth. "Four or five years, yeah." He struck a match and put it to the tip of his cigarette before waving it out. "I don't really recall. We bumped into each other and struck up an acquaintance."

I found it difficult to believe that he could not remember the origin of their friendship, especially when it had not been so very long since they met. I realized with a vaguely uneasy feeling that it seemed that everyone had only known Tom for a few years. I had yet to hear anyone, including Tom himself, mention what his life had been before he'd moved to New York.

"You mentioned that he was going to live the straight and narrow now that he's met Tabitha," I said with a smile, hoping to draw him out. "I suppose you two got into some trouble together."

"Did I say that?" Mr. Palmer asked, his dark eyes meeting mine. "I don't recall."

I was certain he did recall, and I wondered why he had decided to change his story now. There was something very underhanded about Grant Palmer.

I wavered for just a moment between politeness and curiosity and then decided to confront him about it.

"Come now, Mr. Palmer," I said with a laugh that was not quite sincere. "I don't expect your memory is as shoddy as all that."

He smiled at me, and it was not quite the same flippant smile I had come to expect. "I think you're a smart lady, Mrs. Ames."

This was not the answer I had expected. "How so?"

"You've got that society elegance about you, but I don't think you're fooled by a lot of it. That's smart. It's always best to have your guard up. I learned that a long time ago."

I was unsure of how to respond, and before I could, the music had ended and the others returned to our table.

"Oh, hello, Grant," Tabitha said, doing a convincing job of appearing glad to see him.

"Came to enjoy a night out with us?" Tom asked. I noticed that he, in contrast to Tabitha, seemed a bit stiff at the sight of his friend's unexpected arrival.

"No, I need to talk to you about something, if you don't mind."

I watched Tom Smith carefully, but he appeared perfectly at ease with the request, and some of the tension even seemed to leave his shoulders at the suggestion they should leave the group. "Sure. Let's go out into the foyer. I need to buy some more cigarettes anyway."

The two men turned and left as Jemma Petrie and Tabitha took their seats. If Tabitha thought it strange that her fiancé had been called away by Mr. Palmer, she didn't show it.

"I think we're going to leave soon," she told me.

"Oh?" I was a bit surprised, as it was still early.

"We're going to the Stork Club." Jemma leaned forward, voice lowered and brows raised. "They serve alcohol. Would you like to come with us?"

"Oh, I don't think so." I was ready to call it a night, but I knew that Milo might be glad to spend a bit more time on the town. I glanced at him. "Perhaps Milo would like to accompany you."

Jemma looked at him hopefully, but he shook his head. "I'll accompany Mrs. Ames back to the house, I think."

We said our good-byes and Milo and I took our leave. As we walked out into the foyer of the nightclub, I caught sight of Tom and Mr. Palmer having a discussion near a potted palm in the corner.

I was surprised to see that, in contrast to his normally pleasant countenance and his easy manner a few moments before, Tom's face was a picture of barely controlled anger. His jaw was tight and his color high. He gestured toward Mr. Palmer in quick, jerky movements that somehow gave me the impression of suppressed violence.

Mr. Palmer looked, as always, as though

nothing was of much importance to him, listening to Tom then replying calmly, that careless smile on his lips.

I couldn't hear much of what they were saying, but Tom's voice rose suddenly and I caught a few words. "I won't let the past keep following me."

"Ready, darling?" Milo arrived with my coat, drawing my attention away from the two gentlemen. It was then I noticed Jemma Petrie standing off to one side, unnoticed by Tom and Grant Palmer. She seemed to be observing the argument with interest, though she made no move to interfere. I thought it would probably be better if we didn't interrupt the scene to make our good-byes.

I leaned against Milo as we settled into the back of the cab, making our way slowly through the crowded, dazzling streets. It was a feast for the eyes, this city, and I could feel the energy humming around us. It was late, but it seemed the night was just beginning for the people of New York.

"You needn't have accompanied me back to the Aldens' home, you know," I said. "If you wished to go out with the others I could have gone back alone."

"I'd much rather spend the evening with you," he said, sliding his arm around me and pulling me a bit closer.

My head was filled with thoughts of a warm bath and a soft bed, and so I was unprepared for the scene that met us as we alighted the cab and walked along the pavement toward the steps. The front door of the house was suddenly flung open, the sound of loud voices flowing out into the night air. Milo touched my elbow and we held back a moment, shielded from the doorway by shadows and the trunk of an elm tree.

"Get out of here and don't come back!" a loud voice shouted. It took me a moment to realize that it was Mr. Alden, so distorted with anger was his tone.

"You don't know what you're doing," the man replied.

I glanced at Milo, wondering if it would perhaps be best for us to beat a quiet retreat. Milo, however, was listening to the exchange and appeared in no hurry to leave the men to their privacy.

I was about to nudge him, motion for us to walk away from the house for a few moments at least, but before we could move, a man came tumbling down the front steps, landing practically at our feet, and Mr. Alden appeared at the top of the steps, coming into view.

I was startled by the expression on his face, illuminated by the porch light. The tone of his skin was bright red, his eyes blazing. "No one threatens me and gets away with it. If you come back here again, I'll kill you," he said in a strangled voice.

It was only then that he caught sight of us. Mr. Alden stopped, an expression of surprise momentarily supplanting the fury in his eyes.

The man rose to his feet, dusting himself off. I glanced at him. He was young and small of stature, but there was something dangerous about him. It was almost as though I could feel the anger and hatred emanating from him.

"I'll talk to you later, Alden," he said, and I was certain the words held a threat.

The man disappeared down the pavement and into the shadows, and the three of us were left standing in our odd little tableau.

Mr. Alden looked as though he was trying valiantly to collect himself. He was still angry, but he was also now required to regain control of his emotions. He had not expected to see us there, and he was left with either acting as though nothing had happened or coming up with a plausible excuse for what Milo and I had just witnessed.

For my part, I was mortified. I very much wished we had come home just five minutes later and avoided all of this. It was Milo, who never found anything embarrassing, who was the first to break the silence.

"Not a friend of yours, I take it," he said easily.

I let out a little sigh of dismay.

Mr. Alden looked abashed for just a moment, as though he had been caught in something that he shouldn't have been. I thought that he would issue an apology, and then it seemed as though he built his bluster back up and decided to power through as though nothing was amiss.

"That was . . . a business associate," he said, offering us a tight smile. "He was a bit overwrought. It happens occasionally."

"Yes, I can imagine," I said politely, though it seemed to me that Mr. Alden was the one who had been a bit overwrought. I tried to remember if I had ever been involved in any circumstances in which one gentleman had thrown another bodily from his home and came up short.

I had always taken Tabitha's father for a cheerful, mild-mannered gentleman. Clearly, there was a part of him that was capable of more than that.

Mr. Alden drew in a breath. "I'm afraid I

have some matters to attend to. If you'll excuse me?"

He turned and walked into the house without another word, leaving the front door open for us to enter behind him.

"What did you make of that?" I asked Milo in a low voice. "I never would've imagined Mr. Alden capable of such anger."

"Mr. Alden isn't the first man to have a heated disagreement with a business associate, but it seemed there was an undertone of violence in that encounter. Of course, we are talking about Americans."

I shook my head. "I saw the look in Mr. Alden's eyes for that instant before he saw us. He looked positively murderous."

"I dare say a man may look murderous without being intent upon doing anyone any real harm."

I thought of the threat and how he had thrown the man from his house with ease. "We shouldn't have stood there gawking."

He shrugged. "When one resorts to brawling in the streets, I'm afraid one forfeits one's right to privacy."

He was right, of course. Whatever had Mr. Alden been thinking? This was just the sort of stir that was likely to draw attention. A scandal was the last thing Tabitha needed before her wedding.

7

The next morning was clear and warm as we mounted horses and rode onto the bridle trail in Central Park. I had not imagined there would be much opportunity for riding in New York, but once Milo had found that the Aldens stabled horses nearby, he had been very keen to investigate the trails afforded to city dwellers.

And so we made a small party of it. Tabitha declined to come, saying she had wedding details to attend to, and Mr. Alden had begged off to tend to business matters. He had seemed his usual jovial self this morning, as though the events of last night had never happened, but I couldn't help but wonder if the incident was a precursor to more trouble.

"I inquired of Mr. Alden if that visitor was anything I should be concerned about, but he assured me it had no bearing on our venture," Milo had said when we had a brief moment alone, but I doubted he was any more convinced than I was.

The Aldens otherwise engaged, then, Milo, Tom, and I had gone to the Claremont Stables shortly after breakfast, and in no time at all we were riding into the park.

It was amazing to me that this enormous park existed in the middle of such a metropolitan city. I could almost imagine that I was back in the English countryside as we rode along under the shade of the trees that lined the bridle path. The foliage had begun to turn vibrant shades of yellow, orange, and red, and the crunch of fallen leaves provided a pleasant addition to the usual backdrop riding sounds of hoof beats, creaking leather, and the horses' breathy exhalations.

After a short while, Milo, a serious horseman setting a brisk gait, had ridden ahead of us, and I decided it would be an ideal time to get to know the groom better. I nudged my horse closer to Mr. Smith.

"Do you ride often, Mr. Smith?"

"You promised to call me Tom, remember?" He flashed a smile. "I know you Brits are used to formality, but we Americans are more casual."

The world of the Aldens was not, I thought, so much less formal than my own.

Perhaps it was, in fact, society that was foreign to Mr. Smith. Once again, I wondered about his history. Tabitha hadn't been able to tell me much, and the vagueness of his background had left me a bit uneasy.

"But to answer your question, no," he went on. "I don't ride often. In fact, I had hardly ridden at all before I met Tabitha. I hadn't expected there to be much opportunity for it in New York."

"Then you're not from here?"

"No. I hail from the Midwest."

It seemed to me that he hesitated before he spoke, and my curiosity was aroused. Why was he so reticent to speak about his background?

I knew it was really none of my business. All the same, I also knew what it was like to be swept up in a whirlwind romance with little thought for the future, and I didn't want Tabitha to be caught off guard by something she learned after the vows had been said.

"Do you have family in New York?" I asked, hoping for more information.

"No," he said. "My parents are dead, and I don't have any siblings."

"I haven't any siblings, either," I told him. "I always envied my friends their brothers and sisters."

"I'd say growing up alone gave me confidence," he replied lightly. There was something in his manner, something in the careful responses, that let me know this was not a subject he wished to pursue.

It could be, of course, that he just didn't want to talk about what was likely a painful subject. After all, I didn't particularly enjoy discussing my somewhat strained relationship with my parents with strangers. Yet I sensed it was more than that. I remembered what I had overheard him say to Grant Palmer, that he didn't want the past to follow him. What was it he had to hide? It might be a simple matter, of course, but what if it was something darker?

I felt a bit guilty for my train of thought as I turned my attention back to Mr. Smith. My past experience with mysteries had led me to develop a suspicious mind, and now every wary deflection seemed to me to be an indication of something sinister.

Not that there was anything in the least sinister about Mr. Smith. I looked over at him as he rode, his handsome profile set in a pleasant expression, the dappled sunlight shining through the leaves above us and flecking his hair with gold. He looked young, happy, and carefree.

My instincts told me that Tom was a nice

young man. But they also told me that something about him wasn't exactly what it seemed. I thought of Grant Palmer's vagueness about their friendship, and then I remembered what Tabitha had told me.

"Well, it's nice that you've made such good friends in New York," I said. "Tabitha tells me Mr. Palmer even saved your life at one point."

He looked at me, a bit sharply, I thought, but then a warm smile flickered across his face and I wondered if it had been a trick of the light. "Yes, I was in a tough spot once, and he helped me out of it. I'll always owe him for that."

I was preparing to ask more questions, but I would not have the chance.

"I think I'll join your husband, if you'll excuse me," he said. "There are a few features of the path I'd like to point out to him."

And with that, he spurred his horse and rode ahead.

"I don't know what to make of Tom," I said to Milo as we entered a bustling Automat for lunch a few hours later. This had not been Milo's first choice of venue for our meal, but I had been eager to try the popular and lively dining establishment.

109

When Tom had left us at the Aldens' door, promising to meet Milo again later that afternoon to go to the races, I had convinced Milo to accompany me to the restaurant after we had changed from our riding clothes.

The building was crowded for the lunch hour, the diners filling the tables around us, talking in a mixture of accents and languages that rose above the clatter of utensils on dishes and the clinking of cups on saucers. I spotted businessmen, laborers, sailors, and saleswomen all enjoying their noon meal with equal gusto.

I stood for just a moment, looking around to get my bearings and watching the other diners for cues as to how it all worked.

The walls were covered with small, glass-fronted compartments, behind which rested food of every description. Divided into categories labeled as sandwiches, soups, salads, cakes, pies, and a host of other items, one had only to insert nickels into the slot and turn a knob for the compartments to open, granting access to the food, which was then replenished by employees in the kitchen behind the wall. It was all rather informal, but there was something pleasant about the idea of picking and choosing the items one wished to eat based on some combination of sight and whim.

When at last I thought I was ready to proceed, I went to the cashier behind a counter at the center of the room and exchanged a dollar for nickels.

I held out half of them to Milo.

"I don't see the appeal of carting one's food about oneself," he said. "I'd much rather pay to have someone else do it."

"Oh, hush, Milo. Try to enjoy the experience."

He sighed, but dutifully accepted the nickels and took up a tray, following me to the nearest wall. This one was filled with various hot dishes. Beside each compartment was a little plaque denoting the contents. I spotted two kinds of stew, three varieties of chicken, steak, pork, and an assortment of meat pies. It was all a little overwhelming.

"What do you mean you don't know what to make of Tom?" Milo asked as, undaunted by the myriad choices, he inserted nickels into one of the slots, turned the knob, and lifted the glass to take out a steak.

"I tried to make conversation with him, asking him about his life before he came to New York. He seemed overly cautious when answering my questions, as though he didn't want to give away too much about his background. He has no connections, very few friends. For all intents and purposes, he has no history before he arrived in New York."

I made my selection at last, inserting my coins and placing the chicken potpie on my tray.

"That doesn't mean he has anything to hide." Milo selected potatoes and then beans, his nickels rapidly dwindling. "Some people just have no past to speak of."

"You don't think it odd that he hasn't any family?"

"Not necessarily," Milo replied. "After all, I have no family, aside from you."

"Yes, but everyone knows your family name. It's not as though you appeared suddenly from nowhere with no links to the past."

"New York is different from London," Milo said, leading me to the coffee counter, where the dark, steaming brew was dispensed from silver faucets. "This is exactly the sort of place where people show up without a history and make a name for themselves."

"But everyone has a history," I said. "Why should Tom want to hide his?"

"There may be any number of reasons. Perhaps he comes from humble beginnings and wants to appear worthy of Tabitha."

"I just wish that Tabitha knew a bit more about him." As I added a fruit salad to my tray, I was unable to shake the feeling of uneasiness that was beginning to grow the more — or rather, the less — I learned about Tom Smith.

"He's rides well and is a good judge of horseflesh." I knew this was an endorsement as far as Milo was concerned. "Besides, she has the rest of her life to delve into his past. Women enjoy that sort of thing."

I could see I wasn't getting anywhere with him. He was in good spirits after our ride today, and he was not in the mood for a serious conversation.

He added a piece of pie to his tray, his reservations about dining at the Automat apparently long forgotten. "Don't fret, darling. It'll be all right." He smiled and then ambled with his full tray to a recently vacated table.

Despite his reassurances, I felt there was more to be learned about Tom Smith, and I had not given up on finding out what it was.

We returned to the house after lunch, and shortly thereafter Milo went off with Tom. I hoped Milo might be able to glean some information about the young man's personality from their interactions. In the meantime, Tabitha had left me a note asking me to meet her at a shop to complete some wedding errands.

Before leaving the house, I stopped at the mirror that hung on a wall in the foyer. I patted down a few hairs blown astray by the wind. Then I pulled my lipstick from my bag and applied a fresh coat. The lid of the tube slipped from my hand, and I leaned to pick it up. Rising too quickly, a wave of dizziness hit me suddenly and the lipstick faltered in my hand. I dropped it and reached out to catch it, creating a streak of red across one of the fresh, pale peach-colored gloves that complemented my cinnamon-hued belted suit.

The dizziness faded almost as quickly as it had come, and I chided myself that my clumsiness should manifest itself at the expense of my new gloves.

I sighed as I replaced the lid on my lipstick and put it back in my purse. Winnelda had overseen the packing, but I knew that this was the only pair of gloves in this color that I had brought with me. I also didn't feel quite like going upstairs for a fresh pair, especially after the feeling of wooziness that had just come over me. Perhaps if I rinsed the glove in the washroom I would be able to remove the stain.

I went into the little room off the foyer and turned on the brass faucet, wetting a cloth. Then I took the cloth and began to work at the crimson smudge. After a bit of difficulty and the application of some soap, the lipstick began to come out. It seemed as though it was going to be all right, after all.

The red hadn't ruined the pale fabric. I was glad, for I had wanted these gloves particularly, and Winnelda fussed when I ruined my gloves.

"Gloves don't grow on trees, madam," she had told me once with uncharacteristic severity when I had snagged one of very delicate lace. Indeed, she was right.

As I worked on restoring the glove, I heard the sound of the front door opening, and wondered who it might be. I certainly hadn't heard the bell. Perhaps Tabitha had decided to meet me here rather than at the shop. I would find out as soon as I had completed my impromptu laundering.

I was nearly satisfied that I had removed the stain in a way that would pass even Winnelda's rigid standards and turned to leave the washroom, but it was just then I heard footsteps coming from the direction of Mr. Alden's study.

"Palmer. Good," Mr. Alden said. "I want

to talk to you while no one is here." So it was Mr. Palmer who had come in. What was he doing here? Perhaps he had come to finish last night's conversation with Tom, but I was a bit surprised that Mr. Palmer had come in without ringing the bell. Then again, he seemed to enjoy informality.

I was just about to make my presence known, but Mr. Palmer's next words stopped me short.

"I came as soon as I got your summons. But aren't you afraid we might be caught?" There was something mocking in the words, but I recognized the truth in them. Mr. Alden did not want the two of them to be seen together.

"It will only take a moment. It's urgent." There was annoyance underlying his tone, but he was doing his best to suppress it. I found this interesting. From all I had seen, these two men had a casual relationship at best. Why, then, did they want to avoid being linked in some way?

"Very well. I'm all ears, Mr. Alden."

I had expected them to move into Mr. Alden's study, but it seemed that they were going to conduct business right there in the foyer.

I was effectively a prisoner in the washroom. I couldn't make my exit now without letting them know that I had already over-heard part of this delicate conversation. There was nothing for me to do but stay still and remain quiet until they had gone. I shifted backward, retreating a bit farther behind the door so I wouldn't risk being seen.

"It's got to be kept quiet," Mr. Alden said in a harsh whisper. "I've been hearing things, that word is getting around, and that's not going to work."

"I don't have any control over that."

"Well, you'd better find some way to control it, or both of our livelihoods will be on the line." His voice had risen as he spoke, and I remembered how angry he had looked last night when he had thrown the strange man from his house.

"Don't get worked up, Mr. Alden. Things are going along much as we planned, despite the setbacks." Grant Palmer sounded more amused than alarmed, though there was nothing humorous in Mr. Alden's voice.

"Listen to me, Grant. I'm serious. If there is trouble, it's going to be you who pays for it. Not me. Do you understand?"

My eyes widened at what sounded very much like a threat. Of course, I didn't know what sort of business these men had been conducting.

I could hear the smile in Grant Palmer's voice as he answered. "Tabitha's been warning me to stay away from you, you know. She thinks I'm a bad influence."

"You leave Tabitha out of this."

"I'm just telling you, she knows more than you think."

"Let me worry about her. Come here, to my office."

They walked down the hall then, and I slipped out of the washroom, feeling uneasy. What had that conversation meant? It had all been very vague, but there had been the definite hint of something sinister in their interaction. Was Mr. Alden indeed involved in a bootlegging operation? Things seemed to point in that direction.

I very much wished I hadn't overheard the conversation, but there wasn't much I could do about it now. I wondered if I should mention it to Tabitha or keep it to myself for the time being.

I moved back to the staircase and moved quietly halfway up before making my way back down with a heavy tread.

I heard footsteps approaching and Mr. Palmer appeared at the foot of the staircase just as I reached the foyer.

"Oh, hello." I fancied I sounded just the right amount of surprised to see him.

"Hello, Mrs. Ames. You're looking very nice this morning. Pretty as a ripe peach."

"Thank you. I'm just going to meet Tabitha."

"She's let Tom out of her sight for a few hours, eh?"

"Mr. Smith and my husband have gone to the races, I believe."

"Ah, yes. Tom's fond of horses. The racing variety, at least."

It was then that Mr. Alden made his appearance. Apparently, he had heard Grant Palmer and I talking and had come to investigate why the young man had not yet left the premises.

"Oh, hello, Grant. What are you doing here?" In my opinion, Mr. Alden did not sound quite as authentically surprised to see Mr. Palmer as I had.

"We're just having a little chat." Mr. Palmer leaned one elbow against the balustrade, the picture of comfortable ease.

"I suppose you came here looking for Tom," Mr. Alden said. "He and Tabitha aren't expected back until late this afternoon."

"So Mrs. Ames was telling me."

"I suppose you've got things to tend to, Grant?" Mr. Alden said.

He smiled. "Not really, but I know when

I'm not wanted. I'll just go somewhere where I'll be more welcome. Nice talking with you, Mrs. Ames."

"Good afternoon, Mr. Palmer."

Without another word to Mr. Alden, he turned and ambled unhurriedly from the house.

Mr. Alden's eyes followed him, and there was an expression of unconcealed annoyance on his face. I wondered if his dislike of the man extended beyond whatever business dealings they had been discussing. Granted, Mr. Palmer seemed irresponsible and glib, but there was nothing inherently dislikable about him.

At last, he seemed to remember that I was still standing at the base of the stairs and turned toward me. "I hope he wasn't annoying you."

"Oh, no," I said. "He's quite an interesting young man."

He chuckled, but I could tell it was forced. "That's one way of putting it."

"I wouldn't have imagined he and Mr. Smith would be very good friends," I said.

"I don't know what Tom sees in Grant. I told Tabitha we'd be better off not having him around, but she didn't want to upset Tom and I didn't want to upset her."

I could see that he had always been very

careful of Tabitha's feelings. He doted on her and tried to give her everything her heart desired. I hoped, somewhat cynically, that Tom would be up to the task.

"He does seem to be very . . . carefree."

"He's a nuisance. I hope that Tabitha and Tom will have very little to do with him after they're married. But enough of that," Mr. Alden said. "I don't mean to delay you. You're going out?"

"Yes, I'm meeting Tabitha to do some shopping."

"Well, you girls have a good time."

A short while later found Tabitha and me entering a fashionable department store in Herald Square. A steady flow of well-dressed shoppers moved in the brass revolving doors, exchanging the noise of streets, with the rumble of the train on the elevated Sixth Avenue line high above, for the cool, quiet interior where a plethora of sophisticated wares were laid out for our perusal.

We passed through the makeup department, marble floors glowing in the bright light cast by crystal chandeliers, its gleaming glass cases holding a treasure trove of cosmetic products which seemed to twinkle invitingly. Next was the perfume department, the air sweet with the mingled fragrances of a dozen perfumes, elegant sales-girls offering to spritz us with scent as we passed. Tabitha accepted a sample, but I declined as I was already wearing my own perfume, which I had acquired in a recent trip to Paris.

Then we made our way through handker-chiefs and handbags, an astounding array available for the asking, and arrived at last at our destination: the shoe department. It seemed to me that any type of footwear a woman might desire was there on counters and shelves and table displays. Plush leather chairs and sofas were arranged atop a pale pink rug, enticing one to sit and try on shoes before parading them before the mirrors that appeared at intervals.

"Mr. Palmer came to the house this morning," I told Tabitha as we stopped before a tastefully arranged display of evening shoes. "He was looking for Tom."

Tabitha turned from her examination of a pair of satin evening slippers, her eyes narrowed. "Was Dad home?"

I hesitated. "Yes. They spoke briefly, I believe." Mr. Palmer had insinuated to Mr. Alden that Tabitha knew more than she pretended to. Though she had told me that Grant Palmer was trying to draw her father into some sort of business deal, was she aware that their transactions had apparently gone further than that?

I debated on telling her what I had overheard, but I really felt that it was not my place to do so, not, at least, until I knew something definite.

But she needed no encouragement from me to jump to conclusions. "He's up to no good," she said hotly. "If Grant is dragging Dad into something, I'll make sure he pays for it."

She suddenly seemed to realize her level of intensity, for she gave a little laugh and looked around to make sure we had not been overheard by any of the other shoppers. When her gaze came back to me, some of the fire in her eyes had flickered away. "Oh, well. I'm sure it's nothing. As you said, he came to see Tom, though I don't know why he's always bothering Tom when we're so busy. We don't have time for him right now, as well he knows. The wedding will be here soon, and I need Tom to pay attention to all that's happening. I feel like the bridegroom is always terribly inattentive. Was it that way with Mr. Ames?" she asked.

I thought back to that brief, whirlwind period before our marriage.

"Oh, yes. Milo didn't care about the wedding at all. He only wanted to be done with it."

He had tried to convince me to elope with him, in fact. I had been sorely tempted, but I had not wanted to hear my mother chide me about it for the rest of my life, and so the wedding had gone on.

The planning had been a bit complicated, as I had already been in the process of planning my wedding to another man when I met Milo. When I broke off my initial engagement, it hadn't seemed right to me to carry on with the same wedding arrangements with an alternate man. So I had chosen a different dress, different flowers, different music.

It had been a different wedding with a different groom, but in my mind everything was just as I had always hoped it would be.

I was glad now that we hadn't eloped. I looked back on the memories fondly, and the photograph held a place of honor on the mantel in our London flat. My wedding gown still hung in a wardrobe at Thornecrest, our country house.

"I know it must all be terribly boring to Tom," Tabitha went on, drawing me from my reflections, "but I want to feel like he has some sort of interest in things." She sighed as she picked up another shoe from the display. "Half the time I'm excited for the wedding, and half the time I can't wait for it to be over."

We went on to talk about wedding details then, each trying on half a dozen pairs of shoes before we both selected the ones we would wear for the wedding, but the conversation between Mr. Alden and Mr. Palmer was still very much on my mind, as was the look of fury that had passed through Tabitha's eyes when I had mentioned it.

8

As we began our return journey through the busy streets, Tabitha pointed at one of the towering granite skyscrapers a few blocks ahead of us.

"That's where Rudy works," she said.

"Oh, really? It's an impressive building."

"Yes. I know we tease Rudy about his enthusiasm for his job, but he's very good at it."

"Have you ever been to his office?" I asked, remembering how he had invited me to pay him a visit.

"Once or twice. It's very hectic in there, like a beehive or something." An idea struck her suddenly. "Should we stop and see him?"

"May we? I'm intrigued by it all."

"Rudy will love it," Tabitha said. She leaned toward the driver. "Pull over up here, will you, Bates?"

The car pulled to a stop in front of the

building, and Tabitha and I alighted from the car and went inside. The expansive lobby was done in dark marble with Art Deco brass fixtures and grillwork. It was both stately and modern, quiet and busy, as both men and women in well-tailored suits moved with purpose to and from a wall of lifts. Tabitha led the way there, and we entered one that several people had just vacated, Tabitha giving the operator our desired floor.

"We probably won't be able to stay long," she told me as we moved upward for what seemed like an age. "Rudy's bound to be busy. You'll see what I mean. Everyone always looks like they don't have a moment to spare."

Her words were entirely accurate. The lift opened into a vast room full of desks at which men and women of every description seemed to be working furiously at typewriters, speaking into telephones, or rifling through piles of paperwork. There was the murmur of conversation in the air and the clack and ding of what seemed to be scores of typewriters. The room smelled of ink and burnt coffee and freshly sharpened pencils.

Tabitha gave a little wave to a woman who sat at one of the foremost desks, a receptionist of some sort, it seemed. Apparently, she was familiar with Tabitha, for she gave a little nod and a slight smile before returning her focus to whatever task lay before her.

"This way," Tabitha said, moving with confidence down a small aisle that moved through two rows of desks.

We found Rudy Elliot sitting at a desk, much more spacious than the others, in the corner of the room. On the wall behind him were several posters of various very good print ads, including one for Samson's Salad Dressing. I was impressed by the quality of the artwork, but it did not hold my attention for long. His desk was situated near a window that looked out over the stunning New York City skyline. I was rather afraid that, if I sat in such a place, I would get very little work done. Rudy Elliot, however, did not seem to have this problem. He was bent over a stack of papers on his desk, making rapid notes with a pencil.

"Hello, Rudy," Tabitha said.

He looked up, vaguely surprised to see us, and rose at once from his desk, his face breaking into a smile. "Mrs. Ames, Tabitha! To what do I owe this delightful surprise?"

"We were just passing by and thought we'd stop in to say hello," Tabitha said.

"I must say, this is all very impressive," I told him, looking again around the room and then out the window at the city laid out before us. "I do hope we're not interrupting, though?"

"No, no. Not at all. I'm just working on the wording of one of our new radio ads."

He held up a sheet of paper. It was typewritten, but I could see where he had scratched through it in several places with his pencil and scrawled notes in the margins.

"We're airing it this week, during a popular new show called *The Lone Ranger,* and we want it to be perfect."

"Well, hello, ladies."

We looked up, both surprised, I think, to see Grant Palmer. While we hadn't noticed his approach, I saw that several of the women in the typing bank had, for their typing had momentarily slowed as they watched him saunter toward Rudy's desk.

"Hello, Grant," Tabitha said, just a bit stiffly. I could tell at once that she didn't mean to confront him about his conversation with her father now, but it seemed her anger still simmered beneath the surface. "We dropped in to see Rudy."

"Still reeling them in with the salad dressing, eh?"

Rudy smiled. "Some people take an interest in my work."

"As they should, my friend. As they

should."

"And what are you doing here?" Tabitha asked Mr. Palmer.

"The same as you. Stopping by to see Rudy."

I looked at Mr. Elliot. It seemed to me that he looked a bit uncomfortable. I wonder if he disliked being caught up in the undercurrent of antagonism between Tabitha and Mr. Palmer. He seemed the sort of man who would avoid conflict if possible.

"Well, I suppose we'll be on our way," Tabitha said. "We'll see you both soon."

"Sure thing," Grant Palmer said.

"I'll look forward to hearing more about your radio advertisement, Mr. Elliot," I said.

"Thanks, Mrs. Ames."

We left then, and it was not until we reached the lift that Tabitha let out a frustrated sigh. "That Grant," she said. "Always showing up where he isn't wanted."

We returned to the house. I hoped that Milo would be back early enough that I could talk with him about his time with Tom as well as the conversation I had overheard between Mr. Alden and Mr. Palmer, but it seemed that he and Mr. Smith had been having an excellent time at the races, for they didn't arrive back until just before dinner.

The rest of us had just met in the drawing room, and Milo had just enough time to go up and change.

"You're not going to stay for dinner?" Tabitha asked Tom as he made his excuses at the drawing room door.

"I'm not dressed."

"Oh, you know we don't stand on formality around here."

"Just the same. I'd like to go home and freshen up. May I come back and take you dancing tonight?"

She smiled. "I would like that."

He dropped a discreet kiss on her cheek and took his leave then, and a few minutes later Milo returned and we went into the dining room.

Despite her affectionate parting with Tom, there was an air of tension at the dinner table that seemed to originate from Tabitha. I wondered if it had something to do with Tom's declining to dine with us. Surely she wouldn't be upset over something so trivial. Especially not when he was going to return to take her dancing. No, there was something else that seemed to be on her mind.

She was talking too much, as though trying to cover for the silence, and her eyes were too bright with some suppressed emotion.

It took me a while to notice that Mr. Alden, too, seemed preoccupied. Though he smiled and gave the appropriate answers at the right places in the conversation, it was clear that his mind was on something else, for he made no effort to contribute to the topic.

Had he and Tabitha had a falling out? Perhaps she had confronted him about Grant Palmer's visit to the house this morning. I wondered if I oughtn't to have mentioned it to her.

"Did you and Tom have a nice time today?" Tabitha asked Milo when we were on the third course. Something about the overly casual way she asked the question made me wonder if she had some misgivings about their activities.

I glanced at Milo. His expression was, as ever, the picture of perfect unflustered innocence. I knew very well, however, that this did not mean their afternoon had been uneventful.

"We went to the races," he said. "It was an amusing enough way to spend the day."

"I suppose Tom lost a bit of money." There it was again, the fragile cheeriness in her voice. I noticed that Mr. Alden looked up from his plate at the question.

Milo took a measured drink of his wine before answering. "As a matter of fact, I think he was rather successful."

"Well, I'm glad for him. Maybe he'll put some of his winnings toward our wedding trip." She laughed at this and then changed the subject.

The rest of dinner passed quietly, but my mind was still on Tabitha's behavior and her reference to Tom's losing money. Was Tom prone to gambling? If so, I hoped it wasn't going to be a habit that would prove detrimental to their marriage. I reminded myself again that Tabitha had a good head on her shoulders and that I shouldn't be intruding in matters that didn't concern me, but that didn't alleviate my concern.

Milo and Mr. Alden enjoyed their after-dinner drinks at the table, and Tabitha and I listened to the wireless in the drawing room while we drank our coffee. We chatted over more of the wedding details and she spoke in her usual lively manner, the tension at dinner seeming to evaporate now that the two of us were alone.

I had yet to decide how to approach the subject of Tom and gambling when Calvin, the butler, came into the room. "Mr. Smith is on the phone for you, Miss Tabitha."

I saw something flash across Tabitha's face. Worry? Annoyance? I couldn't be sure.

"I suppose he's going to say he can't take me out after all," she said. "Well, that's all right. We can go out dancing any night."

She left the room and I was left to contemplate the vague sense of uneasiness hanging over me. Though I couldn't quite put my finger on the cause of it, I had the feeling that something, somewhere, was very wrong.

A moment later, she came back, her expression one of happiness. "He's been detained. He's going to meet me at the nightclub. Will you and Milo come dancing with us?"

"It's sweet of you to offer, but I think perhaps we'll stay in tonight and let you two have some time alone." I didn't normally speak on Milo's behalf, but I felt confident that he would not be annoyed that I had circumvented another trip to a liquorless nightclub.

"Very well. If you're sure," Tabitha said, making no argument to my excuses. No doubt she would be glad to have Tom to herself for the evening. I didn't blame her, for I well-remembered the thrill of a night out alone with my handsome fiancé, the lingering caresses on the dance floor after the music had stopped and stolen kisses on moonlit balconies. The world had seemed to lay before us, shimmering with the promise of happiness.

I felt again that tinge of uneasiness, but I pushed it down.

"Will you be all right going to the night-club alone?" I asked.

"Oh, yes. I'll catch a cab at the end of the street. I do it all the time."

With that assurance, I said good night, excused myself, and went to my room. My mind was spinning with everything I had learned today: the strange conversation between Mr. Alden and Mr. Palmer, as well as Tabitha's annoyance about Grant Palmer's visit to her father and her seeming preoccupation at dinner. I would be glad to be able to discuss things with Milo.

I had just finished preparing for bed and, too anxious to lie down, had sat on the little sofa near the fireplace when he came in.

"You're up sooner than I thought you'd be," I remarked.

"Mr. Alden was going out."

"Out?" I repeated, surprised. "Where?"

"He didn't say. I thought you'd be in bed, darling."

"I've been waiting to talk to you," I said, my mind still half focused on Mr. Alden's departure. "First, did you learn anything about Tom this afternoon?"

"Somehow I thought that might be your first question. I hate to disappoint you, but he let absolutely nothing slip about his mysterious past."

I ignored the sarcasm in this response and, realizing I was not going to get anywhere with that subject, moved on. "There were a few things I found out this afternoon that are troubling me."

"Oh?" He didn't sound particularly intrigued, but I was undaunted and plunged ahead as he began to remove his evening clothes.

"Yes, first there was a conversation between Mr. Alden and Mr. Palmer." I related the conversation I had overheard as well as the circumstances leading up to my hearing it. "It seemed to me as though they were involved in some sort of secretive scheme together."

"That is a bit strange," Milo admitted. "I've never seen them have anything more than the most superficial sort of conversations, as though they were practically strangers."

"Exactly. So what was it that they were speaking so strongly about? Why keep their relationship a secret?"

"Then again, why make it any of our business?" he asked.

"You made Mr. Alden your business when you invested in his company," I pointed out. "If he's doing something underhanded with Mr. Palmer, it would behoove you to find out about it."

"All right. But I don't suppose we need to worry about it tonight." He had finished dressing in his nightclothes and moved toward the bed.

"What are you doing?"

He paused, looking back at me. "I'm getting into bed."

I glanced at the clock. "Since when do you fall asleep at this hour?"

"Well, I didn't intend to fall asleep the minute my head hits the pillow." He got into bed and pulled the covers back on my side invitingly. "In fact, if you'd like to join me, I'll keep you up as late as you like."

"Do be serious, Milo."

His brows rose. "I am serious."

I sighed.

"You needn't look so cross, darling," he said wryly, settling back against his pillows. "I withdraw all suggestions of seduction."

I gave him an apologetic smile. "I'm very tired, Milo. It's been a busy day."

"All the more reason for you to lie down."

I couldn't argue with this bit of logic, though I felt the unreasoning urge to. With another little sigh of defeat, I went to the bed.

"It's just that I'm so worried," I said, sliding beneath the covers.

"Try not to worry tonight. Get some rest, and we'll examine things in the morning."

I found this to be an appealing suggestion. I lay down, and Milo drew me against him.

I was glad we had decided not to go out tonight. Milo had an excessively social personality, and it was not often we found ourselves spending quiet evenings at home. I was beginning to think that when we returned to England we might do well to spend some time at Thornecrest. It would be nice to sit there with Milo before the crackling fire during the cool autumn nights, sipping our tea and listening to the wireless or reading.

Of course, Milo was likely to be bored by this plan and would no doubt swiftly find some excuse to run off to London. It was nice to imagine it, though.

Unfortunately, I didn't have much time to contemplate the idyllic scene or wonder why I was suddenly becoming so nostalgic for a quiet country life.

Outside the house, there was a sudden loud shout, followed by the unmistakable sound of gunfire.

9

There were four or five shots fired in rapid succession followed by a moment of deafening silence.

I jumped up from the bed, but Milo had beaten me to it, motioning me to stay back while he moved toward the window. The lace curtains suddenly seemed like a very flimsy defense against whatever was lurking out there in the darkness.

He pulled one of them back and glanced outside. I could make out the reflection of his face in the glass, his eyes scanning the street below.

"Do you see anything?" I asked, pulling on my dressing gown.

He shook his head. "No. I can't see much from here."

"I wonder if we should ring the police," I said, a feeling of dread filling me.

"I imagine someone will," Milo replied. "I don't suppose this neighborhood is used to that sort of commotion."

If they were unused to that, then they were probably wholly unprepared for the shrieks that suddenly began to emanate from the streets below. My stomach clenched at the pure terror in them, the hair rising on my arms.

Milo grabbed his own dressing gown and pulled it on as he started for the door without hesitation. "You'd better stay here, Amory."

This didn't deserve a reply, so I said nothing as I followed him from the room.

We hurried down the hall and descended the stairs.

The screaming had stopped by the time we reached the bottom of the stairs, and somehow the silence seemed almost more unsettling. We found Calvin, the butler, standing with the door open, staring at something outside. We crossed the marble-floored foyer to look past him, and I sucked in a breath at the scene before us.

Tabitha, who had apparently been the source of the screaming, knelt on the front steps beside a body that lay facedown. Was it Tom?

My heart seized at the thought, the shock of it hitting me almost like a physical blow.

But then, something began to make its

way through the haze of adrenaline. I realized that the figure lying on the stairs was not tall enough to be Tom.

Who was it, then? He wore a camel-colored coat and a dark fedora. I thought at first that the coat was dirty, but then I realized that it was dotted with black holes. And there was something dark seeping from them, giving the impression that the holes were swiftly widening.

My stomach clenched again.

All of this happened in the space of a moment, though it seemed to me as though time had slowed to an almost excruciating degree.

Then Tabitha looked up at me, tears streaked across her pretty face. "It's Grant."

Grant Palmer? What had he been doing here at this hour? What was more, who might have wanted to shoot him on the Aldens' doorstep?

Milo, ever calm in a crisis, moved beside the body and reached down to feel for a pulse on his throat.

"We've got to help him," Tabitha said, looking from Milo to me to Calvin, then back at the prone figure.

Milo looked up at me and shook his head. So Mr. Palmer was dead. I'd already suspected as much, but the confirmation caused another jolt in my chest.

"We've got to move him inside," Tabitha said, her voice rising slightly, though she was talking to no one in particular. "We've got to call for a doctor."

Milo's eyes were still on mine, calming me with their steadiness, silently communicating what needed to be done. I drew in a breath.

"Come here, dear," I said gently, moving to Tabitha's side. She was obviously in shock — I could see her entire body trembling — and the best thing I could do was to remove her from the scene. We couldn't help Grant Palmer now.

I took one of her arms and Milo took the other, and we helped her to her feet.

"He shouldn't be lying on his face," she said. "He needs to be moved."

"I'll take care of him," Milo said. "Go inside with Amory, Tabitha."

There was something calming yet slightly authoritative about Milo's tone that seemed to break through her stupor. She looked at him and nodded. "All right. Yes . . . all right."

I held her arm as we negotiated our way back up the stairs. Poor Tabitha was forced to step over one of Mr. Palmer's arms, flung out across the top step.

"Ring for the police, will you, Calvin?" Milo asked the butler as we reached the door. He still stood stiffly where he had been when we had descended the stairs, as though frozen, his face ashen. Milo's request seemed to recall him to his duty, however, and he nodded.

"Yes, sir," he said, turning to go back inside.

As Tabitha entered the house, I took one last look over my shoulder.

Grant Palmer lay motionless on the stairs, blood pooling beneath him and dripping down to the next step. The handsome, carefree young man was gone forever.

It seems that my life is a carousel that, instead of brass rings, always brings me back to the moment when stern-faced policemen are asking me questions.

There were two officers in this case. One was a tall, heavyset man of middle age with a dark complexion and even darker eyes who had introduced himself as Detective Andrews. His black hair was sprinkled with silver, and he looked as though he hadn't shaved that morning, or perhaps even the day before. Nor had his suit been pressed. It was a bit rumpled, as was the trench coat he wore over it. Overall, he gave the impression that he had been working for quite some time without rest.

His partner was called Detective Bailey. In contrast to Detective Andrews, he was tall, thin, and fair, his most distinguishing feature the unusual color of his eyes. They were a pale, clear green, like pieces of bottle glass worn smooth by the sea. There was something calming about his gaze, though something searching, too, I thought.

They interviewed us each in turn. Andrews asked most of the questions, while Bailey listened and watched.

I thought neither of them looked at all shocked by what had occurred here. Detective Andrews in particular seemed completely unfazed. If anything, he appeared slightly put out that it had no doubt required him to stay on duty longer than he had planned. His manner was brusque as he asked what seemed to me a series of perfunctory questions.

I really hadn't much to tell. After all, I had only heard the shots. Everyone in the general vicinity had likely done the same. This was apparent by the number of people who had begun pooling from their houses by the time the police had arrived, subjecting Grant Palmer to the indignity of having his bullet-riddled body gaped at by most of the neighborhood.

It was just toward the end of the interview that Detective Bailey asked his first question, something that seemed to hit a bit closer to the mark than Detective Andrews's inquiries.

"Did you know that Mr. Palmer was going to be coming to the house tonight?"

I shook my head. "No. I hadn't heard that he was coming."

"Who might he have been coming to see?"

I looked at him. I wasn't sure why he had asked this question. Surely it didn't matter who Mr. Palmer had been coming to see. No one in the house had killed him . . . had they?

It occurred to me suddenly that no one but Milo and I had been at the house when the murder occurred. Mr. Alden had gone out, and Tabitha had been attempting to catch a cab at the corner when she heard the shots. If someone in the Aldens' circle had wanted to kill Mr. Palmer, they might have done it. I was not going to mention this to these detectives, however. They seemed clever, and I was sure they could work this out for themselves.

I answered tactfully. "He was a close friend of Mr. Tom Smith and a member of the wedding party. It's my understanding that he's been here quite often as of late."

"Even at this hour?" Detective Andrews asked. He had a very casual way of asking questions, as though the answers weren't particularly important. But I knew better than that. He was getting at something. But what?

"I've only been here a few days. I'm not very familiar with the patterns of the house."

He watched me for just an instant longer than he might have had he found my answer unremarkable, and I thought that he must not believe me.

"Is there anything else you have to add?" he asked at last.

"No, I don't think so."

"No idea who might have killed him?"

"Certainly not." I answered the question automatically, but I paused as a thought came to me. "Although . . ."

He waited.

"It was my understanding that Mr. Palmer was involved in some way with bootleggers."

If he found this interesting, he gave no sign of it. In fact, I rather had the impression that he was amused. "Involved how?"

"I don't know. It was just a rumor I heard."

"From who?"

I hesitated. Well, I supposed he would find

out anyway. He was a detective, after all. "From Miss Alden."

"Did she mention any particular gangster?" Detective Bailey asked, those pale green eyes watching me with an unreadable expression. Detective Andrews, meanwhile, smirked.

"Leon De Lora, I believe. But I don't know much else. Perhaps she can give you more details."

Detective Andrews gave a short nod. "Okay. I think you can go, Mrs. Ames. I'll let you know if I have any more questions."

"Very well." I rose to leave and he stood, a bit stiffly it seemed, and walked me to the door. Detective Bailey remained where he was, seemingly lost in thought.

They were an odd pair, and I happily left them and went back to the sitting room where Milo sat with Tabitha on the cornflower-blue sofa.

Milo's eyes met mine in the way he had of assessing my feelings at a glance, and I gave him the barest of smiles to let him know that I was all right.

They were drinking coffee that a pallid but stoic Calvin had brought to us in a silver pot. I wasn't sure we needed any additional stimulation at the moment, but it was nice to have something to do with one's hands.

"I just don't know who could've done this," Tabitha said. She was still pale, and I had noticed the trembling of her hands when she had come from her interview with the detectives. She had not had the past experience with the police that I had, and even I had found the men a bit unnerving. There was something very intense about the combination of Detectives Andrews and Bailey.

I had just taken a seat and picked up my cup of now-cold coffee when Mr. Alden arrived home. We heard him before we saw him, the raised sound of his voice and the heavy footsteps pounding along the hallway.

The body had already been moved, but I assumed the police were mulling about the premises, and no doubt the blood was still pooled on the front steps. In seeing the uproar that was taking place on the stoop of his house, he had hurried inside, calling Tabitha's name.

"I'm here, Dad," she called, rising from her seat.

"Tabitha . . . thank God." His face was white, and he reached out to grip the door frame of the sitting room as though to steady himself.

"I'm all right, Dad," she said, going quickly to his side. He embraced her, and I thought that he looked limp with relief.

"What's going on?" he asked at last. "What happened?"

His eyes moved to Milo and me over Tabitha's shoulder, looking to us for answers. It was Tabitha who broke the news to him, however.

"It's Grant," she said, drawing back to look up at him. "He's been killed. Oh, Dad . . ."

She dissolved then into the tears that she had been holding back since I had found her kneeling by Grant Palmer's body. Mr. Alden held her close, patting her back in a distracted way.

I had watched his face carefully as she said the words, but there was very little reaction. He did not seem shocked.

Detective Andrews came in behind him a moment later, no doubt drawn by the commotion.

"You're the owner of this house?"

Mr. Alden looked over his shoulder. "Yes," he said distractedly, releasing Tabitha and turning to face him. "Yes, I'm Benjamin Alden."

"I need to have a few words with you."

Mr. Alden drew in a breath, summoning his focus, and nodded. "Of course."

"I think that'll be all for now, Mr. and

Mrs. Ames, Miss Alden," Detective Andrews said, glancing at us. "I don't need anything more from the rest of you for the time being. You can go to bed now if you wish."

With that, he turned and left the room. Mr. Alden cast one last glance over his shoulder at Tabitha, gave her a somewhat bewildered smile, and then followed the detective from the room.

It was Milo who broke the silence. "Well," he said, rising from his seat. "We may as well try to get some rest."

"I don't know how we possibly . . ." Tabitha's voice broke as fresh tears filled her eyes.

I moved to her side, sliding an arm around her shoulders. "I know it's been a terrible shock, dear, but things will look better in the morning. There's nothing more that can be done tonight."

"I . . . I suppose you're right. I wish . . . I wish Tom was here." She looked as though she wanted to cry again, but she managed to suppress it.

"Shall we telephone him?" I asked.

We had considered doing so immediately after the tragedy but, given the lateness of the hour and the fact that the police had been ever-present, as though watching our every movement, Tabitha had decided to wait to deliver the news that his best man had been murdered. I was surprised, however, he had not telephoned or come to the house when Tabitha hadn't met him for dancing as planned.

"No," she said. "I'll call him in the morning."

"Do you want me to come and sit with you, then?" I asked. Truth be told, what I wanted more than anything else was to lie down in my own bed without moving for the next twenty-four hours. But if Tabitha needed my company, I would give it to her. I knew well the trauma of discovering a body.

She considered for a moment and then shook her head. "No. I'll be all right. Thank you."

We all went up the stairs together and Tabitha gave me a quick hug before she disappeared into her room.

It was nearly three o'clock in the morning as Milo and I returned to our bedroom. I felt weary to the bone. Weary and terribly sad. It was not the first time I had been witness to a senseless death, but no amount of exposure to such a thing could lessen the impact. I wondered how policemen did it, seeing death day after day. They always seemed so unaffected by it, but I supposed one never knew what went on beneath the surface.

I dropped into the little sofa with a heavy sigh. What a dreadful evening this had been.

I felt sorry for Mr. Palmer. He had been a scoundrel, perhaps, but he certainly hadn't deserved this. What was more, I was certain there had been some hint of a vulnerable young man beneath that careless, carefree façade. Now we would never have the chance to discover what else he might have been.

"Are you all right, darling?" Milo asked, coming up behind me and putting a hand on my shoulder.

"Yes, I'm all right." I reached up to cover his hand with mine, relishing the contact, the steadiness I somehow felt I was deriving from the warm pressure against my shoulder.

"Do you want to go to bed?"

I shook my head. "Not just yet. I won't be able to sleep."

He came around the sofa to sit beside me, his arm sliding around me, and I leaned into him, resting my head on his shoulder. For a moment, neither of us spoke.

"I wonder if someone has told Tom already," I said at last. I knew the young man was likely to be very upset by the death of his friend. I hoped that Tabitha would be the one who was able to give him the news, rather than some unsympathetic policeman.

"I imagine he'll find out soon enough."

"I wonder what this will mean for the wedding." It was the first time this aspect had crossed my mind. Would they go on with things now that the best man was dead? I wasn't exactly sure what the proper etiquette might be in this situation.

I supposed that wasn't the most pertinent thing to consider at present, but I couldn't help but think about it. I stared into the fireplace, the implications of what had happened swirling through my head in a kaleidoscope of jagged, ugly thoughts.

"Amory, look at me," Milo said gently.

I pulled my eyes from the fireplace to look into his. "The weight of all of this is not yours to bear."

"But . . ."

"No," he said. "You don't have to take it all on yourself."

I knew he was right, in a way. But that didn't stop me from feeling that I needed to do something.

"I'm too tired to think about it anymore," I said, feeling as though I was on the verge of tears.

"Yes, I think you're overwrought. Come. Let's go to bed."

He stood and helped me to my feet. I felt suddenly as though I was very old.

"Poor Mr. Palmer." A stray tear slipped down my cheek. "I'm sorry for him."

Milo reached over to wipe my tear away, his hand resting on my face. "Whatever else it was, it was quick."

I nodded. That was something at least. From the position of his body, it appeared he had lain where he had fallen. At least he hadn't suffered.

"Why do you suppose bodies are always turning up wherever we go?"

"I suppose the most likely answer is that we are unknowing harbingers of the Grim Reaper."

"Don't joke, Milo. I can't bear it."

"Death happens, darling. We just happen to travel along the same path occasionally."

I supposed that was as good an answer as any. He was wrong about one thing, though. I did feel as though I needed to take this on myself. I hadn't the energy to argue with him about it tonight, but I knew already that, in one way or another, I was going to have to help discover who had killed Grant Palmer.

We got into bed, and I moved close to

Milo, who drew me against him. Feeling safe in his arms, I pushed the horror of the evening from my thoughts and fell into a deep sleep.

10

I slept very late the next morning, though I imagined everyone had after being up for the majority of the night.

Milo was, surprisingly, no longer in bed when I awoke.

I was just about to force myself to get up when there was a tap on the door.

"Come in," I called.

"Oh, madam," Winnelda breathed, hurrying into the room. "I can't believe there was a murder here!"

I had hoped to avoid thinking about the matter for a few minutes at least, but it seemed it was not to be. I sat up, pushing back my hair from my face. I was trying to think of how best to go about telling her what had happened, but it seemed that Winnelda had no need for my explanations. Apparently, the household gossip network had already been at work, and if there was ever anyone attuned to gossip, it was Winnelda.

She plunged ahead without waiting for me to share any of what I knew.

"They think it has to do with Leon De Lora." She said this with some authority, and I wondered if she already knew something I didn't.

I pushed ahead with my question before she could continue. "What are they saying about Mr. De Lora?"

"Well, Mr. Palmer worked for him, everyone knew that, but then he went away to work for another gangster, one called Frankie Earl, and people think Mr. De Lora may have wanted revenge. And, after all, this is just the way gangsters go about killing each other."

Winnelda had been in New York for all of four days and already appeared to be well-versed on American criminal culture. Of course, I shouldn't have been surprised that she already had a working knowledge of the subject.

I was, frankly, impressed. After all, I had heard nothing of Frankie Earl, or that Mr. Palmer had left Mr. De Lora's employ. Disloyalty did seem as though it might be a valid motive for murder, especially from a gangster's perspective.

"What do you know about Mr. De Lora?" I asked her.

Winnelda had a finely tuned sense of scandal. I suspected she had already picked up the latest New York gossip rags and had begun to familiarize herself with them. I avoided the scandal sheets myself, but I could always count on her for the very latest information and, indeed, information from well into the past. She had an almost encyclopedic knowledge of the rich and famous and all their transgressions.

"Oh, all sorts of things," she said casually.

"You've certainly taken the lay of the land quickly."

"Even back in England I followed a lot of the stories about him. The gossip columns talk about him often. He's very handsome, you know. Like a cinema star."

This I had not expected. The knowledge of the man's illicit activities had conjured up in my mind a menacing figure with sinister features and a cigar clamped between his teeth. Of course, handsomeness and villainy were not mutually exclusive.

"Or perhaps more like a character played by a cinema star," she mused. "A pirate, perhaps. He has a scar on his face, you know. Here." She drew a line with her finger across one cheek, just below the eye. "But I think it gives him a dashing air. A great many cinema stars have been seen in his company, in fact," she said. She then began to recite a list of well-known ladies in the film industry who had been photographed with Mr. De Lora.

"Do you know anything about his past?" I asked, when she had paused for breath.

"They say he grew up very poor and that he was in the war. After that he started bootlegging and became very rich from all his illegal activities. He's credited with a long list of crimes, and his criminal enterprises have caused law enforcement in this city considerable trouble." I began to think she had memorized the articles she had read word-for-word.

"Then why hasn't he been arrested?" I asked.

"Oh, he's much too clever for that," she said. "Everyone seems to know that he's responsible for a great many wicked things, but there is never any way to prove it. He always has someone else do the deeds, you see."

"Yes, I do see," I said. I wondered if he had had someone else do the deed of killing Grant Palmer.

"He owns a speakeasy called De Lora's," Winnelda went on. "That's where they sell illegal alcohol. All the famous people enjoy going there."

I tucked this bit of information away, feeling it might prove useful in the future.

"And the feeling is that he might have wanted to kill Mr. Palmer for leaving his employ?" I said.

She nodded as she went about taking a forest-green dress from the wardrobe. "Gangsters do that sort of thing, madam."

It was, on the surface, a rather loose theory but, I supposed, as good a place to start as any.

I paused to consider as a plan began to take shape in my mind. Perhaps this wasn't the wisest course of action. I was in a foreign country, and the murder victim was not anyone with whom I had had a personal connection. All things considered, it might be best to stay out of things and let the police do their job. Especially if it was related to the criminal underworld. I had the feeling that Detectives Andrews and Bailey were perfectly competent men who would do all they could to see that Grant Palmer's killer was brought to justice.

And yet. The instinct to do something was strong.

I pushed aside the satin bedspread and got out of bed, a plan beginning to form.

It couldn't hurt to visit De Lora's. After all, a great many people did so on a regular basis. It was almost de rigueur among the society set. It seemed unlikely that I would be able to find out the truth from one night spent there, but I didn't think any harm could come of it.

Besides, I was curious about this Leon De Lora, the gangster with the film-star looks and the fearsome reputation.

"I wonder what he's really like," I mused.

She shrugged as she began to lay out my clothes. "I imagine he's coarse and dangerous. I certainly wouldn't care to meet him on a dark street. Or anywhere else, for that matter."

There we differed. I was very much interested in meeting Mr. De Lora. In fact, I thought the sooner I was able to make his acquaintance the better.

Though the thought of food wasn't necessarily appealing, I dressed and went downstairs to see about breakfast. The house had a somber quietness to it, as though the tragedy of last night still hung in the air. I went into the dining room and found Tabitha and Tom sitting at the table. They sat very close, talking in low tones, their food apparently untouched on their plates.

Tabitha seemed much more composed than she had been last night. Tom, on the other hand, looked dreadful. He was pale and there were dark circles around his eyes. His normally youthful face seemed to have aged overnight.

He started to rise as I came back into the room, but I held up a hand to stop him. "Don't get up. Please."

He sank tiredly back into his chair.

"I'm very sorry about Mr. Palmer," I told him. "I know he was a very good friend of yours."

"Thank you. It's such a shock."

"Tom came to the house last night when I didn't arrive at the nightclub, but the police wouldn't let him in," Tabitha told me, a frown creasing her brow. "I wish I had known. I would've come out and made them . . ."

"I was just glad to know you were all right," Tom said, reaching out to cover her hand with his. "It was enough to know you were here, safe, with the others."

"What did the police say?" I asked as I went to the sideboard and poured myself a cup of coffee and selected a piece of toast.

"Just that there had been a young man killed. I told them I was Tabitha's fiancé, but they said they were conducting interviews with the family and that I should come back this morning. I didn't know who it could've been. It never occurred to me that it might be Grant . . ."

He swallowed hard, tamping down his emotion, and Tabitha reached out to squeeze his arm.

I sat down on the opposite side of the table and took an automatic bite of my toast and sipped my coffee, thinking it was strange to go about the same morning rituals after someone had lost his life on the doorstep last night.

"I'm glad you came down, Amory," Tabitha said. "We've just been discussing what we should do about the wedding, and we could use someone to talk to. We're both a bit upset at the moment and nothing seems to make sense."

"It would be kind of heartless, wouldn't it?" Tom asked me. "If we went ahead with it as though his death didn't mean anything."

I hesitated. I wasn't sure I wanted to wade into this particular discussion. This was a very private decision, one that would best be made between the two of them.

"Then again, we've already got everything prepared," Tabitha said, preparing to state her case. "We've sent out the invitations. If we change now . . ."

I could see her point. I knew how much

went into such preparations, and it would be very hard to make adjustments at the last moment. However, if Tom didn't feel that he could go on with things after one of his friends had been brutally killed, I didn't think it would do their relationship any good to press him.

"Perhaps it might be best to wait a few days to make that decision," I said at last. "You've both had a shock, and now probably isn't the best time to think about such things."

"You're right, of course," Tabitha said, rising from the table. "Let's go somewhere, Tom. I need to get out of the house. You don't mind, do you, Amory? I don't want to be a bad hostess, but I feel like I'm going to scream if I don't get away for a while."

"I think it would do you good," I agreed.

"Just let me run upstairs and get my coat and purse."

"But those newspapermen . . ." Tom said.

I hadn't considered the possibility that the murder might have drawn the press, but I supposed I was silly to have overlooked it.

"There are reporters outside," Tabitha told me. "They've been taking pictures of the house all morning. It's disgusting."

"They'll follow us if we go out," Tom said. "I had a hard time getting in. They were asking me all sorts of questions."

I felt sorry for the young man. He looked as though a great weight had descended upon him and he wasn't sure how to go about carrying it.

"We'll slip out the back," Tabitha said. "We'll take the old car in the garage and go driving. Please, Tom. I can't bear to stay here all day."

He sighed. "All right. I suppose I could use some fresh air."

"Thank you. I won't be a minute." She dropped a grateful kiss on his cheek and then hurried from the room.

Tom turned to look at me, his mouth forming a wobbly smile. "I suppose it'll do us good to get out for a while. I . . . I almost feel as though I'm in some kind of a bad dream. It's like my head's in a fog."

I nodded. "I know just what you mean. I think it feels a bit unreal to all of us, all the more so to those that were close to Mr. Palmer."

"Yeah," he said. He hesitated for a moment and then added, "I . . . I kind of wonder how Jemma's doing."

I looked up at him. "Jemma?"

He nodded. "Tabitha called her this morning and said she took it all right. That is, Tab said she was surprised and horrified like the rest of us, but not too upset. But I wonder . . ."

"Were she and Mr. Palmer . . . close?" I asked, seizing upon this bit of information. I had had the impression there was something between Mr. Palmer and Miss Petrie, or had been at one time, and it now seemed that perhaps I had been correct.

He looked suddenly uncomfortable. "I . . . I really shouldn't have said anything."

"I won't tell tales," I said lightly.

"Oh, no! That's not what I meant," he replied quickly. "It's just that . . . well, it's a delicate subject. I should've thought before bringing it up."

I smiled at this somewhat outdated sweetness. "I'm not so delicate as all that."

"I think you're a very fine lady," he told me sincerely. That was all well and good, but it wasn't getting me the information I was after. I fought down my impatience.

He seemed to correctly interpret my silence as encouragement to continue, for he cleared his throat and then went on. "They . . . they never seemed to care much for each other, at least as far as I could tell. There was always kind of an antagonism between them. But, a few weeks ago, I dropped Tabitha off at home after a late night out and decided to stop by and see

Grant. I pulled up at his apartment and . . .
I saw Jemma leaving."

I waited for more, but he appeared to be
waiting for my reaction.

Was that all? I was disappointed.

"Perhaps it was all quite innocent," I suggested.

"It was very late," he repeated, and I
understood the implication.

"You never mentioned it to him?" I asked.

He shook his head. "I didn't want to cause
embarrassment. What I mean is that I don't
know why they would hide a relationship
from us unless it was something very . . .
informal. Grant ran around with lots of girls
and often hinted vaguely about his . . .
conquests. If he was trifling with Jemma, I
didn't want to let on that I knew, for her
sake. And that's why I hope she's all right."

"I'm all ready," Tabitha said, appearing in
the doorway. She had donned a gray coat
and green felt hat and had a large black
handbag on one arm. "If we go out through
the back door, I think we can get away
without being seen."

Tom rose from his chair. "You're sure you
don't mind us leaving you here, Amory?"

"Not at all," I assured them.

They said their good-byes and left the
room then and I sat in the silence, nibbling

at my toast. Truth be told, I was glad to have a bit of time alone. My head was swirling with thoughts of all that had already happened, and it seemed that things were getting more complicated by the minute.

It was not until afternoon that Milo returned.

"Where on earth have you been?" I demanded as soon as he found me in the drawing room, where I had been writing letters for want of something better to do.

I had made it my habit not to be the sort of wife who required my husband to constantly account for his whereabouts, but being left alone after a murder had just taken place seemed like a worthy exception.

"I had some business matters to attend to."

"What sort of business?"

"Banking, sending wires, all to do with my investment with Mr. Alden's company. Very dull stuff, darling. It's not as though I've been out amusing myself."

"You might have left me a note," I pointed out, not appeased by this explanation.

"Yes, I might have," he agreed. "Are we alone in the house?"

"I think Mr. Alden is somewhere about." I had not yet seen him today, though I had once or twice heard footsteps in a heavy tread I had taken to be his. He didn't seem to be in the mood for company, and I didn't blame him.

"Will you come upstairs, darling?"

My eyes narrowed at this suggestion. "Milo, I'm not at all in the mood to . . ."

His smile flashed. "To what?"

"To put up with your amorous advances when I am still quite cross with you."

"That's not what I meant, but I welcome the challenge of changing your mind."

I let out an impatient breath. "I'm not going upstairs. I haven't finished writing my letters."

"Suit yourself, darling," he said, turning toward the door. He stopped in the doorway and lowered his voice. "However, I did neglect to mention that I heard a few rumors that might be pertinent to Mr. Palmer's murder, and I thought you'd be interested to hear them."

He left the room then, and I sat obstinately at the writing desk, staring unseeing at the half-finished letter to my mother. I knew very well that Milo was trying to bait me; I did not intend to give in so easily.

I sat there for perhaps five minutes before I roughly folded up the letter in a display of temper no one was there to witness and made my way upstairs.

I reached our room at the same time as Parks, who held the door for me.

"Oh, hello, Parks," Milo said as we entered. "I'm going out tonight, so I'll need you to see to my evening clothes."

"Very good, sir. I was unsure if you'd been needing my services today as you did not ring for my assistance this morning." There was a very definite reproof in Parks's toneless comment, and I was gratified that I was not the only one who found Milo's behavior today to be reproachable.

"I beg your pardon, Parks. I left quite early and didn't wish to disturb Mrs. Ames."

Parks nodded, but it seemed as though he had not yet voiced all of his complaints. "I understand that there was a bit of trouble last night."

It took me a moment to realize he was talking about the murder. Parks was given to understatement.

"Yes, I'm afraid so."

"I heard the commotion but assumed it to be merely some sort of traffic altercation — the backfiring of a car or some such thing — and fell back to sleep. I wish you had awakened me, sir. I might have been of help."

"I appreciate that, but there was really

very little to be done."

"Just the same, sir. I might have been of use. It is my understanding that Mr. Calvin was not at all collected during the crisis." I suspected this was tantamount to treason in Parks's estimation.

"You can't hold him to your own high standards, Parks," Milo said.

"Quite so, sir. Nevertheless, I do wish that next time a crisis occurs you would make me aware of it."

"I shall certainly do so in the future."

"Thank you."

"Have any of the staff had anything interesting to say about what happened last night?" Milo asked.

"I don't much care for gossip, sir," he said with great dignity.

"Of course not."

"However, I couldn't help but overhear some of the discussions, and it seems that the general consensus is that Mr. Palmer was on the wrong side of a criminal gang."

This was much the same as what Winnelda had told me, but his next words caught me by surprise.

"There is, however, a small faction that believes he may have been killed by someone in the household."

"Someone here?" I repeated. "Why should

someone want to kill Mr. Palmer?"

"Mr. Palmer has made some enemies in the house."

"Who, for instance?" Milo asked.

"As to that, I'm afraid the talk was rather vague, sir. It was just a general feeling that he was not much liked and that his murder might be easy to disguise as a, ah, 'gangland killing.' "

"That's very interesting," Milo said. "Thank you, Parks."

"You're most welcome, sir."

Parks turned then and went noiselessly from the room.

When he had gone, I turned to Milo. "Do you think there's anything in that?"

Milo shrugged, sinking into a chair and removing his cigarette case from his pocket. "It's certainly not outside the realm of possibility."

"But surely if someone had wanted to kill him, they might have found a subtler way to do it."

Even as I said the words, I realized how clever it would be to disguise a killing as the result of a dispute with a gangster. Grant Palmer's death would be written off as another crime statistic, attributable to some nameless, faceless assassin, and the real killer would go free.

"I suppose the police will investigate the link to Mr. Palmer's underworld activities," I mused.

"Yes, though I imagine it might be difficult to prove."

"You know," I said slowly, "it could have been someone in the house. After all, he was killed on the Aldens' doorstep. That seems to indicate a connection."

Milo looked at me, his gaze intent. "Did you have someone particular in mind?"

"I don't know," I said, considering. "I think there may have been something between him and Jemma Petrie, perhaps a bit less serious on his side than on hers."

"I would have thought Jemma Petrie would've gone into such a relationship with her eyes open."

Perhaps he was right. We didn't know anything for certain, after all.

Another possibility occurred to me then, an unpleasant one. "I did hear him arguing with Mr. Alden."

I didn't like to think that Tabitha's father might be responsible for such a thing, and he had certainly seemed shaken when he had come into the drawing room after the murder. Nevertheless, we couldn't discount his troubled relationship with Mr. Palmer.

"He wasn't home at the time," I added,

thinking again that it was a bit odd he had decided to go out at that time of night.

"None of them was here," Milo pointed out.

It was the same thought that had occurred to me last night. If we assumed that it was one of the wedding party, then none of them had been at the house when Grant Palmer had been killed. I wondered if any of them could provide outside alibis.

"I also saw Tom and Mr. Palmer quarreling as we left the Topaz Club," I said. That was nothing conclusive, but it would not be the first time that hidden motives had led to murder. "Perhaps things between them were not as friendly as they made them out to be. Of course, the same might be said of Mr. Elliot. Miss Petrie told me they'd argued over a woman."

"It could even have been Tabitha, for that matter."

I looked up at him, surprised. It had never even crossed my mind that Tabitha might be a suspect. "She was at the end of the street, trying to hail a cab."

"So she says. But you recall that her screams began after the shots. Calvin said he heard the screams before he went to open the door. She could easily have shot him and then set about feigning hysteria."

I stared at him. "You don't mean to suggest that Tabitha might have had something to do with it?"

"I don't mean to suggest anything; I merely point out that she might have had the same opportunity as anyone else."

It was, unnervingly, true. I remembered how strongly she had reacted to the idea that Grant Palmer was trying to influence her father, the impression I had had that she would go to great lengths to protect him. But no. I couldn't believe that Tabitha would have done this.

"If only there had been a witness, someone who had been looking outside when the shots sounded . . ." I said.

"Yes, that would have been very convenient," he agreed. "Alas, not everyone enjoys being involved in events that don't concern them."

I didn't miss the little jibe implicit in this comment. Milo often lectured me on getting myself involved in matters that were no concern of mine, but I couldn't seem to help that I was always falling into such things.

Then again, I did go into them willingly. Perhaps other people encountered the scent of mystery in everyday life but opted not to follow the trail. The problem was, I couldn't just ignore it. I had to know what lay at the root of acts of evil. As my mother had once pointed out, there were police to do that sort of thing. However, I had, in the past, been able to provide the police with insights they might not otherwise be able to access. This instance might very well prove the same.

I expected the lecture about how we should let the detectives do their job and not get involved, so Milo's next words surprised me. "I suspect the police are going to focus on Mr. Palmer's underworld connections, but it might benefit us to see if we can clear the members of the wedding party of suspicion."

I realized what he was saying. "You think that we should try to find out who the killer is."

"I am now involved with Mr. Alden's business; I have an investment to protect."

That reminded me. He had enticed me upstairs with the promise of information. "What was it you discovered today?"

"I wired Ludlow and he referred me to a bank here. There was a very helpful young lady there. I found her to be most forthcoming."

"I'm sure you did." I could well imagine the pretty young bank teller whom Milo had charmed. "What did she have to say?"

"She told me that Mr. Alden has been making a great many deposits as of late, but they have all been in cash so there is no record of who they came from."

Leave it to Milo to have gleaned such personal information in such a short amount of time.

"That wasn't all," he continued. "I found out that one day he came to the bank with a young man, withdrew a large sum of money, and gave it to him."

I felt I knew what he was going to say before he said it. "It was Mr. Palmer."

He nodded. "The description sounds very like him, anyway. The young lady didn't catch his name."

"And did she tell you anything else, this most obliging young lady?" I asked.

He gave me the expression of utmost innocence that I knew was entirely disingenuous. "Nothing of interest."

I shot him a look before continuing. "So it seems they were in some sort of business relationship together. Do you think Mr. Alden is involved with bootleggers?" I had, from the beginning, found it difficult to imagine Tabitha's father involving himself with gangsters, but the more we learned, the more it appeared that Mr. Alden might be participating in some sort of illegal activity.

"I think the matter bears more looking into. If it is Mr. Alden who killed Grant Palmer then perhaps I might have to rethink my investment," he said dryly.

I felt a hint of excitement, and also a bit of relief that I was not going to have to fight Milo on this. It would be nice to be partners in this endeavor. We worked much better when we weren't at odds.

I walked to where he sat on the sofa and took a seat beside him. "Now, where to begin?"

My mind began to turn. First and foremost, I thought we should find out if Mr. Alden had a link to Leon De Lora through Grant Palmer. If that was the case, things would be even more complicated.

"You're not going," Milo said, drawing my attention back to him.

I frowned, more because I comprehended him than because I didn't. "Going where?"

"You know perfectly well 'where,' " Milo said. "You want to go to that speakeasy and nose around to see if you can find out who might have killed Grant Palmer. I think I should go alone. You don't need to put yourself in danger."

I oughtn't have been surprised that Milo

knew what I was thinking. After all, this wasn't our first time being involved in a mystery of this sort, and we had often ventured into what might be considered dangerous territory. Milo, I had to admit, was better suited to some aspects of such investigations than I.

This time, however, we were both on unfamiliar ground. Milo, in his bespoke suit, with his elegant manners and public-school accent, was likely to stand out among the rougher elements.

He seemed to guess what I was thinking. "I've been to gambling clubs all over the world; it's not as though I haven't rubbed shoulders with dangerous men before."

It made sense what he said. Between his love of gambling and horse racing, there was little doubt he could easily insinuate himself with the criminal classes. Besides, Milo was never at a disadvantage. He seemed to slip seamlessly into his surroundings, and I had never seen anyone he was unable to charm.

Still, I wasn't sure I wanted to be left out of the matter. "It's a popular nightspot, after all, so it's not as though our presence would draw attention."

"I'm sure asking questions would most assuredly draw attention from a man like

Leon De Lora. It would be better if I go alone."

I considered the options and begrudgingly had to admit that he had a point. Milo would be far more likely to be able to introduce the topics that needed discussing. Nevertheless, the situation galled me.

"I suppose you may be right, though I don't see why you should be the one to have all the fun."

"Is it so wrong for me to want to shield you from some of the more unsavory aspects of life?"

I didn't know whether to appreciate this sentiment or be annoyed by it. I didn't want protecting. I wanted to have adventures. There was something sweet about his words, however, that made me feel a bit ungrateful for wanting to accompany him. I wondered if that had been his aim all along.

"Very well," I conceded at last. "You go to the speakeasy, and I'll see what I can learn from the others. But I want to know everything as soon as you return."

"Of course. I'll go tonight after dinner."

11

Dinner that evening was a solemn affair. Tabitha and Tom had not yet returned from their outing by the time we sat down to eat, and I was a bit uneasy about their absence. I supposed they simply wanted to be alone after the tragedy that had occurred here, but I was still on edge.

Mr. Alden seemed to have recovered some of his poise from the night before, but there was an artificial heartiness in his tone that revealed that he was still struggling to regain his equilibrium. I did notice that he glanced repeatedly at the clock and wondered if he was waiting for Tabitha to return.

"I apologize for neglecting to be a good host today," he said as the soup was served. "I had a lot of things to tend to. I had to speak to my attorney, as well as fend off a great many people who wanted information on what happened here last night."

"Think nothing of it," I said. "I know all

of this has been rather appalling."

"I don't know what to make of any of it," he said. "I knew Grant was in with a rough crowd, but I never expected anything like this."

I wondered for a moment if he might let something slip about their business relationship, but he focused on his food then, and we lapsed into silence.

I hoped dinner would be quick. The sooner we returned to our room, the sooner Milo would be able to slip out of the house. I didn't know exactly what I expected him to discover, but I couldn't help but feel that he was going to learn something at De Lora's.

We were midway through the second course when Tabitha and Tom came into the dining room. I looked up and was surprised to see that Rudy Elliot and Jemma Petrie were with them.

"Tabitha, I've been worried about you," Mr. Alden said. He seemed as though he was trying to pass his tone off as casual, but there was definite strain beneath the words.

"Sorry we're late, Dad," Tabitha said, seemingly oblivious to his concern. "We were driving for most of the day, trying to think things over. And then we went and picked up Rudy and Jemma. We've got a lot to discuss."

"I can't believe this has happened," Mr. Elliot said. "To think that we just saw Grant at the Topaz Club. Who would have ever thought . . ." His normally cheerful countenance was grave. I knew he and Mr. Palmer had been close, and I could only imagine this had been a great shock for him.

My gaze moved to Jemma Petrie. It was more difficult to tell what she was feeling. She appeared to be perfectly composed, but some of her natural exuberance had dimmed since we had seen her last. She was pale and her eyes were dark and red-rimmed. I wondered if Tom had been right, if she was secretly grieving for Mr. Palmer.

"Tom and I are going to go ahead with the wedding," Tabitha said, drawing my attention back to the conversation.

Mr. Alden looked up at her. "Tabitha, do you think . . . ?"

"I know everything is difficult, but I think it's for the best. All the plans are in place, the guests are coming, and Amory and Milo have come all the way from London."

"You needn't make any decisions on our account," I said. "We can stay longer if necessary."

Tabitha shook her head, an obstinate set to her chin. I recognized at once that she had made up her mind. The wedding was going to go ahead, and that was that.

Mr. Alden seemed to recognize it, too. He sighed. "Very well. Whatever you think is best."

"I think you're right," Jemma said. "I know Grant's death is a tragedy, but that doesn't mean that the two of you should suffer for it. You may as well continue with things as you had planned."

Rudy Elliot said nothing.

"We'll all miss Grant, but I'm sure he would've wanted the wedding to go on." This was the first that Tom Smith had spoken since they had come into the room, and his tone was somewhat unconvinced. The sentiment was understandable, for I had the feeling that Grant Palmer would not much have cared if the wedding went on or not. I had always had the impression that he was not entirely keen on the whole thing.

No one responded to this, and an uncomfortable silence hung in the air for just a moment before Tabitha redirected the conversation, talking of lighter things that allowed us all the pretense of forgetting, at least for the moment, that a murder had occurred on the doorstep of this house not twenty-four hours before.

■ ■ ■ ■

We went to the drawing room for after-dinner coffee, which many of our company took liberally infused with whiskey from a bottle Mr. Alden had fetched from his office. The mood was quiet and restrained.

I had told Milo that I would do my part to see what I could learn from the others since he was going to the speakeasy, so I determined to do my best to begin some sort of conversation with those present, to find out if any of them had a motive to kill Grant Palmer.

I decided to talk first to Mr. Elliot. I doubted very much that he would have wanted to kill his friend, but I did remember what Jemma Petrie had told me, how he and Mr. Palmer had quarreled over the attentions of a woman. Was it possible that he had killed out of jealousy?

"I'm very sorry about Mr. Palmer," I said, as I took a seat beside him on the sofa. "I know you were good friends."

He nodded. "I almost can't believe he's gone."

"It always feels so useless to try to offer comfort in these situations. I know that nothing really helps but time."

"It's just such a shock. I guess at our age we think we're going to live forever. I certainly never expected something like this to happen to Grant. He was the kind of guy who seemed invincible."

I knew what he meant. Grant Palmer had carried himself with that careless disregard for the vagaries of life. It always seemed more surprising, somehow, when someone so wildly alive met with an untimely end.

"This isn't the first time I've lost someone who was important to me," Mr. Elliot said slowly, his eyes trained on the floor in front of him.

I didn't know if I should mention that Tabitha had told me about his father, so I gave a simple answer. "I'm sorry."

"I suppose you've heard about my dad," he said, looking up at me.

"Yes," I admitted.

"It was a tough time. I didn't know things had gotten that bad. He hid it . . . from all of us."

"I'm sorry," I said again.

He glanced at me then, managing a smile. "I try not to think about it. Dad wasn't the sort of man who would've wanted people crying over him. He would have told us to get on with our lives. That's what I've tried to do."

"You've made quite a success of yourself, I understand."

He shrugged. "I've done all right. I enjoy what I do, so that's something."

"I'm sure your father would be very proud of you."

He flushed a little and changed the subject back to the one that was foremost on all of our minds.

"I suppose Grant's death had something to do with De Lora," he said.

"It seems the most likely explanation," I said. "I've heard a good deal about Mr. De Lora. Did you ever meet him?"

He gave a quick shake of his head, smiling ruefully. "I always tried to steer clear of that part of Grant's life, though he nearly pulled me in a time or two. But I'm not much of one for danger and excitement."

"But he enjoyed taking risks?"

He nodded. "He was always like that. He did whatever he wanted, devil take the consequences. Although, lately, I think maybe he was having second thoughts."

This piqued my interest. "How so?"

"He said something to me a few days back, about how maybe it was time for him to be on the side of law and order."

That was curious. He had said something similar to me that night at the Topaz Club, that he was finding it difficult to walk a tightrope. Had Grant decided to leave his criminal endeavors behind? Perhaps Mr. De Lora had decided he couldn't allow this.

I hoped this was the case, that Mr. Palmer's death had nothing to do with anyone in this house, but I couldn't leave that unsavory avenue unexplored.

"I don't suppose anyone else had a reason to kill him?" I asked Mr. Elliot.

I expected a quick denial and was a bit surprised when none was forthcoming. If he thought my question was unusual, he gave no sign of it.

"Those detectives came around asking questions today, almost as though they thought I might have had something to do with it. 'If you don't mind my asking, where were you at the time of the murder, Mr. Elliot?' The swarthy one was especially pushy." Mr. Elliot said this lightly and appeared perfectly at ease. It was difficult for me to believe that he might have had something to do with the cold-blooded murder of Grant Palmer. He just didn't seem the type to me that would want to kill a man over petty jealousies. I remembered the good-natured way he had accepted Mr. Palmer's teasing that first night at the dinner table. There had been no anger in his eyes, no sense that he resented his friend's casual insults.

What was more, I could tell that much of his calm tonight was an act. He seemed to me as though he was genuinely distressed and trying hard not to appear so. His foot was tapping on the carpet, his fingers drumming against his leg in a frantic rhythm. It was never easy to lose a friend, and I suspected his grief was still raw.

This assumption was proved with his next words. "I don't know why the police might have assumed that I might have wanted to kill Grant," he said, and this time his words were addressed to the whole room. "I know we didn't always get along, but I didn't want him dead. He was my best friend."

"Oh, I know, Rudy. I know," Tabitha said gently. "I don't think any of us think that you might have done it."

"We've been friends for years." For a moment I wondered if he might cry. It seemed that his eyes glistened.

"How did you meet?" I asked him as the others went back to their conversations.

He smiled. "Grant had plans to rob my father's bank."

My brows rose in surprise, and he laughed.

"It wasn't a well-thought-out plot. We

190

were probably only twelve at the time, but he was running with some pretty tough kids. One of the older boys had convinced him that he should try to rob the bank alone with a toy pistol. I happened to be on my way to visit my father that day and spotted him at the corner as he was trying to build up his nerve. I don't know what made me go and talk to him, but I did. For some reason we hit it off. He abandoned his plan to rob the bank and we went off to the soda shop instead.

"After that, we never stopped being friends. I was always trying to talk him out of schemes, keep him from doing things he shouldn't. It didn't always work, and I think half the bad things he did he never told me about. There was a secretive side to Grant. But he never did anything as reckless as try to rob another bank." He smiled. "As an adult, I even got him a job working for Dad. We had a good laugh about that, him earning money from that bank, after all, years later."

"I'm glad he had a good friend like you," I said.

"It doesn't seem to have helped much in the end," Mr. Elliot said softly. "It was still crime that brought about his downfall."

I lowered my voice. "Perhaps it wasn't the

bootleggers who killed him. You said the police were asking you for your whereabouts. Do they suspect it might have been someone other than Mr. De Lora, do you think?"

"I suppose it's possible." His brow furrowed as he considered. "I've been thinking it over, trying to work out if anyone else might have had a reason to do it. Grant wasn't always the most likable guy." He looked up, stammering as he tried to amend this statement. "That is . . . I mean . . ." He sighed. "Well, that's the truth of it. He rubbed people the wrong way sometimes."

"And you think that might have been a motive for murder?"

He shrugged, then his shoulders sagged as he looked down at the coffee cup in his hand. "I don't really know what to think."

This seemed a signal that I had pressed the matter far enough for the time being. He was clearly going to be mulling the topic over for some time, and I felt that I had created enough of a conversational opening that he might be willing to revisit the subject after he'd had more time to consider it.

"Perhaps it's best not to think about it anymore tonight," I said. "Perhaps we might talk about other things."

He looked over at me, and I saw on his

face the look of someone who had suddenly been given permission to do something they desperately wanted to do. He suddenly looked very young, like a child who wanted reassurance. "Do you think that's insensitive? To just push it all away?"

"No. In fact, I think that sometimes forgetting for a while is necessary."

An expression of powerful relief crossed his face, and he nodded. "I think you're right. After all, Grant would have been the first one to go on with his life if something had happened to one of us."

Before I could comment on this assessment of his friend, Calvin came to the drawing room.

"I'm sorry to interrupt, Mr. Alden, but Detective Andrews and Detective Bailey are here."

Silence descended over the room. None of us was quite sure how to respond to this unwelcome bit of news. No doubt they had more questions with which to pepper us, and I was sure I was not alone in feeling unequal to the task tonight.

"Show them in, Calvin," Mr. Alden said at last.

A moment later the two detectives made their way into the drawing room. They were both wearing their trench coats, Detective

Andrews looking slightly disheveled, Detective Bailey looking more composed.

"Sorry to interrupt at this hour," Detective Andrews said, "but we've been looking for Mr. Smith."

Tom rose from his seat, a frown on his handsome brow. "I'm here. What . . . why are you looking for me?"

"We just wanted to talk to you," Detective Bailey said mildly.

"We've been looking for you all day, in fact," Detective Andrews added, a hint of accusation in his voice.

"Tabitha . . . Miss Alden and I spent the day together. Needless to say, we were both pretty shaken up about what happened to Grant and we needed some time alone."

"Sure, sure," Detective Andrews said. "That's fine. We just need to talk to you for a few minutes, if you don't mind. Alone."

"I don't mind at all," Tom said, though I thought he didn't look entirely at ease.

"But I don't see . . ." Tabitha began, an edge of worry in her voice.

"It's all right, Tabitha," Mr. Alden said. "These men are only doing their job."

"I appreciate that, Mr. Alden," Detective Andrews said. "We're just all trying to be sure that justice gets done. We're talking to everyone who was close to Mr. Palmer." He nodded vaguely into the room. "We already spoke with Mr. Elliot and Miss Petrie."

I glanced at Jemma Petrie. She hadn't mentioned that the police had called on her, but perhaps that wasn't the sort of information one cared to share, especially if she had revealed her secret relationship with Mr. Palmer to them.

"We're just trying to sort everything out," Detective Bailey said. There was something almost friendly in his manner. He was the calming, quiet complement to his partner's forceful intensity.

"Narrowing out the innocent so you can find the guilty," Rudy Elliot said.

"Yeah, something like that." Detective Andrews scratched the dark growth of whiskers on his cheek. "When it comes right down to it, none of you have alibis."

There was a moment of stunned silence.

"Except Mr. and Mrs. Ames, of course, who were seen coming down the stairs by Calvin the butler."

"I was at my office," Mr. Alden said.

"Sure, but it was late and no one saw you," Detective Andrews said. "That's not to say you're a suspect, but it isn't the same as if you were in a room full of people."

"I gave you my alibi," Jemma Petrie said suddenly, her tone a bit too bright. "I was home in bed, as I told you."

"Alone, you said?"

Jemma blinked, a flush spreading to her cheeks. "Of course."

"Not much of an alibi, then, is it? Not that I'm accusing anyone, mind you. But we like to get everything all straight so we spend our time the right way."

He smiled, which only seemed to add to the attitude of menace I was certain we were all feeling.

"Well, then I'm eager to be cleared of wrongdoing," Tom said lightly.

"Right this way then," Detective Andrews said, motioning toward the hallway with his hat in his hand. Tom followed him out, and Detective Bailey nodded at the room in general. "Good evening, everyone."

When they were gone, I excused myself from my seat beside Mr. Elliot and moved to where Tabitha and Jemma were sitting in a corner of the room, talking in quiet voices. As I approached, Tabitha held out her hand and pulled me onto the settee beside her.

"What do you think they want?" she asked me, her eyes worried.

"I'm sure they're just looking for information on Mr. Palmer's whereabouts before he died," I said reassuringly. "As he said, they questioned Mr. Elliot and Miss Petrie as well."

"And were very insulting about it, too," Jemma said with spirit. "Imagine! Asking me if I was alone! I should've said something scandalous and shocked him."

I smiled, wondering if she was protesting too much, but Tabitha was staring across the room, still lost in thought. "I just don't know what they think Tom will be able to tell them. Surely they don't think . . . I mean, Tom and Grant were great friends. He wouldn't have had any reason to do something . . ."

"No, no. I don't think there's anything to worry about."

I wasn't entirely sure, however. There was something about these detectives that made me uneasy.

"If you'll excuse me, I just need to powder my nose," Jemma Petrie said suddenly. She rose and left the room. I wondered if she was more upset by the detective's brusque questions than she let on.

I turned to Tabitha, trying to draw her out of her doldrums: "Don't fret, Tabitha. I'm sure it will all be all right."

She looked at me, frowning slightly, and lowered her voice. "It's just that . . . I called Jemma last night before I left the house.

She didn't answer her phone."

"Oh, I see," I said, pondering this interesting bit of information. So perhaps Jemma Petrie had not been home when Grant Palmer was killed after all.

"Of course, she might have been sleeping soundly," Tabitha said quickly.

"Yes, that could be," I agreed. But I wondered.

I could see the strain all of this was putting on Tabitha, so I decided not to press the issue for the time being.

"What were you girls talking about?" I asked lightly. "Before we were so rudely interrupted."

"We were talking about the wedding," Tabitha said in a hushed voice, as though it was some sort of secret. I felt sad that such a happy occasion should have been so tainted with tragedy.

"Then fill me in, won't you?" I said, trying to draw some enthusiasm out of her.

She nodded, seeming to return to the normal, cheery version of herself with great effort. "I was talking about the bouquets. The florist isn't sure she'll be able to get the exact arrangements I wanted now, though I suppose it doesn't really matter as long as the colors are right."

She went on then, and I found my mind

drifting slightly, thinking about what Detective Andrews had said. None of the group had an alibi. I had known, of course, that none of them had been in the house at the time, but this new information meant that any one of them might have had the opportunity to shoot Grant Palmer on the Aldens' front steps. And now I had learned that it was possible Jemma Petrie had lied about her whereabouts.

Tom came back into the room perhaps half an hour later, his face grim. I imagined that he had had a thorough going-over by Detective Andrews.

"What did they want?" Tabitha asked at once.

He smiled, almost managing to banish the strained expression from his face. "They just had a lot of questions. They . . . I suppose they're just trying to do their job. They're awfully stern about it, though. They almost made me want to think of something to confess."

Tabitha looked alarmed, and I wondered why. "What sort of things could you possibly want to confess?" she asked with a forced little laugh.

"I . . . well, for some reason I told them that Grant and I had been arguing the night before he was killed."

I remembered the heated exchange I had witnessed between them in the foyer at the Topaz Club. Perhaps it was good that he had told the police before someone else had.

"Tom! Why would you say that?" Tabitha said. "They'll only think . . ."

"Oh, I explained it," he said. "I just didn't want word to get back to them. They might think I was hiding something."

"But what were you arguing about?"

"Oh, only a little money matter," he said. "It was nothing serious."

What I had seen of their argument had not seemed to be a small matter. I remembered the heated expression on Tom's face, as well as something he had said about not letting the past follow him anymore. Where, then, had money come into it?

I pulled my attention back to what Tom was saying. "And, anyway, everything was fine between us. Grant was coming to see me. He had phoned me before I phoned you and said there was something he wanted to tell me."

"Did he say what it was?" I couldn't resist asking.

He shook his head. "It could've been anything."

"Was that why Grant was coming here at that time of night?" Tabitha asked.

"Yes, I . . . I'm afraid that's my fault," Tom said. "He was going to come to the nightclub with us. He said he had something he wanted to talk to me about, but I forgot to phone him to meet us at the club instead. I suppose if I had remembered to call him things might have . . . ended differently."

"Oh, I don't think so," Tabitha said quickly. "After all, whoever did this to Grant could have done it anywhere."

"Yes," he said. "I suppose you're right."

"Well, now that the police are gone, I say we have some fun," said Jemma, coming back into the room. She seemed in high spirits, as though a weight had lifted off of her now that the detectives had left. "Does anyone want to go dancing?"

But the energy seemed to have gone out of the rest of us, and we could no longer sustain the pretense of cheeriness for which we had all been fighting valiantly for most of the evening. Something in the atmosphere had changed with the detectives' visit, and I felt more uneasy now than ever.

Back in our room, I began to prepare for bed as Milo, who was waiting to go out until after the household had retired, took a seat and smoked a cigarette as he watched me undress. His gaze was passively appreciative, and I knew that he had set his sights on other amusements this evening.

"I'm a bit uneasy about you going out tonight," I said as I pulled a dressing gown of rose-colored satin over the matching nightgown.

"Darling, there's nothing to be concerned about; it's not as though I'm going to march into De Lora's and start demanding of assorted criminals which of them killed Grant Palmer."

"I know, but what if someone recognizes you? There was a notice in the society columns about our arrival."

"I somehow doubt that De Lora reads the society columns."

I knew that, no matter what my objections, I was not going to dissuade him from going to the speakeasy tonight. It was not so much the mystery that interested him as the prospect of spending the evening in some sort of illicit establishment. Milo thrived on behaving badly.

He rose from his seat and came to me, sliding his arms around me. "Don't look so glum, darling. I daresay I've spent nights in much more dangerous circumstances than this one."

"Is that supposed to make me feel better?"

He smiled and leaned to kiss me. "Don't wait up for me."

Then he released me and had slipped out of our room before I could reply.

I very much feared I must wait up for him. I was certain I would be unable to sleep a wink until he returned.

Moving to the bed, I threw back the covers and settled beneath them with a book I intended to read until Milo was safely in the bed beside me.

I was very annoyed, then, to wake up at dawn and find Milo asleep at my side. Morning light filtered through the curtains across the peaceful lines of his handsome face. I shifted slightly and was met with a jab from the corner of the book I had been reading, which lay between us.

I put the book on the nightstand and sat up. I couldn't believe that I had fallen asleep or that, at the very least, I hadn't heard him come in.

"Milo."

He stirred slightly.

"Milo, wake up."

"I've only just gone to sleep," he murmured without opening his eyes.

"What happened at De Lora's?"

"Nothing."

"What do you mean?" I demanded.

He opened his eyes with a heavy sigh and looked up at me. "De Lora wasn't there, and I didn't discover anything of interest. I had a few drinks, played a few hands of cards with a sinister-looking and tight-lipped gentleman, and then came home."

I looked at him. For some reason, I had the impression that he was lying to me. There had been a time in our marriage when it was very difficult for me to tell, for he was a consummate liar, but I was becoming more adept at sensing dishonesty in him.

My gaze narrowed as I studied his face.

"I find that very difficult to believe," I said at last.

He met my gaze with guiltless blue eyes. "I hate to admit failure, darling, but I'll go back again in a night or two and see if I can find out anything. In the meantime, I think we should consider our other suspects."

There was something that he wasn't telling me. I had learned to distrust that easy dismissiveness, and now I was certain.

I considered what it might be. It had been Milo's idea that we pursue this investigation, so I didn't think it was merely a matter of trying to dissuade me from investigating. The noblest answer — if indeed lying to one's wife can be considered noble in any circumstances — was that he was trying to protect me from something. Perhaps he had discovered Leon De Lora was more dangerous than Milo had assumed, and he didn't want me to pursue him as a suspect.

This seemed unlikely, however. I felt there was something else that he was hiding. It was irritating in the extreme, but I knew from long experience it would do no good to press him. He would never tell me anything he didn't want me to know.

Well, so be it. If he was going to keep secrets from me, I was just going to have to go to De Lora's and get the answers for myself.

12

Much to my annoyance, Milo was up not long after I was and departed the house shortly thereafter. He had business with a banker and an American lawyer, he told me, though I was fairly sure I didn't believe him.

There was no one in the dining room as I had my tea and toast and thought over the events of the past few days. Though I was trying not to think of it in such grim terms, I found that this trip had devolved in my mind from a joyous occasion to one of suspicion and fear. There was a sense of melancholy that hung over me, and I was sure it was not going to dissipate until Mr. Palmer's murderer was caught.

To make matters worse, someone had left a newspaper on the table. Apparently, Mr. Alden had been reading the morning news, for the paper was folded to an article with a photograph of the Alden home next to a photograph of Grant Palmer, that sardonic smile flashing in his handsome face.

Against my better judgment, I picked up the paper and read.

The shooting death of Mr. Grant Palmer at the home of shipping tycoon Benjamin Alden remains under investigation. So far no suspects have been named, but rumors persist that the method of the killing points to a gangland connection. Mr. Palmer was well-known in underworld circuits, though he had never been officially linked to any crimes. It is unknown whether the Aldens were aware of this connection, though Mr. Palmer was to serve as best man in the wedding of Miss Tabitha Alden to Mr. Thomas Smith. The wedding is due to take place in a fortnight.

I pushed the paper away with a sigh. It was just as I had feared: rumor and speculation were already beginning to spread. I had hoped that Tabitha and Tom would be spared some of that, but it seemed that, no matter what side of the Atlantic one was on, gossip still spread like wildfire. I determined not to dwell on them for the moment. Mr. Palmer's murder was a tragedy, to be certain, but I had dealt with tragedy before and had overcome it.

No one had come downstairs by the time I finished my meager meal, and I wandered out of the dining room into the silent hallway. Though distracted by the newspaper, I had thought I heard someone at the front door, but there was certainly no one there now. Perhaps it had been another reporter dispatched by Calvin.

There was a large grandfather clock in the hallway and I glanced at it. It was nearly ten o'clock. I wondered where everyone was this morning. It seemed as though Mr. Palmer's death had sent them scattered into the winds. Not that I could blame them.

I knew, despite her stiff upper lip, Tabitha was no doubt trying to come to terms with the death of Grant Palmer. It had been terrible for her to see him lying there, his blood spilling out on the steps, and I knew she was likely more affected by it all than she'd let on. I hoped she was somewhere with Tom. I was optimistic that the bonds of love could do much to help her make her way through the trauma.

I suddenly felt an odd little longing for Milo. Ours had never been the sort of relationship where I relied on him for emotional support. Indeed, I had spent most of the first five years of our marriage concealing my feelings from him. It was only recently that I had begun to look upon him as someone in whom I could confide when feeling morose, the steady arm to lean on in trouble. Despite my feelings that he was concealing the truth from me, it would be nice to talk to him now.

Brushing off this silly bit of melancholy with the reminder that he would likely return before lunch and, in all probability, do something to annoy me by dinner, I considered my plans for the day. I was feeling a bit at loose ends. I didn't particularly want to venture out into the city. Even if my heart had been in it, I knew there were still reporters outside and I didn't care to have my picture splashed across tomorrow's papers.

It was then I remembered that I had not finished the letter to my mother. While I was already feeling gloomy, I might as well accomplish the task.

I made my way into the sitting room, considering news I might share while sidestepping the fact that there had been a murder on our doorstep. Knowing my mother, she would hear about it soon enough without my informing her. I was, in fact, a bit surprised I had not yet received a terse wire or even a transatlantic telephone call.

I walked to the drawing room and stopped in the doorway. Detective Andrews was standing before the fireplace, looking at the large painting that hung above the mantel, a cigarette between his lips.

I had not particularly cared for the man's brusque manner last night, and I had no desire to talk with him again now. I wasn't even sure what he was doing here. Was it usual in America for the police to appear so often without warning?

Unfortunately, he apparently had heard me approaching, for he turned before I could slip away.

"You much of an art lover, Mrs. Ames?" he asked, by way of a greeting.

I wasn't sure what to make of the question, but I answered it straightforwardly. "I enjoy art. I wouldn't say I'm particularly knowledgeable on the subject."

"Oh, I bet you have a good eye. What do you make of that painting?"

He nodded toward the painting that hung above the mantel.

I looked up at it. It was a portrait of a man on horseback. The colors called to mind the countryside, and, though the rider's face was not visible, his dress and the set of the shoulders gave the impression that he was a man on a journey. There was something vague yet vivid about the picture; it gave one the loose impression of a story while encouraging the mind to fill in the details.

"I think it's very good," I said, though something told me there was more to his question than simple curiosity.

"It's an Eakins," he said. "Painted in Philadelphia around the turn of the century."

I knew I oughtn't to have made judgments, but I would not have taken Mr. Andrews for an art aficionado, and I was caught off guard by this knowledge of the piece in question.

"That's very interesting. You seem well-versed on the subject of art."

He shrugged. "Everyone has their hobbies." He moved over to the crystal ashtray on the chair by the sofa and stubbed out his cigarette.

"Yes, I suppose you're right."

"I used to work in the robbery division. We saw a lot of art come through there, and I developed an interest. This is an expensive piece. A lot of families are having to sell off these sorts of things now."

I didn't know what sort of information he was hoping to glean from me. Surely he didn't think I was privy to the Aldens' financial situation.

His next question struck closer to home. "You come from money, I suppose?"

I was a bit put off by the question, not just for the fact that it was considered ill-mannered to discuss such things, but because I felt as though he was coming at things from an angle I didn't understand. I was at a disadvantage, and I didn't like it.

That didn't mean, of course, that I would refuse to answer his question. After all, there was no crime in having been born into a wealthy family.

"I've been fortunate enough to live a very comfortable life," I admitted.

He nodded. "I grew up poor, but we had a happy little family."

"A happy family makes a good deal of difference."

I glanced into the room, wondering where Detective Bailey was. I had somehow had the impression that the men did not often go places apart.

"Money makes a difference, too. I can applaud a man who does what he needs to get ahead."

"Mr. Alden has always worked very hard," I said carefully, unsure of what he was getting at.

"You can come into the room, you know,"

Detective Andrews said suddenly. "I may look mean, but I don't bite."

He said the words without any apparent humor, but I could tell he was trying to lessen the impression of an attack. I hadn't even realized that I was still hovering in the doorway. Perhaps it was my instinct for self-preservation that had kept me there, the feeling that I ought to be wary of this man.

I didn't intend to let him see that, however.

"I thought you might be waiting for someone," I said as I moved into the drawing room and took a seat.

"I came back to talk to everyone again. I didn't want to overstay my welcome last night, but I thought another go-round today might be a good idea. Things are always a bit hazy after a tragedy. I thought people's recollections might be a little clearer today."

"I'm afraid I don't have many recollections," I said. "After all, I didn't see anything."

"Yes, so you said. But perhaps some new details have emerged? Maybe you've thought of something you didn't think to mention?"

I had again the impression that he was trying to get me to reveal something. There was no reason to be uneasy. After all, I didn't know anything.

"I'm afraid I told you everything I could think of that night," I said.

"You were in your room upstairs when you heard the sound of gunfire."

I nodded.

"And you didn't see anything?"

"No. I didn't even go to the window. I heard Tabitha scream and went downstairs immediately. That's when I saw Mr. Palmer lying on the steps."

"The butler had the door open."

I nodded.

"And Miss Alden was kneeling by the body? Almost as though she had been there when it happened."

I felt a hint of unease. Was he going to suggest that Tabitha might have had something to do with it?

"I'm not sure exactly how long she'd been there. You'd have to ask her."

"Yes, I came to speak to Miss Alden. It seems she's not here."

I wondered why he had come into the drawing room if he knew that Tabitha wasn't here. I didn't have much time to contemplate the question before he moved on to another topic.

"No one in this house seems much disturbed that Grant Palmer is dead." I wasn't sure whether it was a question or an observation.

"I didn't know him at all well," I said, "but I'm sorry that he was killed."

"I didn't mean you," he replied.

"Tabitha took it very hard. She was almost hysterical." I recalled how I had led her, pale and trembling and smeared with Mr. Palmer's blood, into the drawing room after the shooting. Her hands had been shaking so hard she had been unable at first to hold her coffee cup. No, I was certain that her horror had been genuine.

"She took the circumstances hard," Detective Andrews corrected. "But she isn't overly sorry that he's dead. I imagine she's practically recovered by now."

I thought of Tabitha and Tom sitting at the breakfast table yesterday morning, their decision last night to go on with the wedding. Certainly they were sorry that Grant Palmer was dead, but I could see how her appearance might give the impression that it had not caused any lasting distress.

The more he talked, the more Detective Andrews seemed to me to be a very cynical gentleman. Unfortunately, he also seemed to be fairly astute. I imagined that Tabitha was not going to enjoy her interview with him, and I almost wished Detective Bailey was here. Somehow it seemed that his presence softened some of Detective Andrews's rough edges.

"Did you look into Mr. Palmer's relationship with bootleggers?" I asked.

It seemed to me that he smirked ever so slightly, as though he found me to be very amusing. "We're investigating all the angles."

"It seems much more likely to me than any other scenario."

"Well, I'll keep that in mind."

I gritted my teeth at his patronizing tone. I wished suddenly for the comforting, familiar presence of Detective Inspector Jones of Scotland Yard. Though we had started out on less than friendly terms, our relationship had developed into a warm and trusting one. Somehow, I didn't imagine I would be developing such a relationship with Detective Andrews.

"Did you learn anything from Mr. Smith?" I asked.

His sharp eyes came to my face. "Why? You think he's the guy if the gangsters didn't do it?"

He almost made me wish I had said nothing, but now that I had I needed to make myself clear. "I don't know Mr. Smith very well," I said. "But I have a hard time imagining that he would do anything like this. No, what I meant was, perhaps he knows about Mr. Palmer's involvement with bootleggers. The two of them were good friends, after all."

"He didn't seem to know much about that," he said, turning his back to me and walking along to look at the next painting on the wall.

I waited to see if he would reveal any more of what Tom had had to say, but I ought to have known better.

"This one's a copy," he said, stopping before a painting.

I looked at it. Admittedly, I was no art expert, but it looked genuine enough to me. My curiosity got the better of me.

"How do you know?"

"Just little things here and there. It's not always easy to spot a phony."

He turned back to me.

Just then there was a movement in the doorway behind me. It was Calvin, the butler.

"Mr. Alden says he will see you now, Mr. Andrews. He's in his study."

"Great. Tell him I'll be there in a minute."

Calvin nodded and disappeared. Detective Andrews moved toward the doorway, but he stopped in front of me. "It's been nice chatting with you, but, if you'll excuse me, I have a few more questions for Mr. Alden."

"I still think you'd have better luck looking into Mr. Palmer's business associates than any of his friends," I said.

"You ever seen a Venus flytrap, Mrs. Ames?"

Once again, he had caught me off guard. "No, I don't believe I have."

"They're strange little plants. Shaped kind of like this." He formed his hand into a claw. "Harmless-looking things, really. They just sit there, minding their own business. And then along comes a fly and —" He closed his fist with a crackle of thick knuckles.

He gave a shrug. "Sometimes it just takes a little patience."

I was beginning to see that it would be a very unwise thing indeed to underestimate Detective Andrews.

13

It was that afternoon that I set my plan into motion. I had been thinking about it for most of the day, and I had come up with what I thought would be a feasible plan for making Leon De Lora's acquaintance.

The first step in the process would call for a bit of assistance.

"Winnelda," I said when she came into my bedroom carrying an armload of clothes she had just pressed. "I need you to help me with something."

She looked up from where she was depositing items in the wardrobe. "Certainly, madam. What is it?"

"I need you to help me cultivate an American accent."

She looked at me strangely, and I couldn't exactly blame her. It was, after all, a rather outlandish request.

"I am going someplace where I want to blend into my surroundings," I said, by way of explanation.

She nodded, accustomed, I supposed, to my eccentric ideas. "It's not really that difficult of an accent to imitate once you get an ear for it," she said. My eyes widened. Gone was all hint of her London origins. She sounded exactly like an American. Had I met her on the street, I never would have guessed she hailed from my homeland.

"Winnelda, you're wonderful!"

She smiled, reverting to her natural voice. "I do think I have rather a knack for it, madam."

Winnelda was a woman of hidden depths.

"Say something else," I encouraged her.

She closed the wardrobe and turned to me. "I've watched a lot of American films, you know. The trick to it is not paying any special attention to your a's and o's. You treat them just like any of the other letters."

Again I marveled at how very American she sounded.

"Now you try," she encouraged me.

I unaccountably felt a bit shy. I hadn't had much practice at altering my voice, and I was quite certain I would not do as good a job as she.

"Say 'I'm American, and it's really nice to meet you,' " she instructed.

" 'I'm American, and it's really nice to

meet you,' " I repeated.

"Very good! Say it again."

We practiced for a while, and I began to feel a bit more comfortable with the pattern of speech. I found that I had a decent ear for the accent, though I feared I would never master it as Winnelda had. Furthermore, though getting the cadence was not so difficult, I worried somewhat about particular phrases that might give me away.

"The most important thing to remember is not to say 'blimey' or 'cheerio,' " she said helpfully.

"Yes. Thank you, Winnelda."

"And a 'lift' is called an 'elevator.' "

Winnelda continued to coach me on some of the finer points of American vernacular that she had picked up from her wide reading of periodicals and frequent trips to the cinema. I only hoped I would be able to remember them all.

Our lesson eventually concluded, I thanked her and gave her the night off.

There was just one more thing I needed to mention. "You mustn't tell Mr. Ames anything about this," I said to her before she departed.

"Certainly not, madam," she said. "I never tell Mr. Ames any of the wild things you do."

I didn't know quite how to take this comment.

"If I don't come home by morning, of course, you ought to let him know that I've gone to investigate. He'll know where."

She looked stricken at the thought, so I hurried to reassure her. "I don't anticipate any trouble, but just in case."

"Madam, are you sure . . . ?"

"Quite sure. Everything is going to be fine."

Even as I said the words, I began to wonder if my idea was entirely preposterous. I supposed there was only one way to find out.

Chief among my concerns for the evening was escaping Milo. As it turned out, that matter took care of itself.

He returned late in the afternoon with no explanation of his whereabouts, and I did not press him about where he'd been. I thought the less questions I asked, the better.

I did, however, want to discuss my encounter with Detective Andrews that morning. I related our conversation and the impression I had had that he was beginning to suspect a member of the wedding party.

"What do you think he's getting at?" I

asked Milo.

"He's much cleverer than he looks," Milo said.

I had had the same impression. There was something in his manner that belied his unkempt and careless appearance.

"I'm uneasy about him. I think he's going to try to fix the blame on someone in this house."

Milo looked at me. "Well, perhaps he's right."

"I could see how it might look that way, given that Grant Palmer was killed here at the Aldens' house, but I still feel it must have been those gangsters he was involved with. If not Leon De Lora, then perhaps that rival of his, Frankie Earl."

"You think so?"

I stared at him. "Don't you?"

"I think that's what you want to think, but I'm not sure you do."

As usual, he knew me almost as well as I knew myself.

"You're right," I said. "The longer I remain in this house, the stranger it seems to me that everyone is acting."

I had seen for myself the cracks in the relationships between Grant Palmer and others in the house. Was it possible that one of them had orchestrated his murder? It seemed fantastic, but it would not be the first time I had seen such a thing happen. If nothing came of my ventures tonight, then I would pause to consider it.

"What are your plans for this evening, darling?"

I turned toward my jewelry box, so I wouldn't have to look him in the face. I was certain he would be able to read the guilt in my expression. "I'm a bit tired. I was hoping to retire early."

It wasn't precisely a lie. I was tired and would certainly retire early if I had the opportunity . . . after I had visited De Lora's.

"Then you don't mind if I go out with Tom? There's a gambling establishment he's been telling me about."

It was all I could do not to let out a sigh of relief. I had hoped that some form of New York nightlife would call to him, and I was in luck. What was more, if he was out with Tom, then he wouldn't be at De Lora's when I went there.

"I don't mind at all," I said.

After dinner, he and Tom took their leave and we ladies had been left to fend for ourselves. Tabitha had not seemed opposed to going to bed early, and I had made my excuses and hurried to my room to change for my adventure.

I chose one of the more daring evening gowns I had brought with me. It was a dress of smoky blue satin with a low-cut back that hugged my torso and hips before pooling down in shimmering folds around my legs. I put on a necklace made of paste diamonds and sapphires and, with a hint of guilt, removed my wedding rings and put them in my jewelry box.

Then I pulled on my fur and quietly made my way down the stairs, hoping not to draw any attention to myself. I would have a difficult time explaining why I was going out alone dressed for a nightclub.

I made it outside without encountering anyone, and stood for a moment on the front porch, looking down the street. The moonlight was bright and the streetlamps glowed warmly, so, when I looked down, it was easy to see where the blood still stained the steps. A cool breeze blew, and I drew my coat more tightly around myself.

I made my way down the front steps and along the pavement — sidewalk, Winnelda had reminded me as she made her way through a startlingly comprehensive list of American terminology. It was not long before I spotted a cab and waved him down.

"Where to, miss?" the driver asked as I

got into the car.

I hesitated, realizing I didn't know where I was going. Milo hadn't told me where the speakeasy was located. I suppose there was really no reason for him to have mentioned it to me when we had agreed I wouldn't go there. I hoped this oversight was not indicative of the viability of my entire plan.

"I don't suppose you know the location of De Lora's?" I asked hopefully, trying my American accent on for size.

He shot me a smile in his mirror. "Sure I do."

"Then to De Lora's, if you please."

This was much easier than I had anticipated. The driver pulled away from the curb, and I sat back against the seat.

I supposed I should feel a bit guilty keeping this from Milo, but I was also quite sure that he was keeping something from me. I needed to know more about Mr. De Lora, and I didn't think there was any harm in going to his establishment on my own. After all, he had a reputation where women were concerned, and I felt that I might be able to succeed where Milo hadn't. I wasn't going to put myself in any danger.

Granted, I didn't know what I intended to do should it appear that he might be involved in Grant Palmer's death, but the least I could do was get some sort of information to bring back to Detectives Andrews and Bailey. I had to admit that I would very much like to prove to them, especially to that smug Detective Andrews, that I wasn't just some silly society lady.

We drove along for a while, twisting our way through glowing streets and then to a less populous part of town. The car at last drew to a stop in front of a brownstone building that looked no different from any of the others in the neighborhood. There was no sign and no indication that we had arrived anywhere other than a quiet residential area. I didn't even see anyone about on the streets.

"This is it?" I asked.

"Yes, ma'am," he replied. "Go right up the stairs there."

I had read somewhere that it was the custom to have some sort of special phrase, a password, to gain admission. "Is there . . . some secret code needed to enter?" I asked.

He laughed. "Just go on up to the door and knock. They'll let you in."

I supposed I might as well try my luck. I paid the driver, tipping him handsomely for his invaluable aid, and alighted from the car, making my way up the steps. I tapped on the door, and a sliding slat of wood in it opened from whence I was observed for a moment. Before I could say anything, the slat was closed and then the door was opened to admit me.

A gentleman stood beside the door. He was dressed in evening clothes, though it appeared he might have been more at home in a boxing ring than a nightclub. He had deep-set eyes in a puffy face, and his nose looked as though it had been broken several times and had healed correctly none of them.

"That way," he said, his head indicating a blue velvet curtain.

I supposed it would not be wise to linger too long on the precipice, so I pushed aside the blue curtain and stepped through. I had expected to find myself on the ground floor of the building, but instead I stood at the top of a flight of stairs descending into the smoky haze of the room below. There was a band playing a mellow jazz tune and the air was heavy with the smell of cigarettes, perfume, and alcohol.

As I made my way down the stairs, it was almost like descending into another world. The music swelled louder and the lighting seemed to glow in the smoky air. I had expected a somewhat raucous atmosphere, but everything was fairly subdued at the moment, as though the crowd had fallen under the spell of the languorous tune played by the band.

I glanced around and saw men in dinner jackets, women in glittering evening gowns, as well as people in much less formal attire. In one corner, two uniformed police officers were drinking from glasses filled with amber liquid.

I realized that, standing there agape, I was probably giving off the impression that I was completely out of my element. I tried to put on an air of nonchalance as I made my way down the rest of the stairs.

Milo had said that Leon De Lora had not been there the previous night, but I hoped I would find him here tonight and be able to speak with him.

I had gone over in my head what might be the best way to approach him. I didn't want to try to make an introduction based simply on being a woman. That might give him the wrong sort of impression.

That was what had led me to reason that it would be best not to appear British. Milo had already been here asking questions, and I thought it would likely draw attention if another British person appeared and began to do the same thing. I only hoped I would be able to do a credible job of maintaining my American accent. In any event, New York was a mélange of cultures. Surely my accent wouldn't be particularly notable.

I realized suddenly, as I often did when plunging headfirst into mysteries, that I wasn't exactly sure what my next step was going to be. I had come here to speak with Leon De Lora, but I really had no idea if he was even going to be present tonight. Did gangsters spend a good deal of time at their own establishments? Or did they just let the speakeasies run their course and collect the proceeds? Somehow the latter seemed more likely, and I was a bit crestfallen at the idea.

Of course, that didn't mean there weren't other ways that I might acquire information. If Mr. Palmer had worked here, surely someone was bound to know something about what had happened to him.

It seemed that there were waiters moving amongst the tables, but there was also a bar at one side of the room. I thought this seemed as good a place as any to start. After all, the barkeep was at the social nucleus of any such establishment.

I walked up to the bar, which was made of highly polished mahogany. The shelves behind it were filled with a vast array of bottles. A quick glance showed a good many expensive liquors and impressive vintages.

It appeared that De Lora's did not deal in the sort of low-quality bootleg alcohol I had heard plagued many speakeasies.

"What'll it be?" the bartender asked. He was a tall, broad man, and, like the gentleman at the door, gave the impression that he might be equally comfortable pouring drinks as slitting throats.

"I don't want a drink at the moment," I said. "I'm looking for someone."

"You're free to look." The tone in which he said this seemed to distinctly discourage looking, but I pressed ahead anyway.

"I thought you might help me. I'm looking for Leon De Lora."

The bartender watched me for a moment, his features expressionless. "What do you want with Mr. De Lora?"

I smiled, trying to appear perfectly at ease. "I've heard a lot about him, and I'm very interested to meet him."

Until that moment, I had not paid much attention to the gentleman at the end of the bar. He was leaned against the sleek surface on one elbow, angled slightly away from me, but when he heard my question, he turned.

He was the sort of man who instantly drew one's attention. He was tall and very handsome with slicked black hair and eyes so brown they looked almost black in the dim light. A scar ran along one cheek, but somehow it didn't detract from his looks. Instead, it complemented his appearance with the aura of danger. Not that he needed a scar to do that. There was something about the way he carried himself, about the watchfulness in his unreadable dark eyes that set one immediately on edge. I knew who he was at once.

I offered him a smile. "Mr. De Lora, I presume?"

14

His eyes swept over me in a slow, assessing way before returning to my face.

"You have an advantage over me," he said. "That doesn't happen often."

Despite the light tone in which he spoke, there was an intensity in his gaze that was a bit disarming. I would have to be on my guard.

"Rose Kelly," I said, using the name I had chosen as my American alias. Winnelda had assured me it evoked just the right image.

"I'm pleased to meet you, Rose," he said. He moved toward me, taking my hand in his. I could feel the warmth of it through my glove. The pressure held for just a moment and then he released it, leaning against the bar. As he shifted his elbow against the bar's edge, his jacket moved, and I caught sight of the shoulder holster he wore beneath it and the gun that rested there. I looked away quickly, though my heart rate had increased ever so slightly at this very visible reminder of what was at stake.

"What brings you here?" he asked.

"I came to meet you," I said.

He smiled. "So I heard. It's not every day a beautiful woman comes into this place looking to meet me."

I found this hard to believe. I imagined there were any number of young society women who made their way to this club for a look at him. He was terribly handsome, but, more than that, there was a hard edge to him, a glint in his eyes that belied the easy smile on his mouth. He looked smart in his impeccably tailored evening clothes, but he wore that gun just as easily as he did a dinner jacket and I could sense the energy tinged with menace that was barely contained beneath the polished exterior he presented. Leon De Lora was just the sort of trouble a great many women would enjoy getting into.

"I imagine you're more popular than you let on," I said.

He shrugged. "I try to avoid attention whenever possible. Though you knew who I was readily enough."

"Your picture often appears in the paper," I said.

"But yours never has."

"How can you be certain?" I asked.

"I'd remember a face like yours."

Whatever his reputation, he had a way with words. Having lived with an expert charmer for several years, however, I was certainly not going to lose my head over his flattery. What was more, I was glad to realize that he hadn't seen me or Milo in any of the society columns.

"Can I offer you a drink?" he asked.

"Not just now, thank you."

"No bad bathtub gin here at De Lora's, if that's what you're worried about."

I smiled. "I'm not much of a drinker."

"Ah, yes. I forgot. You came here to meet me. Well, come and sit down."

He took my arm and led me to a booth in the corner, inserted into its own little private alcove in the wall. The seats were made of a dusky dark blue velvet and the surface of the table was a gleaming dark wood that reflected the light that hung above us. I realized, as I slid into my seat, that we were shielded from view from the rest of the room in this secluded corner. This was not the only such booth in the club, but it was a little disconcerting to be tucked away, out of sight, with this notorious man. Of course, I had put myself in his power the moment I had walked into his establishment, so there was no reason to start worrying about it now.

Besides, we were not really alone. As we settled into our seats, I did not miss the movement of two large men who stood with their backs to the booth, their watchful gazes moving restlessly around the room. I wondered if there was some particular danger from which they were protecting him or if this was merely a necessary precaution in his line of work.

I let my fur slide off my shoulders and tried to maintain an air of ease even as he leaned toward me slightly, his arms on the table between us.

"Now, sweetheart, what did you want to talk to me about?"

I was slightly caught off guard by this casual endearment, but I reminded myself that I was meant to be an American comfortable with this sort of crowd.

"I hesitate to tell you," I said coyly.

"Why's that?"

I gave a little laugh. "It's a bit embarrassing."

"I don't embarrass easy."

My eyes caught his. "No. I don't imagine you do."

I realized that I might be precariously close to some sort of boundary. I had not come here expressly to flirt with Mr. De Lora. In fact, I had been determined not to do so. I had to admit, however, that, if one wasn't careful, it might be shockingly easy to fall into the habit.

"Perhaps I should start at the beginning," I said.

"By all means."

He took a gold cigarette case out of the inside pocket of his suit and offered one to me. I declined, and he lit his up.

"I've just moved to New York," I said.

He waited. It was one of the quickly discernible traits that marked him as dangerous, I realized: this calculated way he waited and watched. He might look like a man at ease, but there was in him the latent menace of a tiger poised to pounce.

"From Maine. Things have been difficult, and I hoped that I would be able to make a better life for myself here." I had to remind myself not to volunteer too much information. It seemed to me that filling the silence with useless detail was the best way to get in trouble later.

"Whereabouts in Maine?"

I realized again in that moment how poorly thought out my plan had been. I knew very little about Maine, and if he knew more than I did I was going to be found out.

"Augusta," I said, seizing upon the only city in Maine I could think of. "Though I grew up a bit on the outskirts. I'm afraid I'm something of a country girl at heart."

He smiled, though his eyes remained unreadable. "You don't look like a country girl to me."

"Thank you." I drew in a breath as though building up the courage to make a confession. Then I plunged ahead with the story I had formulated. "The truth is, I'm a reporter. That is, I want to be. I'm trying to get a job with the society columns, but anyone can write about parties, and plays, and society events. I thought it might be interesting if I wrote about something a bit more . . . exciting."

He smiled. "You thought they'd be interested in the criminal element."

"Well, you're awfully interesting, Mr. De Lora."

He blew out a stream of smoke, watching me with those dark eyes of his. "I think you're pretty interesting yourself."

I affected a flustered smile and then continued. "I knew it was a gamble coming here, but I thought I should up the ante," I said, silently thanking Winnelda for recommending that I include some gambling parlance in my dialogue. "If you'd just give me a bit of information, I'm sure I could make an interesting story out of it."

"I usually have reporters thrown out of here on their ear," he said. His eyes ran across my face. "But your ears are too pretty for that."

"I don't believe I've ever had someone compliment my ears," I said with a laugh.

"Well, I've always been a bit unconventional."

"Why don't you tell me about it," I said.

"Why are you really here?" he asked suddenly.

I looked at him, wondering if he had discovered something about me. Had my accent given me away? I had been relatively confident that I could keep up a consistently American cadence, but perhaps he had noticed that something was amiss.

"There are any number of — shall we say — reputable places in this city where a nice young woman might have gone for a story," he went on. "Why is it that you came here, trying to fit in in an element that doesn't suit you?"

He was perceptive. Somehow, I hadn't expected that. Of course, I imagined one didn't grow to become a successful criminal without having good instincts. As with any other enterprise, there was an element of talent involved.

"I . . . I don't know. I just . . ."

I was saved by a sudden movement at the door nearest the band, and a woman stepped out onto the dance floor, illuminated by a single light.

She was a beautiful woman with flawless dark skin, marcelled black hair, and lustrous brown eyes. She wore a beaded gold evening gown that set off a marvelous figure.

And when she began to sing, I was mesmerized. Her voice was low and sultry, every note perfectly pitched, but there was more to it than simple training. There was something in her tone that could not be learned. I felt as though I was being transported to a different place, as though her voice was carrying me into a dream.

For a moment I forgot where I was and listened as she sang the lyrics — a sad song about love and loss — infusing them with depth and meaning that I had never heard in this song before. It was a rare gift.

"She's good, isn't she?" Mr. De Lora said.

I dragged my attention from the singing woman to look back at him. "She's marvelous."

"Her name is Esther Hayes. People come

a long way to hear her sing."

"I can see why."

We sat in silence after that until the song ended. Esther Hayes finished her song and disappeared from the room amidst a swell of applause. I was brought back to the present by Mr. De Lora.

"Look, baby. You're a sweet kid, and I'd like to help you, but I don't know that I should tell you anything." I didn't seem to be getting anywhere with him. In fact, I had the impression that he was very close to bringing this interview, such as it was, to a close. I needed to do a better job of charming him.

"I don't expect you to tell me about what goes on behind closed doors around here," I said. "But isn't there some sort of a story you could give me? Some angle that may be of interest to my society readers? Please, Mr. De Lora. Won't you help out a country girl?"

He took a drag from his cigarette and seemed to contemplate the question. I wondered if he was considering throwing me out of his establishment after all.

At last he spoke.

"I do have a bit of a scoop for you."

"Oh?" I wondered just what it was he was going to reveal. I hoped that he would not ever ask me what paper he could find this story in. I had the feeling he would be annoyed if he were to discover I had been lying to him.

"Yeah, I've been looking into getting a new line of business."

I found this surprising, and it must have showed on my face.

He smiled. "Well, 'new' in a manner of speaking. I'm looking at opening a few nightclubs. Prohibition's on its last legs. I've known that for the last couple of years, and I've had my eyes on bigger and better things. The real money has never been in bootlegging, at least not for me."

"Which is why you don't serve moonshine and bathtub gin?" I asked with a glance toward the well-stocked bar.

"You've got a sharp eye for a country girl," he said, leaning back in his seat. There was something calculating in his gaze, but he went on without a pause. "I've served my share of moonshine, but competition's stiff and I find it tedious. No, I've found there's a market for the good stuff. And it can be had for the right price. Once Prohibition ends, there'll be a lot of people looking to have a good time out in the open."

I found myself a bit disappointed. It was not that I had expected him to suddenly reveal that he had had something to do with the death of Grant Palmer, but I had at least hoped for something that might be able to lead the conversation in that direction. Telling me that he was considering going into legitimate business was not very exciting at all.

"This is all very interesting," I said, hoping I sounded as though I meant it.

"Maybe you should write some of it down. Don't you carry a notebook?"

He was watching me carefully, and I wondered if he had realized that this was all a ploy. I had thought it was an excellent ruse, but I was quickly learning that Leon De Lora was no one's fool.

"I thought it might make me conspicuous."

The corner of his mouth tipped up. "Baby, it's hard to be conspicuous in a place like this."

I glanced around. I supposed he was right. It seemed that there were people from all walks of life congregated within these walls.

I turned my attention back to him. I knew he had been purposefully putting off my questions, but I was determined to play the part of a dogged reporter and that meant pressing him for answers. If we had to start with his idea for a nightclub, so be it.

Perhaps then I could win some of his trust and he would let something slip.

Looking at those dark, unreadable eyes, I somehow doubted he was the type of man to ever give something away unintentionally, but I could always hope.

"I don't need a notebook at present," I said. "Tell me more about your nightclubs."

"I plan to open the first one here in New York, of course, but I'd like to expand beyond that. Maybe even internationally, if it works out."

This was not at all what I had been expecting. I had come here to talk to an American gangster, not a handsome entrepreneur with an eye for expanding his existing enterprises.

Perhaps it was a good thing. Perhaps it meant that he could be cleared in the death of Grant Palmer. After all, if he was indeed set on leading a legitimate life once Prohibition had run its course, it wouldn't do for him to commit a murder at such a pivotal time.

Then again, I had the feeling that Leon De Lora always did exactly as he pleased with very little worry about consequences. And there was always the possibility that Grant Palmer had posed some impediment to this plan, created enough of a problem that Mr. De Lora thought it must be eliminated.

"Have you . . . selected a site for the new nightclub?" I asked. I was trying very hard to think of questions a newspaperwoman might have under just such circumstances, but I was finding it a bit difficult. I realized I was disappointed that this man might not be the murderer I was seeking, and I had to reconfigure my existing preconceptions.

"I've got a few places I'm eyeing," he said. "Nothing set in stone at the moment."

"Do you really think Prohibition will be repealed?" I asked.

"It's as good as done. The whole thing'll be over by the end of the year."

"Then I suppose you'll be glad to be able to live a life without the threat of the law hanging over you."

I wondered, as I said the words, if I was pushing things too far, but he didn't seem to think so.

A smile tugged at his lips. "The law has never made much difference to me one way or the other."

I wondered what it was like to live life that way, with a careless disregard for propriety or societal boundaries. I had always been the sort of woman who tried, for the most part, to stay within the lines that had been drawn for me. But I had encountered a great many people who had challenged those boundaries, and some of them had been murderers. Was this man a killer?

"I suppose that will be very profitable for you," I said, trying to keep my questions focused.

He shrugged. "I'm making money, and I'll keep making money."

I opened my mouth, prepared to formulate another question, when a man made his way to the table. He had the same weathered, dangerous sort of face I'd noticed on the other employees here at De Lora's, and I was reminded that Leon De Lora might give the impression of handsome sophistication, but there was still something a bit less refined beneath the surface.

Mr. De Lora looked up at the approaching gentleman. "What is it?" he asked in a tone that indicated he didn't appreciate the disturbance.

"We . . . uh . . . got a little issue, boss," the man said, his gaze flickering to me and back to Mr. De Lora. "Something you might need to take care of."

I glanced in the direction from which the man had come, to catch a glimpse of the "issue": someone in a state of advanced inebriation, perhaps, or a fistfight, which seemed somehow likely in a place like this. But there was nothing, no disturbance visible through the haze of cigarette smoke.

I glanced back at Mr. De Lora. It was difficult to tell what he thought about this request. He seemed neither alarmed or, indeed, interested, but after a moment's pause, he reached to grind out his cigarette in the ashtray on the table and slid out of the booth.

"Sorry to run out on you, Rose, but duty calls."

"But I . . ." I tried to think of some way to finish the sentence. After all, he had already given me more information than he would likely have given to anyone else, the "scoop," he had called it.

He stood there a moment, waiting. When I said nothing more, his brows went up ever so slightly. I realized this might be my only chance; if he slipped away from me now, perhaps I might not have another opportunity to speak to him.

And so I decided to be bold and push ahead. "I was hoping to get more details from you . . . for my story."

He seemed to consider this for a moment, and then he gave a short nod. "Come back tomorrow night. Maybe I can tell you more then."

"I . . . all right," I agreed.

It was just then that Esther Hayes came back into the speakeasy from a door set to one side of the wall. I saw her eyes settle on Mr. De Lora, and he motioned her over.

"Good evening, Mr. De Lora," she said when she reached us. Then she nodded at me. "Ma'am."

"This is Esther Hayes," he told me. "Esther, this is Rose Kelly, a new friend of mine."

"How do you do, Miss Hayes," I said. "I really enjoyed your performance. Your voice is so lovely."

"Thank you," she said quietly.

"Rose is writing an article. Answer some questions for her, will you?"

"Of course, Mr. De Lora." Miss Hayes's expression didn't change, but her eyes flicked to him briefly, as though trying to ascertain his motives. There was something very guarded about her, and I had the impression she wasn't very pleased with the idea of speaking with me.

He turned then without another word and was gone, following the other man through the maze of tables, the men who had stood near our booth trailing out after them.

Esther Hayes stood looking at me.

I motioned to the seat he had vacated. "Sit

down, won't you?"

She sat, a few of the gold beads on her gown clattering softly against the wooden table as she slid into the booth.

"What questions can I answer for you, Miss Kelly?" she asked. Her speaking voice was as pleasant as her singing voice, low and soft.

"How long have you been singing here?" I asked, trying to break through the barrier that seemed to exist between us.

"A year. Maybe a little longer."

"And you enjoy working here?"

"Very much."

"As Mr. De Lora said, I'm writing an article about him for my society column," I said, pushing ahead. "What can you tell me about him?"

She looked at me warily. I wondered if she might be afraid of her employer. If so, I couldn't exactly blame her. From everything I had heard, he was a dangerous man. I knew that loyalties in this world were not just a matter of employment in a difficult economy; they were a matter of life and death.

"He's very handsome," I said. "I'll admit I wasn't expecting someone so young and attractive." I thought this might, perhaps, give the impression that I was a somewhat silly young woman who wanted a gossip piece. While it was not exactly the impression I wished to cultivate with Mr. De Lora, I thought it might be the best way to build camaraderie with another woman.

Again, her eyes searched my face. She seemed to be considering her answer, and when she spoke I was surprised by her reply. "He's a better man than he's given credit for being."

I might have suspected this was a lie, or the careful answer of a woman who had a good deal to lose, but there was something about the tone of her voice as she said it that made me think she believed what she was saying.

"He's been kind to me," she went on. "I haven't had an easy life, and Mr. De Lora gave me a job when a lot of places wouldn't."

"But your voice is magnificent," I said without thinking. "I can't imagine anyone not wanting to hire you."

She looked at me, her expression wry. "To a lot of people, the color of the skin is more important than the quality of the voice."

"Of course," I said, realizing the stupidity of my comment. It was sometimes easy for me to forget the privileges of the life into which I had been born.

"But Mr. De Lora hired me as soon as he heard me sing. And he's looked out for me. A lot of men wouldn't do that."

"Yes, I see what you mean," I said, my opinion of him improving based on this information. She was certainly right that there was more to him than met the eye.

Of course, this did not excuse his criminal activities. But it made me think that, perhaps, there was something kinder beneath the menacing persona he presented to the world.

I considered asking her about Grant Palmer but decided against it. I didn't think she would be likely to tell me anything. After all, I was a strange woman asking probing questions. What was more, I had a feeling that Mr. De Lora would ask her later about the content of our conversation, and I didn't want to show my hand just yet.

"He tells me he's interested in opening some nightclubs. Would you continue to sing in one of his establishments?"

"Maybe," she said vaguely.

I realized that the conversation had lagged. She was watching me, waiting to see what I would say next, and I suddenly found I wasn't sure how to proceed.

She seemed to sense this. "If you'll excuse me, Miss Kelly," she said. "I have to prepare for my next number."

"Oh, yes. Of course. Thank you for taking the time to talk to me."

She nodded, the corners of her mouth rising slightly in what was not quite a smile. And then she rose and walked slowly away.

I sat alone in the booth for a moment, considering everything. I hadn't exactly learned anything of importance, but I couldn't help but feel that I had definitely made progress. After all, he had agreed to see me again. I would just have to come up with some way of steering the topic around to Grant Palmer tomorrow night. Perhaps I could even say that I had read it in the newspapers. It was a risky thing to do, but it might be a chance I would have to take.

I pulled my coat up over my shoulders and slid out of the booth. Now that Mr. De Lora was gone, I didn't think I should push my luck by asking any more questions this evening. If he found out, it would likely annoy him. I would just have to wait until tomorrow.

I made my way out of De Lora's and into the cool night air. The cold, silent street, when contrasted with the noisy, smoky atmosphere from which I just exited, was startling, even a bit disorienting, and I stood still for a moment, wondering how I was going to find my way back to the Aldens' home. I pulled my fur tightly around me, both tired and exhilarated by the progress I had made in forming a relationship with Leon De Lora.

It was then my attention was caught by a sharp cry from the alleyway between De Lora's and the apparently vacant building next door. I looked around, wondering if I should try to locate some help, but the street was empty. A soft thud and a muffled groan from the same direction were enough to convince me the matter bore looking into.

I moved to the edge of the building and peered into the alleyway. It was very dark, but the moon was shining into the space enough for me to make out three figures standing there. I couldn't see their features distinctly, but I was fairly certain that two of them were Mr. De Lora and the gentleman who had come to fetch him from my table. The latter gentleman was holding a third gentleman against the wall by his throat. I barely stifled a gasp as I realized some violence was being done to the man.

"I'm not going to give you a second warning," Mr. De Lora said in a calm voice. "You stay away from here. If I find out you've come back, you won't get off so easy."

He turned then and his employee released

the man, who slumped to the ground. The two gentlemen, if such a term was applicable in this situation, turned without a backward glance and disappeared farther into the alley. A moment later I heard the sound of a door closing somewhere toward the back.

I slipped back to the front of the building, trying to decide what I should do next. It was very possible the man was badly injured and needed help. Should I phone for the police? It was then I realized ruefully that the officers that patrolled this particular neighborhood were likely the same ones who were, even now, enjoying mugs of beer in the basement of this establishment. Thankfully, I was saved from this conundrum when the man stumbled out of the alley and, without a glance in my direction, walked stiffly down the street.

I stared after him, wondering just what I had gotten myself into.

It was late when I reached the house. I slipped inside, glad no one had locked the door in my absence, and made my way across the dark foyer, feeling my way up the stairs with a hand on the banister. The air was cool and still, and all was silent save for the ticking of the grandfather clock in the foyer and the brush of my skirts against the steps as I ascended.

I slipped into the bedroom, closing the door quietly behind me. When I turned back toward the room, I started.

Milo was sitting in one of the chairs, still in his evening attire, smoking a cigarette.

It had not even occurred to me that Milo might be back from his outing with Tom. I had expected it to last until dawn, as his gambling forays often did, and had assumed that I would have plenty of time to get back into the Aldens' home without Milo having known I was gone. This unexpected development was disconcerting.

I felt very much like a naughty child who had been caught doing something they oughtn't, but I did my best to hide it. "Oh, hello, Milo."

"Hello."

I came into the room and tossed my fur across the back of a vacant chair.

"You're still dressed," I said nonchalantly, as I moved toward the dressing table to remove my jewelry. "Why aren't you in bed?"

"I didn't undress as I was wondering if I might have to comb the city looking for you."

I turned to look at him, feeling a bit guilty,

255

though I knew it was ridiculous as he had left me wondering about his whereabouts countless times over the years.

"I didn't think you would be back so early," I said lamely.

"I've been back for over an hour."

"Oh." It didn't seem at all fair that he was always catching me doing underhanded things when I could never catch him at anything.

"We didn't stay out very long, as Mr. Smith said he had lost enough money for one evening."

I sighed. "Do you suppose he's getting himself into debt?"

"As to that, I couldn't say. He hadn't the finesse of a long-term gambler and didn't extend beyond whatever limit he had set for himself, but that doesn't mean he hasn't done it before. He was disappointed with his losses, but no one likes to lose. I do hate to change the subject, darling, but do you mind terribly if I ask where you've been?" He asked the question in a perfectly casual way, as though my answer made little difference one way or the other. Perhaps it did. I had the sinking suspicion he already knew where I had been.

I hesitated. I had little doubt that this conversation was going to lead to an argument, and I was very tired. Then again, I supposed we might just as well have it out now as later. "You're going to be angry with me," I said at last.

"Oh, I have no doubt."

"I went to De Lora's tonight."

He swore beneath his breath, but I pushed ahead.

"I wanted to see what it was like, to see if I could find out anything about Mr. Palmer's involvement there. I was very careful not to do anything dangerous. After all, a great many society people go there every evening."

"So that's why you didn't protest when I went last night, so you could go alone tonight, putting yourself in danger without anyone knowing what you were up to."

I started to tell him that Winnelda had known to inform him if I had disappeared, but I thought better of it. There was no sense dragging her into this.

"I wasn't in danger," I protested.

This was a conversation we had again and again, Milo wanting me to stay safely at home while he did the things he considered unsafe. While I appreciated his attempts to protect me, I didn't see why I should be prevented from doing things just because I was a woman. I was smart and capable, and

I didn't think I should be excluded from taking small risks just because I had not been born a man.

He interrupted this inner tirade. "Did you learn anything?"

I looked up at him, surprised, even a bit confused, by the question. "What?"

"Did you learn anything? At De Lora's."

"You're not going to read me a lecture first?" I asked.

"I obviously can't stop you," he said. "You're going to do just as you please, so I might as well just resign myself."

I was glad that he was taking this realization so well.

I moved to take a seat in the chair across from him. "I had a long talk with Leon De Lora."

His eyes met mine.

"You just waltzed up to Leon De Lora and introduced yourself."

"In a manner of speaking."

He shook his head. "I don't know what I'm to do with you."

It seemed I had not escaped the lecture after all.

"You needn't do anything with me," I replied tersely. "I'm not incompetent, and there's no reason you need treat me as though I am."

"I know you're perfectly competent," he replied mildly, apparently unwilling to be drawn into an argument on the topic. "But you're my wife, and I think I've a right to be concerned for your safety."

I let out a breath. "I appreciate your concern, but I was perfectly safe."

"You agreed to let me go there alone."

"And you did," I pointed out. "When you didn't learn anything, I decided to try my hand at it."

He gave a sigh and motioned for me to continue.

"I told him that I had recently moved to New York from Maine and was trying to find work as a reporter and asked if he would answer a few questions."

"So you invented a reason for being blatantly inquisitive. I suppose that's one way to go about things. And how did you explain your accent?"

"I used an American accent."

His brows rose. "You're becoming more and more incorrigible with each passing day, my love."

I had the vague suspicion this was not a compliment, so I went on. "He was very pleasant and gave me information on a new nightclub he intends to open. It didn't exactly lead to any information about Mr.

Palmer's death, but . . ."

I broke off, feeling instinctively that now was not the time to mention that Mr. De Lora was expecting me for another visit tomorrow night. I expected Milo to prod me on, but it seemed he had focused on the beginning of my sentence rather than the end of it.

"Very pleasant, was he?" His eyes moved over me. "I suppose that dress didn't hurt anything."

I shrugged, the strap slipping off my shoulder as if in answer to his remark. "He didn't seem to take any particular notice of my dress."

It was not entirely true, perhaps. I had seen his eyes run over me once or twice in an appraising sort of way, but there had been nothing untoward in his manner. In fact, I had been treated much worse by gentlemen of my own social circle.

He stubbed out his cigarette and rose from his chair. "You can convince me of a lot of things, darling, but you're not going to convince me that a man like Leon De Lora took no notice of your . . . physical attributes."

I made a show of considering this. "He did say I had pretty ears."

"Ears?" Milo repeated. His eyes swept

over me. "You were wearing that, and it was your ears he noticed? I would have expected De Lora to have a bit more finesse."

"He has a certain sort of rugged appeal," I mused.

"I don't mean to appear overly inquisitive, darling, but are you intent on seducing Leon De Lora?"

I frowned at him. "Of course not."

"Does he know that?"

"I didn't make any improper advances to him, if that's what you mean," I replied, vaguely irritated. It was true that Mr. De Lora had been a bit flirtatious, but that was in his nature. There had been nothing to indicate that he was interested in me beyond my role as a reporter, and I certainly hadn't given him the impression that I was receptive to such a thing.

"Yes, but I was wondering what you plan to do when he decides he wants to do more than give you information."

"That's not going to happen. I've made it perfectly clear I was only interested in writing an article."

Milo sighed. "I cannot believe it's possible for you to have been married to me for six years and still retain that breathtaking naïveté."

"I'm not as innocent as you think," I

retorted.

His brows rose. "Oh? Do tell."

"I only mean that I am perfectly capable of divining the nefarious intentions of gentlemen, and I can tell you that Leon De Lora isn't thinking of me in those terms. He's handsome and charming, yes, but I know how to deal with men like that."

"I see I shall have to put all thoughts of him from your mind," he said, taking my hands and pulling me to my feet, his arms sliding around me.

"And how do you intend to do that?" I asked with a laugh, suddenly much less tired than I had been.

"With my own ode to your earlobes, perhaps?" he leaned to murmur, his lips against my ear.

Within a few moments, Leon De Lora was the furthest thing from my mind.

15

It was at breakfast the next morning that Mr. Alden broached the subject of a visit to the center of his shipping operations.

"Perhaps we might take that visit to the warehouse today, Ames?"

I looked up from my plate. This was the first I'd heard of any visit to the warehouse. I glanced at Milo, but he wasn't looking in my direction.

"I'd enjoy that," Milo replied. He took a sip of coffee, and I had the distinct impression he was avoiding my gaze deliberately, as though to ward off my curiosity. He ought to have known better.

"Things have been so hectic as of late that I haven't had much thought about them," Mr. Alden continued, "but I suppose I really ought to make sure that everything is going well. My warehouse manager hasn't telephoned me, but he's the sort of man not to worry until things get out of hand. Besides, it'll be a good time for you to get the lay of the land."

"An excellent idea."

Tabitha sighed. "We don't have to come, do we? The warehouse is such a dreary place, and it's always so horribly hot inside, even at this time of year."

"No, of course not," Mr. Alden said. "I'm sure you and Amory have wedding details to take care of."

I could see where this was headed. I would be packed off for another morning of shopping or some such thing while the men went off to examine the place that might very well hold clues to the motive behind Mr. Palmer's murder.

"I hate to contradict Tabitha, but I'd love to see your warehouses," I said to Mr. Alden.

Milo glanced at me, and Mr. Alden looked up from his coffee with an expression of surprise. "I didn't think it would be of much interest to you, Amory, but, of course, you'd be welcome."

"Thank you," I replied. Now it was my turn to refuse to look in Milo's direction lest he try to dissuade me with his eyes.

"Well, I hope you don't mind if I beg off," Tabitha said. "I'll call up Tom and see if he wants to go driving. It looks like it's going to be a lovely day."

Breakfast finished, we went to gather our coats and hats as Mr. Alden had his car sent round.

"You don't need to come to the warehouse, you know," Milo told me as I pulled on my gloves.

"I want to see it for myself. I've been wondering about those break-ins."

"You'd do well to stop wondering about them," he said. "That has nothing to do with any of this."

"You don't know that. It might very well have something to do with Grant Palmer's murder. If Mr. Alden is involved in some unlawful scheme that led to Mr. Palmer's death, then we might find a clue to tell us so there."

"Even if that's the case, you're certainly not to go traipsing around those warehouses asking questions. If Mr. Alden or one of his associates is the killer, it won't be safe for you."

What he said made sense, of course, but I didn't like it. I felt certain that some key to this matter might be found at Mr. Alden's warehouse. And if I could I was going to find out.

The warehouse was located in an area

known as the Meatpacking District, though Mr. Alden explained to us that many of the industries located there had nothing to do with the meat business. The nucleus of Alden Shipping was an impressive brick building, surrounded by a scattering of smaller, less imposing buildings, not far from the waterfront. The main building was two stories and had one wide, tall door in the front of it, big enough to drive a vehicle into, I imagined. There were windows, too, though they appeared dark as though shuttered from the inside. Outside were stacked large wooden crates that towered upward like buildings of their own. Trucks drove to and fro, smaller crates piled up in their beds. Men moved about, too, with an air of purpose, many of them pushing handcarts or pulling small trolleys loaded with odds and ends. It all gave the impression of busy industry and apparent success. I was beginning to see how Mr. Alden might have recovered from his financial difficulties, and I felt a bit guilty for my suspicions.

We alighted from the car at a smaller brick building, and Mr. Alden led us inside. A man behind one of the battered wood desks stood when we entered. He was an older gentleman, tall and thin, with nondescript features and wearing dusty coveralls, but he had the unmistakable aura of a man comfortable in his authority.

"This is my warehouse manager, Fred Brown," Mr. Alden said by way of introduction.

"Hello," Mr. Brown said with a nod in our direction.

"How is everything, Fred?"

The two of them launched into a brief discussion about the running of the business. I listened carefully, trying to catch any discernible hints of uneasiness in either of them, but everything seemed very straightforward. At last Mr. Alden turned his attention back to us. "Ready for the tour?" he asked.

We walked back outside and were greeted with a burst of cool wind off the water. I pulled my coat tighter and took Milo's arm, hoping to derive some warmth from him. Mr. Alden led us around the stacks of wooden crates and through a warren of wheelbarrows, hand trucks, and other assorted moving apparatus to a door in the side of the warehouse. He took a key from his pocket, inserted it into the lock, and pushed the door open.

"We keep all the doors locked, except the loading dock, which is open during the day.

Cuts down on the chance of thieves getting in."

We followed him inside. The interior of the warehouse was much the same as the outside had been. There were heaps of crates, barrels, and boxes here, too, workers moving about the room with purpose and focus. A line of tin drums sat near the open door of the loading dock, gasoline for the trucks, I imagined. Above us, a catwalk followed the walls of the building, and men moved about there, too, looking down on the industry beneath them, making notes, and occasionally calling things out to the workmen on the floor. No one seemed to take much notice of our presence as we moved farther into the cavernous space.

The temperature in the warehouse was noticeably different than it had been outside. As Tabitha had said, the interior of the building was very hot. Within a few minutes, I thought of discarding my coat, but we were moving at a good pace through the warehouse, following Mr. Alden through a maze of stacked containers, and I didn't like to halt our progress.

Mr. Alden began to explain the workings of his enterprise as we walked. "We do a lot of shipping, but the items often come here to be stored before we have a truck or boat ready for shipping them. It takes a carefully organized system to make sure that everything is sorted correctly and loaded and delivered on time."

"You mentioned someone trying to break in? I suppose that's why, because you keep valuable items here?" I said, hoping to bring the conversation back around to what had been on my mind.

If Mr. Alden thought my questioning suspicious, he gave no sign of it. Instead, he nodded. "Yes, we've had a couple of break-ins. These are difficult times, and there are a lot of people looking to make a little money in whatever ways they can."

He didn't sound overly concerned about it, but I wondered. Surely thieves would be a serious matter?

It was then he spotted a man moving a large stack of boxes. "Hank!" he called, raising a hand to stop the man before turning back to us. "Excuse me for just a moment, will you? I want to talk to him about something."

As soon as he was out of sight, I turned to Milo. "It seems as though it's going to be rather difficult to learn anything." I was disappointed, but I would also be glad to leave the warehouse. It was so very warm here.

"We've only just started the tour. I'll see if I can mention the attempted robberies or if there might be some connection between Mr. Alden and Leon De Lora."

I was glad to see that he wasn't going to fight me on the issue, but it suddenly seemed of second importance as I was rapidly becoming overheated, my vision growing dark at the edges.

"I wish you'd have let me come alone. He's more likely to talk if I . . ." He stopped then, looking more closely at my face. "Are you all right?"

"Yes," I said vaguely. "Why?"

"Your color's gone off."

"I'm very hot."

"Here, take off your jacket." He moved behind me and helped slip it from my shoulders, and I felt immediately cooler.

Milo took my elbow, looking down at me. "Better?"

I nodded.

Mr. Alden came back just then. Either the sight of my face or the way in which Milo was looking at me alerted him that something was amiss. "What's wrong?"

"I'm just feeling a bit overheated, I think," I said. "Would it be all right if I went back to the office?"

"I can have my driver take you home,"

Mr. Alden said.

"No, no. I'll just wait for you."

"Amory . . ." Milo began, but I shook my head firmly and mustered up a smile. "I just need some fresh air. I'll be fine."

His eyes met mine, and I knew he could see my determination in them. This might be our only opportunity to find out something, and I needed him to pay attention.

"Are you quite sure?" Mr. Alden asked.

I nodded, feeling better already at the thought of escaping the stifling heat of the warehouse.

"I'll escort you back, darling," Milo said.

"That's not necessary," I said.

"I'll have to let you out with a key," Mr. Alden said. "The doors are all locked from the inside."

Milo took my arm and we followed him through a warren of cargo until we reached a door at the side wall. He inserted his key into the lock and pushed it open for me.

The cool air that hit my face was an exquisite relief.

"Are you sure you don't want me to walk you to the office?" Milo asked.

"No, thank you. I can find my way. Please, carry on."

I stepped out the door then before either of them could protest.

"What kind of vehicles do you use, Mr. Alden?" Milo asked him.

"We've got several different trucks," he said, clearly enthusiastic about the subject. "And we've got our own little shop here — spare parts, tires, the works — so we can keep everything running smoothly. If you'll follow me this way, I can show you the models."

The door closed behind me then, and I made my way back through the towering maze outside toward the little office building.

I felt instantly better now that I was back in the fresh air, and I drew in deep breaths, clearing my head. My being overheated had not been a ruse, but that didn't mean that I couldn't turn it into an opportunity.

Upon entering the little office, I saw Mr. Brown rise again from his desk. "Can I help you, ma'am?"

"I'm afraid I got a bit overheated in the warehouse. I told Mr. Alden and my husband I would wait for them here."

He nodded sympathetically. "It's hot in the warehouse buildings. Sit down there, won't you?"

He motioned toward a pair of wooden chairs sitting against one wall. I sat in one of them, setting my jacket on the empty seat beside me.

"Can I offer you some water?"

"That would be wonderful. Thank you."

He moved from behind his desk and to a little table in the corner containing a water jug and glasses. As he poured the water, I considered how best I might be able to get information from him. Mr. Brown was Mr. Alden's warehouse manager, after all. He would likely know the ins and outs of everything that was happening here, perhaps even more than Mr. Alden did.

I thought it unlikely he would appreciate questions from a strange Englishwoman, but it certainly didn't hurt to try. I didn't want to seem too inquisitive, but, then again, women were given a bit more leniency where gossip was concerned. It was insulting, perhaps, but that didn't mean that I couldn't use it to my advantage.

He brought the glass of water to me, and I drank it gratefully. I hadn't realized how thirsty I was until I had drained the glass of half its contents.

"Thank you," I said.

Mr. Brown nodded. "Is there anything else I can get for you?"

"Oh, no. I'm quite comfortable now," I said.

He moved back toward his desk, and I

wondered if he was going to carry on with his work and do his best to ignore me. It seemed, however, that he was in the mood for conversation. Perhaps being in this office all day was a bit lonely.

"You're not from around here, I take it," he said settling back into his seat behind the desk.

"No," I agreed with a smile. "I'm from England."

"Nice place, I hear."

"Yes, though I am very much enjoying my visit to New York."

"It's a grand city," he said proudly.

"And this seems like a very nice place to work. I'm quite impressed with the facilities."

He nodded. "I've worked for Mr. Alden for many years, through a lot of ups and downs. He's a good man, and I have a lot of pride in Alden Shipping."

It occurred to me that this was not the type of man to tell tales out of school, as it were. He was clearly very loyal to Mr. Alden. I knew it was important to make it look as though I was a close family friend, privy to some of his difficulties.

"I knew the Aldens when they lived in England," I said. "I'm going to be in Miss Alden's wedding."

"Miss Tabitha's a fine woman. I wish her all happiness."

"And her fiancé, Mr. Smith, is going to join the company, I understand."

"Yes," he answered. "A first-rate young man he is, too."

Now that we had exchanged pleasantries, I decided to push ahead with some more pertinent questions.

"I understand there has been some difficulty here as of late, break-ins and things of that nature," I said. "I do hope it isn't dangerous for you."

I hoped to appeal to his sense of company pride, and it seemed to work, for he drew himself up a bit. "Well, it isn't always safe working here. Mr. Alden owns a great deal of property and there are always thieves about, looking for easy pickings."

"I do hope the thieves don't strike often."

"No, ma'am. We haven't had much trouble of this sort. I suppose after a few failed attempts they'll realize that it's no use and go on to someplace else."

"I suppose you have very good security."

"We hire a few men to patrol at night. The property is fairly large, so they can't be everywhere at once."

"When was the last break-in?"

"Oh, about a week ago." He seemed to

consider. "Yes, exactly a week ago, it was. It was during the middle of the night. Someone broke one of the windows in the alleyway along the big buildings."

"Trying to get inside?"

He shook his head. "I suppose, but it was a lost cause from the start. The windows along the alley are boarded up on the inside. There was no use in breaking the window. They couldn't get in that way. There's no entry from the ground if you don't have a key. The windows up on the second floor aren't boarded up, but the thieves would have a hard time carting things up to the catwalk and then down a ladder. I guess that's why they broke in here."

"Here?" I looked around the spartan office. "Did they take anything?"

He shook his head. "Nothing to take."

"Who might have done it, do you suppose?"

"Young hoodlums, I expect. There are always young boys running around the docks, trying to prove they're tough and make a few bucks."

I wondered. I supposed it was possible that it was just some young thieves, but the timing seemed very strange to me. His next words, however, brought up another intriguing possibility.

"Although I wouldn't be surprised if it was that young man, God rest his soul."

I looked up at this comment. "Young man?"

"That friend of Mr. Smith's. He was a troublemaker, make no doubt. He was here that day with a young lady, shortly before we locked up for the night. He said they were looking for Miss Tabitha and wanted to go into the warehouse, but I wouldn't let them. Not without Mr. Alden here. It isn't safe, for one thing. For another, I didn't trust him."

Grant Palmer had been here, trying to get into the warehouse, on the night it had been broken into? That was certainly an interesting piece of information.

"Did you know the woman?" I asked casually.

"It seemed to me she was a friend of Miss Tabitha's. Miss Peters, maybe?"

"Petrie?" I ventured.

"Yes, Petrie. That's it." He looked at me a bit closer then, as though realizing that I might be friends with Jemma if I was friends with Tabitha.

"I don't know her well," I said, by way of reassurance.

"And I don't know, of course, that the young man had anything to do with it. But

277

I heard things about him."

"His underworld dealings, do you mean?" I had dropped my voice to a conspiratorial tone.

Mr. Brown nodded. "That and his murky past."

"Murky past?" I repeated.

"I hear he came from a rough family." Then he gave a smile and shrugged. "Of course, a lot of us do. I had a bit of my own reputation in my day."

I turned over in my mind what he had told me. So Grant Palmer and Jemma Petrie had come to the warehouse one evening together. I doubted they would have come looking for Tabitha, for she had professed her dislike for the place. What, then, had been the reason for their visit? And what had they been doing together, when Jemma had disliked Mr. Palmer? It was certainly something worth looking into.

"Did you tell Mr. Alden that you had seen Mr. Palmer here the night of the robbery?"

He nodded. "Oh, yes, ma'am. I tell Mr. Alden everything that goes on around here."

I realized two things from this. First, if I was to make things any more obvious, Mr. Brown might feel inclined to relate this conversation to Mr. Alden. I didn't especially want Mr. Alden to know how interested I was in the goings-on at the warehouse. Second, it seemed that Mr. Alden had not been overly concerned with Mr. Palmer's appearance at the warehouse. I thought again of their hushed conversation in the hallway. What had their relationship been?

"Can I get you more water, ma'am?" Mr. Brown asked, nodding at the glass in my hand.

"No, thank you. I hope I'm not disturbing you, Mr. Brown."

"Not at all. Happy to talk to you, ma'am. It's not very often we have ladies of your quality around these parts."

I smiled and shifted the conversation, and we talked about lighter things while I waited for Milo and Mr. Alden to return. But beneath our superficial chatter, my mind was churning. So Grant Palmer, with Miss Petrie in tow, had tried to gain access to the warehouse. What had he been looking for? And what had Mr. Alden's reaction been when he had found out? Did he have something to hide? Something, perhaps, worth killing for?

I had just been handed a new piece of the puzzle, and I needed to determine where it fit.

16

I found, when we returned to the house, that Tabitha had left me a note saying, should we return from the warehouses in time, she would love for me to join her and Jemma Petrie for lunch at Delmonico's.

"Are you sure you're feeling up to it, darling?" Milo asked, as I was about to ascend the chairs to change.

"Certainly. I'm feeling fine now. It was just a bit of overheating, that's all."

And it had been a rather lucky thing, at that. I had had the chance to speak with Mr. Brown. And this lunch presented the perfect opportunity to see if I could learn anything more from Jemma Petrie.

I was curious about her. While she seemed a lively, outgoing girl, I had noticed that she never seemed to reveal more of herself than she meant to. Indeed, the few times I had conversed with her, I had learned very little about her, and I was even more curious having learned that she had been spending time with Grant Palmer shortly before his death. Tom Smith had also seen her leaving Mr. Palmer's flat, so that was twice they had been spotted together.

That didn't mean, of course, that she was involved in his murder. It might simply have been a secret affair, as Tom had speculated. But Jemma had professed her dislike for Mr. Palmer — rather believably, I thought — so it was all a bit curious.

Milo and Mr. Alden had gone off to discuss, presumably, more business, so I left the house without speaking to Milo alone. I would have to tell him what I had learned from Mr. Brown later.

The Aldens' car let me off in front of Delmonico's, an interestingly shaped building on the corner of William and Beaver Streets, and I went inside. The dining room was the picture of luxury, the tables bedecked with white cloths, formal place settings, and gorgeous floral centerpieces.

"I'm here to meet Miss Alden," I told the waiter.

"Of course, madam. Right this way."

He led me to a table, and I was a bit confused for just a moment, for Tabitha wasn't there. Instead, Jemma Petrie sat with two gentlemen, both of whom seemed to be trying to outdo the other in capturing her attention. Jemma was smiling and laughing, encouraging the unspoken competition between the two of them. When she saw me approaching, she waved me over.

"Hello, Mrs. Ames. I'm glad to see you," she said, when I reached the table. She looked pretty in a rose-colored dress perfectly suited to her complexion, and her hair had clearly been recently waved.

The gentlemen on either side of her rose at my approach, and Jemma waved a hand. "Pete and Myron," she said, not giving any indication of who was who. "They were lunching here and came to keep me company until Tabitha arrived."

"Good afternoon," I said.

They nodded at me and Pete — or Myron — pulled out a chair for me to sit.

"Where's your husband today?" Jemma asked, her eyes searching the room behind me for Milo. Was she hoping that he would soon appear to sweep me away from her table? It was the impression I had. The ratio of women to men now being equal, she was no longer the center of attention. Alas, I was afraid I had to disappoint her.

"I'm not entirely sure. I'm sure he'll enjoy lunch on his own. We don't always have the same ideas of what constitutes a good time."

She smiled, a little flash of something like speculation in her eyes. "Being that understanding must make for a pretty good marriage," she said.

"It has its benefits," I replied mildly.

"Would you care for a cigarette?" Pete or Myron asked.

"Thank you, no."

"I don't care for the nasty things either," Jemma said. "But how about a drink, then? A real drink, I mean. They serve the good stuff here."

I found myself surprised, again, at the easy flow of alcohol in a country where it was outlawed. The waiter, who had arrived at the table, had clearly overheard her but made no show of surprise to hear this suggestion openly spoken.

"What will you have, madam?" he asked.

"I think a cup of tea will suffice," I said. In fact, I wanted tea so badly that I could almost taste it. I hoped it was very strong.

"You look worn out," Jemma noted. "I suppose Tabitha has had you running all over town. It seems like she's gone kind of frantic since . . . well, you know." Jemma herself didn't look quite in the pink of health, now that I was sitting a bit closer to her. I had mistaken a liberal application of rouge for a natural rosiness in her cheeks, and she looked pale beneath the makeup. She looked almost as though she might be ill.

Now that she had mentioned the murder, however, I saw no reason not to pursue this conversational opening.

"Things have been rather hectic," I admitted. "Mr. Ames and I went with Mr. Alden to tour his warehouses this morning."

She made a face. "Oh, no wonder. The warehouses are awful."

"You've been, then?" I asked, hoping she would mention her visit there with Grant Palmer.

She nodded. "Yes, but not for years."

The lie came out with perfect ease, and I had a hard time concealing my surprise. I wondered if I should mention what Mr. Brown had told me, but I decided not to do so in front of her friends. Besides, it was sometimes best to keep one's cards close to the chest.

"It was very hot," I said. "But nonetheless, it was nice to forget for a while about all that's happened lately. What do you make of all this?"

"Of all what?"

"The . . . murder and everything, the wedding going on as planned." I meant for the words to come off sounding gossipy, but instead my tone held just a touch too much significance, as though her answer would be weighted and dissected, which I supposed it would.

She shrugged, pulling off a careless air much more convincingly than I had been able to. "I haven't really thought much about it, I suppose. I don't see any reason why the wedding shouldn't continue. It's sad that Grant is dead, but Tabitha didn't know him well, and even Tom doesn't seem much upset by his death, so I don't see why they should postpone their wedding. Their honeymoon is already paid for, after all."

It was a practical approach. And, really, I didn't know why Jemma should be upset by Grant Palmer's death. Except for the rumors that I had heard about the two of them.

"Who do you think might have killed him?" I asked.

She shrugged again. "I expect it was those gangsters he was running around with. Nothing good ever comes of that."

"Have you ever been to De Lora's?" I asked the question casually, but it seemed as if she looked at me rather sharply.

"Maybe once or twice," she said at last. I had the feeling she was rather reluctant to admit it, but once she did she decided to brazen it out. "After all, a lot of people go there. I like a good time once in a while, and it's one of the more popular speakeasies in the city."

"Yes, I've heard that," I said. "I understand Leon De Lora is considered very handsome and charming when he sets his mind to it."

I watched her carefully when I mentioned the man's name, but I didn't see any sign of guilt there. She only nodded, a small smile flickering across her mouth. "Yes, he's very good-looking."

I again had the impression that, despite her confidence, there was something a bit guarded about Jemma Petrie. Of course, that might just be her natural way of going about things. I was much the same myself; I was friendly to a point, but there were few people I let see behind my carefully constructed poise.

"But if it wasn't gangsters," I pressed, "who do you think it might have been?"

She frowned, and I wondered if it was because I had asked the question or because the possibility that there might be another culprit had never occurred to her. "I don't know."

She turned suddenly to her companions. "Why don't you fellows go back to your table and let Mrs. Ames and I talk in peace for a while. Tabitha's going to be here soon, and you'll only be in the way."

Pete and Myron didn't look especially pleased at being summarily dismissed, but neither of them protested. They both rose from their chairs, and I had suddenly the impression of two well-trained terriers following their mistress's command. They made polite good-byes before going to another table in the corner. I wondered with vague interest what Jemma's relationship with these men was, but I thought it in bad taste to ask when I was already trying to pry information from her.

I thought for a moment she might doggedly stick to her original hypothesis that "those gangsters" must be the killers but, the gentlemen gone, Jemma leaned toward me. "I didn't want to say anything in front of them. Neither of them can be trusted with a secret. But I did overhear Grant and Tom having an argument the night before Grant was killed."

I recalled how I had seen their terse exchange at the nightclub. Was this the same argument Miss Petrie had witnessed?

"Really?" I asked eagerly. I thought to keep up the pretense that I was a woman who enjoyed gossip. Jemma didn't know that I was trying to help solve the case, after all.

She nodded. "I didn't think much about it at the time, but I've wondered a couple of times since then if it might have meant more than I gave it credit for meaning."

"Surely you don't think Tom . . ." I let the question trail off, hoping she would fill in the gap.

She shrugged, but there was a flash of something in her eyes that looked like satisfaction at the suggestion.

I didn't have time to interpret this reaction before the waiter arrived then with my tea, and I was momentarily distracted by the steaming liquid.

"Do you know what it was about?" I asked at last, setting aside the teaspoon. "The argument, I mean."

"I only heard a little of it, but I'm fairly sure they were talking about money."

"I suppose that can be an inflammatory subject," I said lightly.

"I think Grant was asking Tom for a loan. He did that more than once, actually."

I didn't know if this was especially surprising. After all, Grant Palmer did not have a particularly stable form of employment, and Tom had mentioned that they had argued about money. I did wonder where Tom

Smith was getting the money to loan to Grant Palmer. From all that Tabitha had said, Tom had very little money of his own. Maybe that was why he was trying to win at games of chance.

"This time, it seemed like it made Tom angry," Jemma went on.

I found it interesting that, when beginning this story, she had barely been able to recall the details, but now they seemed to be returning to her with impressive speed.

"Had they been friends for long?"

"I think so," Jemma said. "I know they knew each other before Tabitha came along. They were often out carousing together, from what I can tell."

I thought of Grant Palmer's comment that Tom had come to the "straight and narrow." Was that what he had meant?

"I suppose they resolved whatever their argument was," I said lightly.

"I don't know. Tom usually gave in and gave Grant money, so I imagine he did this time as well."

But why had he been angry at this particular request for money? I remembered the phrase that I had overheard, how Tom said he wouldn't allow his past to follow him. Had Grant Palmer been demanding money to keep quiet about something? If so, perhaps that was why Tom had asked him to come to the Aldens' house and then asked Tabitha to meet him at the nightclub. He might have killed Grant Palmer and hurried back to meet her, creating an alibi for himself. Only it turned out that Tabitha had still been trying to catch a taxi.

All of these thoughts flashed through my mind in the space of an instant, and I was spared having to determine what to ask next as Jemma went on, leaning a bit closer.

"Though, I will say, it almost sounded to me as though Grant was trying to get money out of Tom against his wishes."

I frowned. "What do you mean?"

"I don't know, of course, but it sounded almost as though Grant was threatening him in some way."

"Surely not," I said, though the theory did coincide with my speculation that Grant might be demanding money to keep quiet about something in Tom's past.

"I could've heard wrong, of course. I didn't linger to listen."

I wondered. It seemed to me that she had heard quite a good deal.

The waiter came to our table then. "Mrs. Ames and Miss Petrie?"

We looked up. "Yes?" Jemma asked.

"Miss Alden has telephoned and said she

was detained. She wishes you to dine without her."

We placed our orders. I selected the eggs Benedict at his recommendation, while Jemma chose a steak. Then she excused herself from the table for a few moments, and I was left alone to ponder these latest revelations. When she returned, I thought it prudent not to resume the conversation. If I pushed too far, Jemma might grow suspicious.

Topics shifted as we ate lunch. The food was delicious, and I found, in contrast to the aloofness I had begun to expect from her, Jemma seemed in the mood to be a pleasant and lively conversationalist. More than once I laughed at one of her stories, and I could see how she and Tabitha might have become good friends.

We finished the meal, and it was my turn to excuse myself to the powder room. As I was returning to the table, I saw that Jemma was speaking with the waiter. I was still out of her line of view, but I couldn't help but overhear part of the conversation.

"I'm afraid your credit has reached its limit, Miss Petrie," the waiter was saying apologetically.

"What?" Jemma was incredulous. "I've kept an account here for years."

"Yes, Miss Petrie, but . . . I . . . I'm afraid the bills have gone unpaid for quite some time."

I turned away then, not wanting to overhear any more of such a private conversation.

I went back into the powder room to wait a few moments before making my reappearance. I had been overhearing a great number of things lately that might be better off left unaddressed.

When I returned to the table, Jemma rose from her seat, taking a silver compact from her purse. "Oh, there you are. Just let me run off and powder my nose, and then we'll be off."

I pulled my own handbag from the chair beside me. "I do hope you'll let me pay for lunch."

"You don't need to do that," she said, with a wave of her hand.

"I'd be happy to."

"Oh, no." She waved a hand. "Myron's already paid for it. Sweet of him, wasn't it?"

It was indeed.

As my cab pulled up before the Alden home, I saw the figure of a man standing on the front steps. I thought for a moment it might be a lone reporter, still holding out for some kind of story. I was surprised, then, to realize that it was Detective Bailey.

"Hello," I said when I reached the stairs.

"Good afternoon, Mrs. Ames," he said, tipping his hat at me.

"Has no one come to let you in?" I asked, glancing at the door. I was surprised that Calvin had not answered the bell.

"Oh, I'm not coming in," he said. "I was just looking over the crime scene again."

I looked down at the bloodstains on the steps that had so far defied all efforts to remove them.

"Is Detective Andrews here with you?" I asked.

"No. This is an unofficial visit, so to speak. I wanted to check something out. I've been thinking."

"Oh?" I asked. I had the impression that he would be more receptive to my queries than his partner had been. "Do you have a theory?"

"I'm working on one."

"Do you think Mr. Palmer's death was connected to Leon De Lora?" I asked, confident he would not sneer at my suggestion as Detective Andrews had done.

Instead, he answered me honestly, which was almost worse.

"No," he said. "I don't think it has anything to do with De Lora."

"What about Frankie Earl?" I suggested, hoping to foist the crime off on someone who had not appeared in our little drama. "I heard Mr. Palmer had gone to work for him after he left Mr. De Lora's employ. Perhaps he ran afoul of him in some way."

He was looking at me carefully, but he shook his head. "No. It wasn't De Lora or Earl."

He said it with a confidence I found troubling. "Oh? Why not?"

"For one thing, he was killed with a pistol. If gangsters want to kill you in the street, they usually use a car and tommy gun."

I was not much familiar with the weaponry of local criminals, but I had to acknowledge that Detective Bailey probably was. Besides, from what I had seen of American gangster films, he was right. A pistol seemed much less effective than mowing someone down in a hail of bullets from a passing automobile.

"And they often shoot you in front of your own house instead of someone else's. And the bullets often go in the back, not the front."

I looked up at him, the implication of this newest piece of information startling. "He was facing his killer."

He nodded. "He was shot multiple times in the chest before he fell facedown on the stairs."

I felt a bit sick at this description and at the idea of what it meant. If he had been facing his killer, it was likely someone whom he knew.

I decided to take the offensive. "You think someone close to Mr. Palmer did it."

He looked at me intently. His pale green eyes were so cool and expressionless, but there was a glimmer of something in them — suppressed warmth or humor? — that kept them from being entirely fathomless.

"Is that what you think?" he asked.

"I don't know what to think about any of this," I said truthfully. "My husband and I came for a wedding. We never imagined that something like this might happen."

He nodded. "I'm sure this has all been pretty rough on you."

"It's just that . . . I can't believe any of these people would have had a good reason to kill Grant Palmer."

Those disquieting eyes met mine. "You just never know who might be a killer."

"Yes. Yes, I suppose that's true."

"I'd suggest you watch your back, Mrs. Ames."

I felt a little chill as he said the words.

"I shall. Thank you."
Then I hurried into the house.

17

I closed the door behind me and drew in a deep breath, utterly exhausted in mind and body. I was upset by Detective Bailey's quiet confidence that Grant Palmer's death was not related to his bootlegging activities. While I had suspected this might be true, I still didn't want to think that it might actually be someone whom I knew.

I discarded my jacket and pulled off my hat and gloves. I couldn't possibly go on thinking about it at the moment. I wanted nothing more than to take a long, cool bath and lie down before dinner. I climbed the stairs and met Tabitha as she was coming down.

"Oh, hello, Amory. I'm sorry I wasn't able to make it to lunch. I . . . I'm afraid something came up."

She seemed to avoid meeting my gaze as we spoke, and I looked more closely at her face. She looked uneasy, distracted.

"Is everything all right?"

"Yes, fine. Did you and Jemma have a nice lunch?"

"It was very nice. I met two friends of hers, Pete and Myron. I'm afraid I didn't catch their surnames."

Tabitha frowned. "Not them again. I don't think they're a good influence on her."

"It seemed to me that she was the influence upon them," I said dryly.

"Yes, maybe . . ." she said vaguely, and I had the impression that her thoughts were already wandering from our conversation.

"Is there something on your mind, Tabitha?" I asked.

She looked up at me. "Oh, I was just thinking about the wedding. It's all happened so fast that sometimes it catches me by surprise to realize that I'll be a married woman in only two more weeks."

This confession made me a bit uneasy. I hoped that she wasn't having second thoughts. Had something happened this afternoon that was making her want to reconsider?

"You don't feel as though you're rushing into things?" I asked carefully.

"Oh, no. Not at all. I feel as though I've known Tom forever."

I hesitated, wondering if I should tell her

that feeling as though you knew someone and actually knowing them were two entirely different things.

"You know that Milo and I married rather quickly after meeting," I ventured.

She smiled brightly. "And look how well it turned out for you."

"It hasn't all been a bed of roses," I said. That was putting it mildly. I didn't know how to go about telling her what a disaster a good portion of my marriage had been. All was well that ended well, I supposed, but I wanted her to pay attention to what she was doing.

"Oh, I know marriage isn't going to be perfect," she said. "Tom and I have our share of disagreements. It's just that I . . . I . . . oh, well. Never mind."

I didn't want to press her, but it seemed that there was hesitation now when she spoke of Tom. Had they argued? I didn't like to press her about her private affairs, but I also knew that she might need someone in whom she could confide.

"I hope you know that you can talk to me if you need to."

She nodded and gave a smile that was fairly convincing. "Everything's all right. Really. But thank you."

She moved past me then and I retreated

to my bedroom.

I still had the uneasy feeling that there was something amiss. I did hope it wasn't Tom who was getting cold feet. That would be heartbreaking for Tabitha. I thought back to the days before my own wedding. In the midst of my desperate love for Milo, there had been a hint of caution, the feeling that I should not put every bit of my heart into the idea of our marriage in case he was to change his mind.

Was that what was happening with Tabitha and Tom? Somehow I doubted it. Tom seemed to have a different personality from Milo. Whatever secrets his past might hold, I didn't sense the same undercurrent of reckless energy about him. Besides, happily, Milo had been there waiting at the altar for me. It wasn't until our conversation as we arrived in the harbor that I had realized he had been feeling the same thing about me. How very vexing love was at times.

I went into the bathroom and ran a bath in the claw-foot tub, adding a liberal amount of rose-scented soap beneath the running water. When at last I sank into the warm, fragrant water, I breathed a sigh. It felt wonderful to have a moment of escape from everything that had been happening.

Even as I luxuriated in the bubbles,

however, my mind wouldn't rest. I was still thinking about the aspects of the case. What had I learned so far? I had been told that Grant Palmer and Rudy Elliot had quarreled over a woman. I needed to find a way to subtly ask Mr. Elliot about the woman in question.

I also knew that Grant Palmer had been asking, perhaps even demanding, money from Tom Smith, perhaps to conceal something that had happened in the past.

Furthermore, Mr. Palmer and Jemma Petrie had gone to the warehouse together one evening, trying to gain access. They were denied and, coincidentally or not, the warehouse had been broken into later that evening. Mr. Alden had been made aware of it, and I couldn't help but wonder if this had brought things to a head between himself and Mr. Palmer.

It seemed that there was a great deal of information, but I didn't exactly know what to make of it.

"Oh, there you are, darling," Milo said, coming into the bathroom. "I've been looking for you."

"I'm trying to relax," I said. "It's been an exhausting day, and I am having a bath, then a nap."

"Good. You weren't looking at all well at

the warehouse."

I had meant to give him the impression that he should leave, but he didn't seem inclined to do so. Instead, he sat on the edge of the tub.

"There are far too many bubbles for you to catch a glimpse of anything enticing," I said with mock tartness.

"Then I shall just have to wait here until the water is cold and you decide to get out."

"Go away, Milo." I laughed. "Let me bathe in peace."

"Very well," he said, beginning to rise. "I only wanted to share with you what I learned from Mr. Alden this afternoon."

"Sit down," I demanded, and he lowered himself again to the edge of the tub. "Did you ask him about the break-in?"

"He mentioned it, in fact. There were more than one. Someone broke into his office, but apparently realized there was nothing worth stealing there. That was after they tried, and failed, to break in to the warehouse itself. He said it was in the little addition in the back of the building that contains a collection of automobile tires and other items used to repair the shipping trucks."

"Automobile tires?" I repeated. "Why on earth should anyone want to steal those? What's more, how did they intend to make off with such bulky items?"

Milo shrugged. "Perhaps they didn't know what was held in that particular area. As I said, it was in the back of the building. They may have thought there would be less chance of their being discovered there."

"Perhaps," I mused. "I learned something rather interesting today."

I relayed what Mr. Brown had told me about Grant Palmer and Jemma Petrie's visit to the warehouse.

"They were denied entry, and when I mentioned the warehouse to Miss Petrie today she claimed she hadn't been there in years. Do you suppose they might have been breaking in for some reason?" I asked.

"It's possible, I suppose."

"Furthermore, it's possible that Mr. Alden knew it was Mr. Palmer and, for some reason, he decided to kill him."

"It seems a bit far-fetched, but I suppose not entirely implausible."

I sighed. "It doesn't seem we're any closer to solving the mystery than we were at the beginning."

"I expect that grim detective will be around soon enough. Perhaps you can charm some information from him."

I gave a bitter laugh. "I very much doubt that." I had no illusions that I would ever be able to form any kind of bond with the dour Detective Andrews. "Although, it's funny you should mention it. I did see Detective Bailey as I came back to the house. He seems to doubt it was gangsters who killed Grant Palmer." I related what he had said, leaving out the vague warning he had given me.

"The speculation about the gun is a bit telling," Milo said. "But don't worry, darling. I'm sure the truth will come to light in time. Clearly, the detectives are doing their job. Try to enjoy your time with Tabitha."

This reminded me of the other issue that was weighing on my mind. "What do you make of Tabitha and Tom's relationship?"

"I don't know that I make anything of it," he replied.

Milo, I had come to learn, was singularly disinterested in the machinations of other people's hearts. He could really not care less whether other people were happily or unhappily married or if they parted ways and their hearts were broken.

I, however, could not so easily dismiss the memory of Tabitha's worried countenance this afternoon.

"I suddenly have an uneasy feeling about them."

He shrugged dismissively. "You've seen

them together. They can barely keep their hands off each other. I think they're going to be very happy."

"There is more to marriage than . . ."

I paused as Milo's brows rose expectantly. "Physical compatibility," I finished.

"Naturally. But it makes the long days of marriage much more palatable when one has the nights to look forward to."

I had half a mind to splash him for his impertinence, but I laughed instead. "You're a wretch, Milo."

"But I'm your wretch, darling."

"Lucky me. Tabitha said she knew the moment they met they were going to marry. Do you think that's possible?"

"I suppose it might be," he said. "What did you think the moment you first saw me?"

"That I would do well to steer clear of you," I replied truthfully.

He laughed. "You see? Your first instinct was probably the right one."

"All the same," I replied. "I'm glad I didn't listen to that instinct."

"So am I," he replied. "Because, your beauty aside, I married you because you're smart and clever and you challenge me in ways no other woman could have."

My breath caught a little at this unexpected declaration. "You do say the sweet-est things, Milo."

His eyes caught mine. "I mean them, you know."

It was unlike him to be blatantly romantic, and when the moments occasionally arose they took me off guard. I pressed my lips together to keep the tears from coming to my eyes.

"I'm glad," I whispered.

He leaned to rest his hand on the opposite edge of the tub and lowered his mouth to mine.

"Here's your robe, madam. I . . . oh . . . oh!" Winnelda stopped in the doorway to the bathroom, turned halfway around, then turned back, holding up the robe like a shield against indecency.

"It's all right, Winnelda," I said, before she spun herself dizzy. I pushed Milo back, leaving a wet handprint on his white shirt-front. "I'll take the robe."

She came in, eyes averted as though we might try to scandalize her further. It wasn't the first time she had walked in to find us kissing, but it never ceased to embarrass her. She was now a bright shade of red.

Milo withdrew his hand from the other side of the tub and rose unhurriedly from its edge. "I shall leave you in peace to take your nap."

He exited then, through the door that led to his room, and I couldn't help but feel just a bit disappointed.

Winnelda held up the robe for me, and I stepped from the tub, wrapping it around myself.

"I didn't mean to . . . to interrupt, madam."

"It's perfectly all right," I assured her.

"I didn't know . . . that is, I didn't think . . . Mr. Ames is always where one least expects him to be," she said.

I suppressed a smile at this apt description. "Think no more of it, Winnelda."

She followed me into the bedroom and laid out a silk nightdress for me to nap in as I went behind the changing screen to finish drying off and put on my underthings.

"Will you be going out this evening?" she asked.

"Yes. Will you lay out the beaded black evening gown?"

She went to the wardrobe and sorted through my gowns as I slipped the night-gown over my head and came around the screen.

"What's he like, madam?" Winnelda asked, turning with the gown in hand.

I was momentarily confused. "Who?"

"Mr. De Lora."

I stared at her, wondering how on earth she knew I was going to see him.

She seemed to interpret my question. "I won't tell Mr. Ames," she said, lowering her voice. "I know he wouldn't approve, but I feel that duty to one's employer is the most important thing. And we women ought to stick together."

I smiled, despite feeling as though I had been caught doing something I oughtn't. "I appreciate your loyalty, Winnelda."

"You will be careful, though, won't you, madam? I should hate to feel that I might have done something to help you if something goes wrong."

"I'll be careful," I said. "I haven't been doing anything dangerous. After all, a great many reputable people visit De Lora's. It's something of an open secret, I daresay."

She nodded. "Well, I shall be glad to keep your confidence, madam. And if you wish to give me a secret word to let me know that you're in trouble, you might be able to telephone and I can then pass the message on to Mr. Ames."

"We'll consider that," I said.

"Is he as handsome as they say?"

"He's very handsome," I admitted. "But there is an air of quiet menace about him, as though he wouldn't mind at all doing something very wicked."

I was embellishing a bit to feed Winnelda's love for the lurid, but I realized that the impression I gave her was not entirely an exaggeration. I knew that Leon De Lora, despite his charm, was a dangerous man. He seemed friendly enough toward me so far, and I could only hope that the trend would continue tonight.

I enjoyed my nap and woke up very much refreshed.

There was still a bit of time before I needed to dress for dinner, so I put on a dark rose-colored blouse and a lightweight gray tweed skirt and went downstairs, looking for company.

I was walking toward the drawing room when I heard the sound of male voices. I recognized the speakers as Milo and Tom. I was just about to go and join them when Mr. Smith's words caught my attention.

"I'm sorry to ask you this, but there really isn't anyone else for me to talk to." There was a pause, and then he rushed ahead. "Have you ever done anything you oughtn't, something that it would hurt your wife very much to discover?"

I paused, torn between discreetly taking

my leave and listening to Milo's answer. Naturally, my curiosity won out.

Milo gave a dry laugh that made my eyes narrow. I suspected that the list was fairly comprehensive, and I listened with rapt attention for his answer.

"I suppose there have been a few things in my past of which Amory wouldn't approve," he said easily.

"And don't you ever feel as though you should tell her?"

"I'm afraid I haven't a confessionary nature."

Tom sighed. "I'm afraid I do. I don't think I'll ever be able to rest until my conscience is clear."

I felt again that hint of unease that was always in the background when I thought of Tabitha marrying Tom. I had sensed that there was something he was hiding, and this seemed proof of it.

"Then that's a decision you'll have to make," Milo said.

"It's just that Tabitha has been acting strangely lately. It's almost as if . . . as if she suspects something. But it isn't just that. It's a matter of principle. Don't you . . . don't you think it's the right thing to do?"

Tom obviously wanted reassurance, the encouragement that confession was for the best, but if he was looking for sound marital advice, I thought he ought to have looked a little further than Milo.

I waited to see what Milo would say. If I hoped that he would tell Tom that an open and honest relationship with the woman one loved was the key to a happy marriage, I was to be severely disappointed.

His answer came at last, his tone light. "The best advice that I can give you is this: what wives don't know won't hurt them."

I didn't want to hear any more. I turned and walked quietly away from the room and went upstairs.

18

I tried very hard not to let the words affect me, but I found it impossible not to be hurt by the flippancy with which Milo treated the question of honesty between partners.

Whenever I began to believe that he had truly put his wild ways behind him, he did something like this to remind me of them. Of course, I understood what he meant, or at least what I hoped he meant: that there was no use burdening one's wife with the sins of the past.

I felt, however, that it had been couched in such terms as to recommend that the young man might do things without ever having to worry about the consequences.

In the early days of our marriage, I might have let the matter drop. I would have hidden my hurt and tried to find excuses to minimize my internal struggle with his behavior.

But those days had passed. As things

stood between us now, I felt that I had to confront him.

When he came up to dress for dinner, I was ready.

"I overheard some of your conversation with Tom this afternoon," I said, as he tied his necktie.

His brow rose sardonically, and I could sense that he was not entirely amused. "Did you?"

As I ought to have expected, he displayed no sign of guilt whatsoever. I had frankly begun to believe that Milo was immune to that particular malady.

"I sometimes forget how very good your hearing is, darling."

"I wasn't eavesdropping, if that's what you're implying."

"It's what *you* implied, I believe."

I knew what he was doing. He was building up his defenses, trying to shift some sort of blame back to me. It wasn't going to work.

I plunged ahead with the real issue at hand. "You know the troubles we've had, Milo. Don't you think it's best not to advise Tom to keep secrets from Tabitha? I would have thought you might have learned something from our own difficulties."

"I didn't tell him to keep secrets from Tabitha. I said that there are some things better left unsaid."

"It amounts to the same thing."

"If there are some misdeeds in his past that would hurt her to learn about, what good is it going to do for him to tell her?"

It was a logical enough question, I supposed, but I didn't like the implication of it. I told myself there was no point in getting angry. It wouldn't make a difference to Milo anyway.

"Did he tell you what his secret was?" I asked.

"No." Was he lying to me? I couldn't be sure, but, in any event, I wasn't certain I wanted to be burdened with Tom's secret.

We looked at each other. Inwardly, I tried to formulate my argument. I did not want things to escalate to a heated row or shouting match. Not that Milo ever shouted. In every argument we had ever had, he was always maddeningly calm. That was the worst part of quarreling with him: the way he became completely devoid of emotion when his temper rose. His anger was never white hot as mine was; instead, the angrier he was the colder he became. The higher his emotions ran, the more tightly he controlled them. It made it terribly difficult to come to a resolution between us.

Thankfully, we had not had many arguments of this nature. Most of the time we managed to disagree very civilly with each other. I was not one to hold a grudge, and Milo's charm made him easy to forgive.

I met his gaze, trying to get some hint of what he was thinking. I didn't want to lose my temper now. I wanted to be able to discuss this in a calm and rational manner. The problem was that I felt precariously close to bursting into tears. I didn't know what was wrong with me. I had never had trouble containing my feelings, especially not where Milo was concerned. Indeed, I had made something of a habit of doing just that for the better part of our marriage.

I felt suddenly very weary. Why must there always be so many secrets? It seemed no matter where I went, people were always hiding things and making them worse with their deceit. Lies never worked out well in the end; they always managed to hurt people more than the truth might have.

"Can't anyone be honest?" I asked Milo suddenly.

His expression was still guarded. "To whom are you referring?"

"Everyone," I said. "I don't know why everything must always be a big muddle. If people weren't always so secretive, life would be much easier."

"You know I'm not much of one for philosophical debates, darling."

He was also not much of one for compulsive truth telling. I was not going to find any sympathy from him. But I felt suddenly that this was very important, that I needed to resolve this issue and couldn't move forward until we did.

"Let's be honest with each other, Milo," I said. "From now on. Let's tell each other the truth, no matter how unpleasant it might be."

His eyes met mine, and I knew that he could see how much this meant to me. "All right, darling. If that's what you want."

"It is."

There was a tap at the door just then, and I didn't know whether to be dismayed or relieved to have this conversation interrupted.

"Come in," I called.

Winnelda came into the room, her face a bit flushed, her eyes bright with excitement.

"Oh, madam. I just heard something I thought you'd like to know. From Annie, one of the maids."

"Yes, what is it, Winnelda?" I was still half-preoccupied with my conversation with Milo, so it took me a moment for her next words to sink in.

"It's about a gun."

"What about a gun?" Milo asked.

She drew in a breath and let the words out in a rush. "Annie says that . . . that Miss Tabitha used to keep a pistol in the drawer with her . . ." She paused, glancing at Milo. "Her . . . unmentionables."

"What about it?" I pressed.

"Well, Annie says the gun is gone now."

It was just the Aldens and Milo and I at dinner that evening. Tom Smith wasn't there, and Tabitha didn't make his excuses. I wondered again if some kind of rift was developing between them, but Tabitha seemed in good spirits and I thought perhaps my imagination was playing tricks on me.

Winnelda's latest revelation was still very much on my mind. What had become of the gun in Tabitha's drawer? Winnelda had said she would attempt to get more information from Annie, but in the meantime the only way I could find out the truth was from Tabitha. I wanted very much to ask her about it, but I wasn't sure how I could go about introducing the topic. Besides, just because she had been in possession of a gun at one point didn't mean she had used it to kill

Grant Palmer.

Nevertheless, I was having a difficult time dismissing the potential significance of a missing gun when a murder had been committed with one. I would just have to find a way to bring it up.

We had just begun drinking our after-dinner coffee when Calvin appeared in the doorway of the drawing room.

"Mr. Elliot is here."

"It's all right, Calvin. I can tell them myself," Rudy Elliot said with a smile, coming into the room. "Hello, everyone. I'm sorry to drop by unannounced, but I thought Tom might be here."

"He's not," Tabitha told him shortly.

He glanced at her with what might have been a searching look. "Yes, I see that. Should I leave?"

"Of course not, Rudy," Tabitha said, her tone lightening. "Come and have some coffee."

Rudy came into the room and accepted a cup and saucer before sinking onto the sofa.

"I called Tom at his house, but he didn't answer, so I thought he might be here." He looked at Milo. "He invited me to go out gambling with the two of you. I'm not very lucky, but that's never stopped me before."

"Everyone's luck is bound to change

eventually," Milo said.

Rudy took a sip of his coffee and looked up, his cheerful expression faltering. "I thought for just a minute about calling Grant before I remembered . . ."

"Yes, it's very sad," Tabitha said automatically.

There was an awkward silence in the room as everyone tried to think of how best to go on with the conversation. It was Rudy Elliot who eventually charged ahead onto a less strenuous topic.

"Anyway," he said, affecting a cheerful note. "How are the wedding plans?"

"Things are going well," Tabitha told him. "Though there is always so much to do."

We chatted about the wedding for a few moments before Milo and Mr. Alden, apparently bored with the topic, launched into a discussion about automobiles. I had no desire to take part in that particular conversation, though Tabitha seemed to find it of interest. She had evidently picked up on some aspects of her father's business, for she talked knowledgably on the subject of the vehicles he used for shipping.

It seemed like a good opportunity to speak with Mr. Elliot again. I took my cup and saucer and went to sit beside him on the sofa.

"How fares the advertising business?" I asked, suspecting this was a surefire way to draw him out.

He smiled. "Fairly well. I opened another large account today. It's for a pretty big company." He launched into a description of the transaction, complete with amusing anecdotes.

I liked Rudy Elliot. Despite Grant Palmer's claim that Mr. Elliot was dull, I found him quick-witted and good-natured. I wondered how it was that he and Grant Palmer had remained friends all these years. They seemed to me to have very little in common.

Grant Palmer was apparently still on his mind as well, for he suddenly said, "It was Grant who said I should try for this particular company. He was always trying to scare up business for me."

Now that he had reintroduced the topic of Mr. Palmer, I thought I might as well plunge ahead with my questions.

"Have you thought any more about who might have killed him?" I asked suddenly.

If he was surprised by this unexpected question, he gave no sign of it.

"I've thought about it and thought about it," he said. He gave a rueful laugh. "Believe me. I've thought of little else."

"Do you think he might have learned something he wasn't supposed to know?"

Rudy frowned. "Like what?"

The more I thought about it, the more it seemed like an ideal solution. Perhaps Grant Palmer had learned something that he wasn't meant to know, and he had been shot to keep him silenced.

"I don't know. Perhaps something to do with the bootlegging business?" I suggested. I didn't think I should elaborate on the fact that I knew Mr. Palmer had switched loyalties.

Rudy shrugged. "It could be. I suppose we'll never know. I don't really think the police are going to solve it. You know the way it is with these mob killings. They're big news for a while and then they're swept right under the rug."

I hoped he wasn't right. He wasn't going to be, if I had anything to say about it.

There was another rumor I wanted to discuss. I lowered my voice, though I was certain that no one else was paying attention. "I heard a rumor that Mr. Palmer and Miss Petrie were friendlier than they seemed."

It seemed to me that surprise flashed across his face. "Grant and Jemma?"

I wondered if I had been mistaken. Perhaps what I had interpreted between them had not been romance but something else. After all, a warehouse visit wasn't exactly romantic. There was also the matter of Tom's having seen Jemma come out of Mr. Palmer's flat late at night, but I supposed there were alternate explanations for that as well.

"It could be a false rumor, of course," I said.

He frowned. "I think Grant would have told me if there was something going on with Jemma. He liked to . . . brag about . . . women. Oh, I know he and Jemma spent some time together, but as far as I know it was just social, nothing romantic."

I wondered if the assessment was accurate, or if Rudy Elliot was just hopelessly naïve.

"He was something of a ladies' man, I understand."

Rudy nodded. "They all seemed to love him."

I smiled in what I hoped was a casually teasing way. "I suppose he tried to steal girls from you in his time?"

He shook his head. "No, we didn't like the same type of girls."

This was in direct opposition to what Jemma Petrie had told me. Which one of them was lying?

I didn't have time to formulate another question before Calvin made his second appearance in the doorway, disapproval clear on his features. "Those policemen are here again, Mr. Alden."

I was surprised by his words. What on earth would Detectives Andrews and Bailey be doing here at this time of night?

I looked at Mr. Alden and saw his jaw tighten. "What do they want?"

"Detective Andrews didn't say, sir. Only that they wished to speak with you."

"Very well, Calvin. Show them to my office. They can wait there." I had the impression that Mr. Alden intended the wait to be a long one, and I realized I was not the only person whom Detective Andrews had rubbed the wrong way.

"I beg your pardon, sir," Calvin said apologetically. "He wished to speak with the entire group."

Tabitha looked up sharply.

Mr. Alden let out a sigh and then gave a nod. "Fine. Show them in."

Calvin nodded and disappeared and Mr. Alden set his cup and saucer down with a clatter in a gesture of impatience. "I don't know what other questions he could possibly have for us. And why show up at dinnertime?"

"He wants to make us uneasy," Tabitha said. "I think that's how the police work. They show up at unexpected times and try to force confessions." The words were meant as a joke, but her tone was strained.

Detective Andrews came into the room then, hat in hand. He looked a bit rumpled, as he was wont to do, but his eyes were as sharp as ever. I realized then what was so disarming about him; it was the way those intense, focused dark eyes looked out at one from that unshaven face.

"Sorry to disturb you all," he said, though I had the impression he was not sorry at all. He glanced around the room, as if taking stock of us.

Detective Bailey stood slightly behind him. He was watchful, too, and I had the sense he was looking for something in particular.

Mr. Alden had risen from his seat. "What can we do for you, Detectives?"

"I just wanted to stop by and tell you that we've arrested Grant Palmer's killer."

19

We all sat in shocked silence for a moment. They had arrested the killer? Surely not.

I wasn't certain why denial was my first impression, but the feeling was strong as I stared at the policemen.

It was Tabitha who found her voice first. "Who . . . who was it?"

"A two-bit thug named Toadie Willis," Detective Andrews said. "He's one of De Lora's goons. When an acquaintance of his got arrested for cooking up moonshine, he sang like a canary to avoid the slammer, ratting on Willis as quick as you please."

While I was still parsing through this unfamiliar jargon, he went on. "Turns out, Willis heard that Palmer went to work for Frankie Earl, rival mob boss to Leon De Lora. He thought that rubbing out Palmer would make Mr. De Lora happy."

"I can't believe it," Rudy Elliot said under his breath.

Detective Andrews looked up at this, and I thought I saw the way his eyes fastened on Rudy. It was so quick a change from his relaxed demeanor that I wondered if that persona was the one he used to give suspects the impression that he was not a threat . . . until it was too late.

"Why's that, Mr. Elliot?" he asked.

Rudy looked up, surprised, I think, that he had been overheard. "I just . . . I can't believe Grant was killed that way. It's so senseless."

"These gangsters don't make a lot of sense. Violence is a way of life to them."

Rudy nodded.

"Did you have another suspect in mind?" This question came from Detective Bailey, calling our attention unexpectedly back to his unobtrusive presence behind Detective Andrews.

"No . . . I. No," Rudy said. "It's just all so surprising."

"Did you find the gun he used?" I asked. Beside me, I felt Tabitha stiffen.

Detective Andrews turned his piercing gaze on me. "Why do you ask that?"

"I only wondered," I said calmly. "A pistol shooting seems unusual for this type of thing. One always hears of gangsters using machine guns." I didn't look at Detective

Bailey as I repeated this bit of information he had told me, but I could feel him watching me.

"We got him, and we got the gun," Detective Andrews said. "I found the pistol in his apartment myself."

"I'm glad to hear it," I said mildly. I hoped he was right. I had read that the last few years had seen impressive strides in the ability of the police to determine if two bullets had been fired from the same gun. If this was the case, I might not have to worry about Tabitha's missing weapon.

"I doubt we'll be able to pin anything on De Lora," Detective Andrews said, "but we've got the trigger man, and I suppose that's what counts. There'll be a trial and we may need some of you for witnesses, but I guess that can all wait until after the wedding. I just wanted to come and tell you."

Mr. Alden cleared his throat, apparently a bit thrown off by this development. He had meant, I thought, to be brusque with the detective, but he had not expected a solution to the mystery that had landed, quite literally, on his doorstep. "Thank you for coming, Detective Andrews, Detective Bailey. I appreciate your letting us know. It's a great relief to all of us that Grant Palmer's killer has been caught."

Though the arrest of Mr. Palmer's murderer should have been cause for celebration, it seemed that the news had sucked the energy from our group. I, for one, had plenty I wanted to discuss with Milo once we were alone, but it seemed that would not be for a while. Several weeks before our trip, Tom had purchased the four of us tickets to a Broadway revue, and, despite the circumstances, we thought it would be best not to let them go to waste. So, soon after Detective Andrews and Detective Bailey had left the house, we gathered our coats and settled ourselves into Mr. Alden's Duesenberg for the ride to the Music Box Theatre.

Given my most recent experiences with the theater in London, I had a few apprehensions as we filed into the columned building and made our way down the aisle to our seats near the stage. At least this was a musical and not a tragedy.

"Do you believe that man really killed Grant Palmer?" I asked Milo in a low voice as we settled into our red upholstered seats. I was quite sure I couldn't wait through the duration of the performance to at least mention it.

"Detective Andrews seems quite sure of it," Milo said. I couldn't help but notice there was something noncommittal in his tone.

I glanced at him. "You aren't convinced."

He shrugged. "It may very well be as he says."

"I don't know if I believe it."

He smiled. "You don't want your mystery to be pulled out from under you."

The music started up then, and I was able to give him only a frown at this accusation. That wasn't the case at all. I just felt, deep down, that there was still something wrong about all of this.

Despite my conflicted emotions, I was determined to enjoy the revue, and I soon discovered this took very little effort on my part. *As Thousands Cheer* had been very popular since its opening in September. Each of the short scenes was heralded by a newspaper headline, proclaiming some recent news item or scandal, and then the event was turned into a song to great effect. I was only glad none of Milo's and my forays into murder investigation had been noteworthy enough to immortalize in song.

The witty sketches and Irving Berlin's musical numbers, some cheerful and some moving, provided a great distraction, and it was not until we had made our way laughing and talking from the theater that I began to focus again on the visit from the detectives tonight.

"I'll get a cab for you, ladies," Tom said as we entered the crowded street, lights from every direction casting a glow over the theatergoers in their evening finery. As he and Milo were bound for another late night on the town, Tabitha and I would go back to the Aldens' together.

He wandered off to try to procure a cab amidst the rush of people pouring from the theater, a difficult feat, I thought.

"Oh, excuse me a moment, will you?" Tabitha said suddenly. "I see someone I know." She moved off into the press, and Milo and I were alone. Or, at least, as alone as we could be on a crowded curb.

I leaned close to him, picking up the conversation where we had left off. "I know you think I'm overanalyzing things, but something about it just doesn't seem right. For one thing, Detective Andrews told me before that the murder had been committed with a pistol, which was uncharacteristic of such a shooting."

"A weapon's a weapon, darling."

"I don't know. I just couldn't help but feel we were onto something. I wonder if Detective Andrews might have made a rush to judgment in his haste to solve the case."

"Comparing him unfavorably to our D.I. Jones, hmm?"

I certainly wished for the presence of my Scotland Yard inspector friend, but that was beside the point.

"It's just that, with all these bootleggers running about, things are bound to get muddled. He has only the . . . singing gentleman's word for it that this strangely named Toadie Willis is the killer. That seems rather poor evidence, especially as the informant was trying to avoid getting in trouble himself." I sighed. "It seems that Prohibition has made a mess of things."

"Well, they won't have to worry about it for much longer. Prohibition is nearly finished," Milo said, echoing what Leon De Lora had said to me. "They're going to repeal it."

Milo, though he never seemed to possess more than a marginal interest in politics, always seemed to know what was going on in the world. He sometimes surprised me with his insights.

"It does seem as though it's been rather a failed endeavor," I said.

"They ought to have known that telling people they mustn't have something only makes them want it more."

I considered the implications of a repeal. While I knew a good percentage of the population would rejoice at such news, I knew there would be others to whom it would seem a disaster, not the least of which those who had seen fit to make Prohibition work in their favor. The police might have an easier time of it, but I felt certain the criminals would have to adapt. They wouldn't all, like Leon De Lora, find some legitimate avenue to explore.

"I wonder what will happen to all these bootleggers when they'll no longer be making a profit from their enterprises," I mused.

"I wouldn't be concerned about the well-being of the criminal classes, darling. There is any amount of money to be gained from illegal activities. They'll get on all right."

"Oh, of course," I said. "I'm only curious."

"I expect a number of well-structured crime organizations have sprung up over the last decade. There are any number of other pursuits in which they might invest: prostitution, drugs, gambling."

It was not exactly an encouraging thought.

All I knew was that I was not entirely satisfied with Detective Andrews's solution to the mystery. I knew that man was clever, but everything about this seemed too tidy. I had had the impression that even Detective Bailey was not entirely convinced. I still wanted to talk with Leon De Lora, especially now that his name had been newly linked to the crime. When Tabitha had gone to bed, I would leave for De Lora's.

"Amory, Tabitha, over here!" I looked up and saw Tom waving an arm. Somehow, he had managed to hail a cab. I saw Tabitha moving in his direction as Milo took my arm, and we made our way through the crowd toward the car, which was parked halfway down the block.

As if knowing what my thoughts had been, Milo suddenly asked, "Am I going to return home to find you gone again?"

"No," I answered honestly, not looking at him as we reached the cab. I intended to be home long before he came back.

"All right. Good night, then." He leaned to drop a kiss on my lips and then turned to walk away.

It was then that I inconveniently recalled the conversation we had had only hours earlier, the one in which I had lauded the virtues of honesty between husband and wife. How very hypocritical it was of me to be lying to him after my earlier feelings of righteous anger at the idea of concealment in marriage.

"Milo, wait."

He turned.

"I'm going back to De Lora's tonight." I wasn't sure what would come of this sudden burst of honesty, but it was done now.

He didn't look surprised. "I expected as much."

I ought to have known I couldn't hide things from him.

"I'll be careful," I said firmly. "But I'm going alone."

"Very well."

I stared at him. "You're not going to object?"

The corner of his mouth tipped up. "Darling, when has objecting ever done any good?"

By a combination of feigned weariness to Tabitha upon our arrival at the house and a fortuitously passing taxi as I snuck from the residence a short time later, I arrived back at De Lora's in good time. As I walked up the front steps of the innocuous-looking brownstone building, my heart picked up the pace a bit at the thought I would soon be sitting with Leon De Lora again, especially now that his name had been linked definitively — by the police, at least — to

Grant Palmer's death. I had put a small notebook and pencil in my handbag this time, so I hoped to make a better impression.

I was unable to locate Mr. De Lora within the smoky confines of the speakeasy, however. I even worked my way through the maze of tables, thinking perhaps he was seated with a customer, but there was no sign of him. At last, I made my way to the bar, where I had met him the previous evening.

"I'm looking for Mr. De Lora," I told the bartender. "I was here last night, and he told me to come back."

The bartender shrugged. "I ain't seen him yet this evening."

I nodded, pushing down my disappointment. Perhaps he didn't mean to meet me after all. "All right. I'll just sit over there," I said, pointing to a table in the corner. "If you see him, will you tell him I'm here? Rose Kelly."

"Sure. I'll tell him."

"Thank you."

I was about to make my way to the table in the corner, but the music started then and Esther Hayes moved to the center of the floor. Tonight she was wearing a gown of silver satin. She began to sing, her voice flowing through the room, subtle changes in her expression conveying the emotion behind the lyrics.

"She's good, ain't she?"

I turned at the sound of the bartender's voice. He was leaning against the bar, watching Miss Hayes. It was the first sign he had shown of any interest in conversation with me.

"Yes," I said. "Very good. Mr. De Lora tells me people come a long way to see her."

He nodded. "She has her share of admirers."

There was something in the way he said it that drew my attention.

"I imagine so. She sings so well."

"We joke sometimes that she casts a spell with her voice. Like one of those sirens from mythology."

I looked at him. With his rough and foreboding demeanor, and the hairy, brawny forearms, smattered with tattoos, leaning against the bar, I would not have thought him a student of mythology. I was reminded once again that it was never prudent to judge a book by its cover.

"Perhaps she'll be famous one day," I suggested.

"Maybe so. A couple of guys came in here once, wanting her to go away and make recordings, but she wouldn't. She's too loyal."

"That's admirable," I said, though privately I wondered if such a thing would have provided her with more opportunities than singing nightly in a speakeasy, however much notoriety it possessed.

"And there are gentlemen admirers, I suppose," I said.

He nodded. "Though the boss doesn't let them bother her. He even had to talk to one of our employees who wouldn't leave her alone."

My ears perked up at this. I wondered if it could possibly have been Grant Palmer. After all, I was coming to learn that the man had been infamous for his relentless pursuit of women.

"I see," I said, hoping that he would elaborate. He didn't, however, and for a moment we stood without talking, listening to the soothing sounds of Esther Hayes's voice coating the room like honey.

I was just about to attempt to find the right way to inquire about the identity of this troublesome employee, when the barkeep straightened suddenly and I heard a voice beside me.

"Hello, Rose."

I had been so absorbed in the music that I

hadn't even noticed Mr. De Lora approaching. Or perhaps it was that he moved with a predatory grace, appearing out of nowhere with little warning. Yes, he was very like a panther, I decided. Sleek, dark, and deadly.

"Hello, Mr. De Lora." I turned to face him, offering a confident smile. "I'm back."

"So I see. I'm glad Eddy here was keeping you entertained."

His dark gaze flickered to the bartender, and I could sense the man had stiffened slightly behind me before he went back to wiping down the bar with a rag.

"We were just enjoying Miss Hayes's singing," I said.

Mr. De Lora motioned to a nearby table. "Shall we?"

I preceded him to the table and he pulled out a chair for me before taking the one across the table and lowering himself easily into it. There was something very elegant about his movements, though there was clearly that menace below the surface.

"I thought maybe Esther would've given you enough for a story."

"I think Miss Hayes is very interesting, but I was looking for a different angle from the entertainment one. People are interested in you, Mr. De Lora."

Mr. De Lora said nothing as he pulled a

cigarette from his gold case and put it between his lips.

He felt his pockets, but it seemed that there was no lighter to be had, so he motioned to a woman who was wearing a low-cut gown and carrying a tray of cigarettes. She came quickly to the table.

"What would you like, Mr. De Lora?" she asked, flashing her dimples at him.

"Some matches."

She handed them over. "Anything else I can do for you?" I had the distinct feeling she wasn't talking about the items in the little tray she carried.

His eyes swept over her. "I'll let you know, baby."

She gave him another smile, then turned and walked unhurriedly away. He watched her retreating figure for a moment before turning back to me.

"Smoke?"

"Thank you, no."

He lit his cigarette and tossed the matches onto the table.

"Now, where were we?"

I looked down at the book of matches. The cover of the book showed a cocktail glass, with the words *De Lora's* written across it in gold letters.

My brows rose. "It's a bit brazen to

advertise your speakeasy on a book of matches, isn't it?"

He smiled. "It's a show of pride, of sorts. Nothing illegal about matches, after all."

"No, I suppose not."

"We've got several different designs. One has a drawing of Esther on them. Another one has just my name printed. Good advertising for my nightclubs."

So we were back to that again. I was going to have to find a way to redirect the conversation from his talk of the De Lora nightclub chain. But then he did it for me.

"One of my competitors, Frankie Earl, even stole the idea for his place, the Lightning Lounge," he said. "That's not the only thing he's stolen from me. No honor among thieves, eh?"

My ears perked up at this mention of Frankie Earl. His name had been hovering in the background of this case, and I was curious to learn more about him.

"What sort of man is this Mr. Earl?" I asked.

"A two-bit thug," Mr. De Lora said succinctly. "A crook and a cheapskate, to boot. I heard a rumor he was too stingy to order enough custom matches to give out at his place, so he's currently giving them only to his 'trusted associates.' He's billing it as some kind of badge of honor." He gave a derisive chuckle. "My guys prefer money to matches."

Esther Hayes had gone backstage by this point, and the band resumed playing. This one was a lively tune, and several couples rose from their tables to make their way to the dance floor.

"Do you dance, Rosie?" Mr. De Lora asked.

Somehow I did not imagine that he meant the waltz. "Not really," I said.

I was worried for a moment that he might press me to attempt some American dance with which I wasn't familiar and my ruse might be discovered, but he didn't suggest we move to the dance floor. He really didn't strike me as the type of man who might enjoy dancing.

"So what do you want to know?" he asked.

I had considered this from many different angles. I had come to realize that Leon De Lora was not going to let something slip unintentionally. He was too smart for that, too wary. If I wanted answers, I was going to have to ask him direct questions.

"There . . . there is something I've been wanting to ask you," I ventured.

He waited, his dark eyes on my face. I imagined that tougher people than I had looked into those eyes and lost their nerve, but I had come this far. I might as well press forward.

"I've heard some rumors," I said.

Still he said nothing.

"I want to know about Grant Palmer." There. I had said it.

His expression didn't so much as flicker. It was enough to make me wonder, just for a moment, if it was possible I had been mistaken and he didn't know Grant Palmer at all.

He said something then in a low voice, but it was growing difficult to hear amidst the raucous music.

I leaned a bit closer. "I beg your pardon?"

"Let's go to my office and talk," he repeated.

I felt a hint of wariness at this suggestion, but it was true enough that it was hard to hear over the music.

He stood and waited for me to follow his lead. I hesitated momentarily, then rose from my seat. He turned and wove his way among the tables, through the crowds, and toward a door located unobtrusively in a wall to the left of the bar. There was a man standing outside, arms folded in front of him, who gave a slight nod to Mr. De Lora as he pulled the door open.

He led me through a door and into a dim corridor. I had the vague feeling that it might not be the best of ideas to follow him to this secluded part of his club, but I also knew that if Leon De Lora had determined I was a threat then there was probably little I could do to protect myself.

It wasn't exactly a comforting thought.

The corridor was not as elaborately finished as the rest of the club. Here the bare brick of the basement walls was exposed and a procession of pipes followed along the ceiling above our heads, branching off in various directions like the roots of some great metal tree beneath the ground. A short way beyond the door, a little alcove was stacked with wooden boxes and crates, the shipping containers for his liquor, I supposed. Beyond the alcove there were several closed doors.

He led me past them to a wooden door near the end of the corridor. Stopping before it, he pushed it open and motioned for me to precede him through it.

I stepped into the room, unsure of what to expect, but I definitely had been picturing something more sinister than the comfortable, well-appointed office that lay before me. The floors were parqueted in an alternating pattern of light and dark wood, which glowed in the light from lamps that sat on tables placed around the room. A pair of deep, green leather chairs sat before a bookshelf that lined one wall and another pair faced a large desk on which sat neat stacks of paper.

Mr. De Lora walked to one of the chairs near the bookcase and motioned to it. "Sit down, won't you?"

I sat, and he moved to the little sideboard that sat against a wall. "You want a drink?"

"No, thank you."

He poured himself something from a crystal decanter then came and took the chair across from me, crossing one leg easily across the other.

"Now," he said, offering me a smile. "Why don't you tell me why you're really here."

There was nothing overtly threatening in his words, but I felt it would behoove me to tread carefully. Nevertheless, I had come this far now, and I did not intend to back down.

I drew in a breath and plunged ahead. "I'd like to know why Grant Palmer was killed."

The smile changed, a certain hardness creeping into the corners of his mouth, and he sat back in his seat. "You working for the police?"

"No," I said.

"Then what's your stake in this?"

I debated on how much of the truth I should tell him. I thought it would be best if I continued the ruse of being an American reporter on the trail of a good story.

"I heard that he was killed and that he worked for you. I thought I would try to get a scoop."

"You're a reckless little thing, aren't you?" I couldn't tell if there was amusement in his tone or an accusation. Whatever it was, it was vaguely annoying.

"I like to think of myself as persistent."

He took a sip of his drink before he answered. "I don't know who killed Grant Palmer."

I could tell that I was going to have to be direct. I recognized that look, the look of a man who was closing himself off from my questions. I didn't intend for that to happen if I could help it. I had worked too hard building a connection with Mr. De Lora. I knew that he appreciated action, and so I decided to be bold.

"There are rumors that someone who works for you might have killed him." I didn't say, of course, that I had heard this directly from the police.

This accusation didn't bring about any sort of intense reaction. He almost seemed bored by it. "Anyone gets iced in the city, chances are it'll be blamed on me or one of my associates. That doesn't mean we did it."

"That doesn't mean you didn't," I countered.

He studied me for a moment, and I took the opportunity to study him in return. The lighting in this room was much better than it was in the dim, smoky speakeasy.

He was just as handsome in the light as he had been in the shadows, but there was an edge to his attractiveness. I judged him to be about Milo's age, perhaps slightly older, but there was something very hard about his dark eyes that made me certain he had lived a difficult life.

"You want the truth?" he said at last. "I've killed a lot of guys."

I wondered if my face betrayed my surprise at this admission. I certainly hadn't expected him to say such a thing.

He studied me for a moment, then added, "Of course, that was a long time ago. In France."

In France? Of course. The war.

"You were in the army," I said.

"American Expeditionary Forces. I saw a lot of action."

He leaned back in his chair, swirling the

liquid in the glass in his hand.

"There are a lot of stories about me, baby. This, for example." He pointed to the scar on his cheek. "The papers have claimed it was a knife fight, or a broken bottle in a barroom brawl. But do you know what it really was? A German bayonet."

"I'm sorry," I said.

He shrugged. "The other guy got the worst of it."

I didn't doubt it. I had met men who presented a front of bluster and bravado, but I felt instinctively that there was no pretense about the danger in this man.

"I did my part for this country," he went on. "When I came back from France, I figured it was time that this country did something for me."

There was a certain logic in what he said, I supposed. At least I could see how one might make that assumption. There were, I had noticed, several different ways men went about dealing with what had happened in the war. Some of them had shut down, closed their minds off from the memories they could not bear to live with. Some had soldiered on, doing their best to forget. And some, as I suspected was Mr. De Lora's case, came away with a determination to make life pay for the hand it had dealt them.

I had not faced the horrors they had faced, so I could not judge the decisions they made.

That didn't make his career in crime right. But I had not come here to pass judgment on his career as a bootlegger. I had come here wondering what he could possibly tell me about the death of Grant Palmer.

"And so it has. I've made a good life for myself, and I don't regret any of it."

"I'm not here to talk about bootlegging, Mr. De Lora," I said.

"No," he replied, a smile touching the corners of his mouth. "I suppose you're not."

He seemed to consider something for a moment, and I sincerely hoped it wasn't "icing" me, the fate he had mentioned befalling other unfortunates who had crossed him. At last, however, it seemed that he had made up his mind.

"Palmer worked for me at one point, but he was never what I would call one of my most trusted associates," he said.

"Why not?"

"Because I have good instincts, and I knew Palmer wasn't the kind of man you could trust."

"Everyone I've spoken to found him very amiable," I said, only narrowly remembering not to say that I had met him.

"Oh, he was likable enough. The ladies liked him, certainly. But I don't think there was anything especially loyal about him. He went to work for Frankie Earl, but he could've just as easily decided to talk to the police if it benefited him. He was the kind of guy that would be willing to sell you out if the opportunity arose."

It occurred to me that perhaps just such an opportunity had arisen and that Mr. De Lora had not taken kindly to it.

"So I gave him a few small jobs. I let him bring in some of his friends. He ran in high circles after he got out of prison."

This caught my attention. "What do you mean?"

"A few years ago he was practically out on the streets. I knew him back in the neighborhood. Then he went to prison for a few months, and when he got out his luck improved. He was spending time with a much classier group of people and he had adapted himself to their world, did a decent job of it from what I saw."

My mind was beginning to turn in an uncomfortable direction. It seemed possible that Grant Palmer's imprisonment might have some connection to the secret in Tom's past. Was that where they had met? It was just possible that Grant had been demanding money to keep it a secret, and that might be reason enough for Tom to have killed him.

"What did he go to prison for?" I asked.

He shrugged. "I never asked."

"But you said he no longer worked for you." I remembered what Detective Andrews had said, that Grant Palmer had gone to work for Frankie Earl, Mr. De Lora's rival. I wondered if he would admit as much to me.

"No, I cut him loose. Like I said, I value loyalty and Palmer wasn't the loyal type. I had no reason to kill him, though, and if I had I would've done a cleaner job of it."

I studied him, trying to determine if he was telling the truth. He was an interesting character, Leon De Lora. There was more to him than met the eye, more than the caricature of a killer that was presented in the papers. I had no doubt he *was* a killer. He talked about killing with ease, and there was no hint of tortured memories in his eyes, the remorse that burdened those of tender conscience after the heat of battle was past. But I was not here to solve New York's crime problems or to accuse him of whatever deaths lay in his professional wake. My focus was much narrower than that.

Despite everything, I had the impression that he was telling me the truth about Grant Palmer.

There was a tap at the door just then and he rose from his seat.

"I've got some business to attend to," he said as he moved toward the door. "But if you want to hang around, we can talk some more later."

I rose from my seat as he pulled the door open, and I was startled to see Milo standing in the doorway.

20

I hoped I was able to hide my surprise. Milo certainly did an excellent job of pretending as though he had never seen me before. It was almost disconcerting how casually he looked at me, as though I were a woman he was seeing for the first time and had no interest in.

"Rose, this is my associate, Mr. Ames. He's new to the organization. Ames, this is Rose."

New to the organization?

"How do you do, Rose," Milo said.

"Hello," I replied.

I turned back to Mr. De Lora and caught him watching me. I wondered if he suspected something. Surely not. There was no way he could link Milo and me.

There was another knock on the door then, which somewhat alleviated the awkwardness of the moment.

"Come in," Mr. De Lora said.

The door opened and Esther Hayes stepped inside. Her gaze moved from Mr. De Lora to Milo, then to me and back to Mr. De Lora again. I could tell she was not entirely comfortable here, but something told me it was more to do with the presence of Milo and me than with Leon De Lora. She didn't seem wary of him, at least not in the same way as the others who worked for him were.

"I'm sorry if I'm interrupting," she said.

Mr. De Lora was watching her with his expressionless dark eyes. "Not at all. What is it, Esther?"

"I . . . could I have just a moment of your time?" she asked.

"Sure thing." He motioned to the door and Esther, with the faintest of smiles and a slight nod in our direction, went out of it.

"Hold on a minute. I'll be right back," he told us. He motioned to the sideboard on the way out. "Help yourselves to a drink."

As soon as the door closed behind him, I rounded on Milo.

"What are you doing here?" I hissed at him.

"I had a meeting scheduled with Mr. De Lora," he replied. He didn't seem the least bit surprised to see me in Mr. De Lora's private office, nor did he appear at all repentant about being here himself.

"You told me you were going to let me come alone," I said accusingly.

"You did come alone," he pointed out.

He was trying to distract me from the matter at hand, and he would not succeed.

"He said you were one of his associates. What did he mean?"

"I don't have time to explain it now, darling. I think you should go back to the Aldens' house and let me worry about Leon De Lora."

"No. I want to know what you're doing here. You told me you never met the man."

"That was not entirely accurate," he said, with no trace of remorse. And after I had been compelled to tell him the truth out of a sense of guilt!

"You met him and didn't tell me." I could feel my anger building, but Leon De Lora's private office was not the place to start a row.

"I didn't want to tell you until I had settled things. I ought to have known better. Instead of your forgetting that matter, I find you interrogating one of the most dangerous men in the city about a murder you think he committed."

When phrased like that, he almost managed to make me feel as though I had done something reckless. However, I didn't intend to let it distract me from the fact that he had lied to me once again.

"So you've forged some sort of relationship with him?"

"He realized I'm from London, and told me about the nightclubs he intends to build there. He's looking for investors."

"I hope you haven't made him any promises," I said. "He's going to be angry when he finds out you don't mean it."

He looked amused. "But I do mean it."

I realized suddenly that he was in earnest. He might have gone into De Lora's on false pretenses, but he now seriously meant to involve himself with Leon De Lora's London nightclub.

"Milo, you don't mean to invest in that man's nightclub?" I asked, though I already knew the answer.

"Why not? It's a sound business proposition."

"He's a criminal. In all likelihood, a murderer."

Milo did not seem in the least bit concerned about this particular detail.

"I've got money to invest, and De Lora is good at making more. I don't see any reason why we shouldn't form an alliance."

"Why should he need your money?" I

355

asked. "It seems to me that he's making more than enough to finance whatever he needs to in London."

"It's connections that matter. He's made a name for himself here in New York, but he needs London backers who know the city and the target clientele."

"Wonderful. So you're going to attach your name to an American bootlegger's."

"It's certainly not the worst thing I've ever attached my name to," he pointed out with maddening logic.

I sighed and tried to come up with an argument that would penetrate Milo's indefatigable confidence. "What if he is responsible for Grant Palmer's death?"

"I don't think he is," Milo said.

I had come to much the same conclusion, but I didn't intend to tell Milo that. Besides, there was no way we could be sure. Leon De Lora didn't seem at all interested or invested in Grant Palmer's death, but that didn't mean he wasn't. There were any number of reasons he might have had to want Mr. Palmer dead, and if there was one thing a man like Mr. De Lora knew how to do, it was keep secrets.

"What if he is?" I persisted.

Milo shrugged. "He's not going to jail for it, as Detective Andrews pointed out. In fact, there have been any number of deaths attributed to Leon De Lora and he has yet to be directly linked to any of them."

He said this as though it was something to be commended.

"Do you mean to tell me that you intend to go through with this arrangement whether or not Leon De Lora might be a cold-blooded killer?"

I had hoped this plainspoken question might bring about the least bit of reflection on Milo's part, but it was not to be.

"It's just business, Amory. I'm not talking about aligning myself with the man's morals."

"I'm talking about justice, Milo. Doesn't it matter to you?"

"Bringing justice and order to the world has always been your cause, darling. Not mine."

I was rendered somewhat speechless as I realized that he was right. He enjoyed mystery as a puzzle, the thrill of finding the answer to a question no one else could, but unless there was some reason for him to be invested, the matter of justice had always been secondary.

"In any event," he went on, "the nightclub is going to be strictly legal. We've already discussed it."

So they had discussed the pros and cons of legality, had they? I could imagine the two of them sitting in this room, drinking expensive scotch and conferring over whether or not their joint venture would be a legitimate business or something less aboveboard. I ought to have known that Milo would be absolutely useless at keeping himself out of trouble in New York.

"It's nothing for you to worry about," he said.

I sighed heavily and disapprovingly. I knew I was not going to win this argument. Milo always did just as he pleased. And, my reservations aside, I knew he was likely to be successful. Despite his reputation for reckless hedonism, he had always done a very good job of maintaining his finances. Whatever his faults, there was quite a good brain behind that handsome face of his.

"Well, I do hope you'll be careful," I said.

"I'm always careful, darling."

The door opened and we stepped apart.

"That's very interesting, Mr. Ames. I would love to visit London someday," I said with a smile, hoping I was doing a credible job of appearing as though Milo and I had not been engaged in any sort of meaningful conversation.

"The boys are waiting for you outside,

Ames. They'll give you the lay of the land. We'll talk later, once I'm finished with Rosie."

Milo's gaze flickered in my direction, and Mr. De Lora smiled.

"She's doing an article on me. She's got aspirations of being a crime reporter. Don't you, baby?"

I thought I saw the faintest glimmer of annoyance in Milo's eyes as Mr. De Lora dropped the casual endearment.

"Something like that," I said lightly.

"Anyway, I'll catch up with you in a while," Mr. De Lora said.

"Excellent," Milo replied. "Until then."

He nodded in my direction. "Good evening, Rose."

"Good evening, Mr. Ames."

Milo left and Mr. De Lora turned back to me. "Sorry for the interruption."

"That's quite all right."

He moved past me toward his desk. Reaching into a wooden box atop it, he took out a cigar. He clipped it and put it in his mouth. Striking a match, he lit the cigar and perched on the edge of his desk, watching me.

"Now," he said. "Is there anything else you need to know for this article of yours?"

I hesitated. I had been derailed by Milo's

sudden appearance, and I knew that Mr. De Lora wasn't likely to share anything else with me.

"No," I said at last. "I think you've answered all my questions for now."

He nodded. "It was nice talking with you, Rose. I look forward to reading that article."

I realized that I was being dismissed, and I thought it best that I accept it gracefully.

"Thank you, Mr. De Lora," I said. "I'll see that you get a copy."

I moved to leave, but his voice stopped me. "A word of warning."

I turned.

"I wouldn't push this issue of Grant Palmer's death," he said. "The people who are involved in it probably aren't as understanding as me."

Was there a veiled threat in the words? I couldn't be sure.

"I have to do my job, Mr. De Lora," I said.

His eyes met mine, and, though it was impossible to guess what he was thinking, his next words were clear enough.

"You're playing with fire, baby. If you're not careful, sooner or later you're going to get burned."

Milo was nowhere in sight as I left Mr. De Lora's office and stepped back into the corridor. Mr. De Lora's warning hung heavily in my mind. Perhaps he was right. Perhaps I should let the matter drop now that the police had their suspect in custody. But somehow I knew that I wasn't satisfied with this solution, that there was some other element that had thus far escaped me, and I wouldn't be able to rest until I knew what it was.

As I started back toward the main room of the speakeasy, I passed an open door that had been closed as Mr. De Lora and I had made our way to his office.

I glanced inside and saw Esther Hayes sitting at a large dressing table with three beveled mirrors. The dressing room, in contrast to the hazy dimness of the main room of the speakeasy and the elegant masculinity of Mr. De Lora's office, was light, bright, and feminine. Gold-and-white-patterned wallpaper covered the walls, and the pattern was repeated on the rug that lay beneath white leather furniture. A number of gold lamps with white shades gave the room a warm brilliance that was absent elsewhere in the building.

Another quick glance around confirmed I was alone in the corridor, so I stepped forward and knocked on the door frame. "Miss Hayes?"

She looked up, surprised, I think, to see me standing in the doorway.

"Yes?"

"I just wanted to tell you how very much I've enjoyed your performances the past two nights."

Her dark eyes searched my face, as though trying to read my intentions in my expression. "Thank you."

"May I ask you something?"

"Of course." I could sense that she was not enthusiastic, but she was too polite to decline.

"Did you happen to know Grant Palmer?"

"Not really." She had hesitated for the barest fraction of a moment, but it was enough. She was lying.

"Mr. De Lora tells me he used to work here." I had hoped that the mention of discussing it with her employer would give the impression it would be all right for her to tell me what she knew. This was not the case. She simply waited for me to go on.

"I heard that he was killed recently, you see, and I was curious."

"Sometimes it's better not to be curious," she said lightly.

I nodded. "Maybe you're right."

"Esther . . ." We both looked up to see a man standing in the doorway. From his general appearance, well-dressed with the countenance of someone who had lived a rough life, I surmised that he was another employee here.

"Yes, what is it?" she asked.

"Can you look at this?" He held out a sheet of paper. From where I stood, I couldn't make out what was written on it, though the paper seemed to be filled with writing.

She rose from the seat at her dressing table and took the sheet of paper from him, her eyes running over it.

"It's right," she said, after a moment.

He nodded. "Okay. Thanks."

He turned and left the room, and Esther Hayes turned back to me. It was clear by this point, however, that I wasn't going to get any information from her.

"Well, I know you must be getting ready to sing again, so I'll leave you in peace," I said.

She smiled. "I'm sorry I couldn't be more helpful."

"Oh, it's all right. Thank you anyway."

I walked from her dressing room lost in thought and was just passing the little bricked alcove that sat off the hallway before the exit when a hand reached out and

grabbed my arm, pulling me into the shadows.

21

"Milo," I hissed, when I realized just who it was that had grabbed me. "What are you doing?"

"This," he murmured. He pulled me against him and leaned to kiss me in a most scandalous fashion.

I succumbed for just a moment and then pulled my mouth away. "What's wrong with you?" I demanded in a whisper.

"I don't like the way he looks at you," Milo said. "I might have known that he would take a fancy to you."

"You're not the only one who can cultivate underworld relationships," I replied, enjoying his displeasure. Milo rarely ever displayed even the smallest hint of jealousy, so I was secretly pleased.

"It's different, hearing you talk in that accent," he said, his eyes roving over me. "It almost makes me feel as though I am wooing a strange woman."

"No wonder you seem to be enjoying it," I remarked. "Nevertheless, you must stop this. If we're caught . . ."

"No one is going to care," he said, drawing me tighter against him. "We'll tell them the sparks flew from the moment we were left alone together in Mr. De Lora's office."

He gave me another kiss to illustrate the point, his mouth exploring mine as though I really were a strange woman he had never kissed before. My pulse quickened, and not just from the threat of being found out. Alas, as enjoyable as this interlude was proving, it couldn't go on.

"We can't risk them making a connection between us," I said breathlessly, catching his roving hands, though I could not quite bring myself to step away from him.

"It's thrilling, though, isn't it?" he asked with a wicked smile. "The possibility of being caught."

I might have known that was it. We could be at a party in London and Milo would spend the night surrounded by beautiful women, completely unconcerned with my whereabouts. Now that it was, to a certain extent, dangerous for the two of us to be seen together, he wanted nothing more. I had to admit there was a certain allure to the forbidden, but I wasn't about to be caught kissing him in this alcove.

"It won't be thrilling if we're caught talking like this."

"Then we'd better make sure they can't understand us."

He whispered something quite shocking in my ear in French, and I pushed back with a scandalized laugh. "Milo, you must learn to behave yourself."

"It's far more fun to misbehave," he said.

I laughed. "You'd best save the rest of your kisses for later tonight."

"I won't be back tonight, I'm afraid."

"Why not?"

"I have to go somewhere with De Lora this evening. He has a meeting with an associate at another nightclub. I have no doubt we'll be there all night."

I found it very irritating how Milo had managed to ingratiate himself into this bootlegging ring to such a level with such startling rapidity. It was quite unfair that women were excluded from so many things. What was even more irritating was that, if I had not taken on a pseudonym, I might have accompanied him as his wife. Oh, well. It was too late now.

"What am I to tell the Aldens when you don't come home?" I asked.

"Tell them I had a business matter to attend to."

"But, Milo . . ."

My protest was cut short by the sound of voices in the corridor. It was two of Mr. De Lora's men. They were engaged in a heated debate about racehorses and walked past without noticing us as we were half-concealed by the stack of wooden crates. I let out a relieved breath as their voices faded away.

"I've got to go before we're caught," I said. Still wrapped in the warm circle of his arms, I was hesitant to leave him, but I knew I must.

"De Lora will probably be looking for me soon," Milo admitted.

"All right. Go then." I stepped out of his embrace and moved back toward the alcove. Pausing, I turned back to him. "Please be careful tonight, Milo."

"I will."

I nodded and then turned and made my way along the rest of the corridor and back into the noise and smoke and music of the speakeasy.

I arrived back at the Aldens' house and made my way quietly up to our bedroom. It felt very quiet and empty without Milo there. I did hope he wasn't going to get himself into any sort of trouble tonight. I was used to his evenings away from home and had never been one to sit and fret, but something about tonight had me on edge. I very much hoped he would arrive back quickly and set my unnamed fears to rest.

As I prepared for bed, my mind ran again over all that I had learned. Mr. De Lora had been rather cagey about his relationship with Grant Palmer, but I had the feeling he had been telling me the truth. At least insofar as his not having anything to do with Mr. Palmer's death. I did have to admit that it had been rather sloppily done. Why had he been killed on the steps of the Aldens' home rather than somewhere else? It was all so strange.

Mr. De Lora had also told me that Grant Palmer had spent time in jail. I wondered how many people knew this fact. This was not to say, of course, that it had any bearing upon his murder, but it just seemed to me that there were too many coincidences.

I wondered if there was any way I could discover what kind of crime Grant Palmer had committed. Surely it would be on record somewhere? Or was it possible that someone might know? Rudy Elliot and Grant Palmer had been friends since childhood. Mr. Elliot would likely know why

Grant Palmer had gone to jail. I would just have to ask him.

I lay in bed for a long while, all of this swirling in my head. I half hoped that the door would open and Milo would slip in, his evening having not taken as long as he had originally assumed. What if something, even at this moment, was going wrong? What were we thinking, anyway, involving ourselves with American gangsters?

I sat up and switched on the light. I was clearly not going to fall asleep now.

Looking around the room, I saw that I had left my book on the table near the fireplace. Perhaps a few pages of reading would calm my mind. I got out of bed, sliding my feet into my slippers, and pulled on my dressing gown. Moving across the soft carpet, I took a seat in the chair and picked up the book.

I began a desultory perusal of its pages, but soon found myself unable to concentrate. It was a good-enough story, a mystery, in fact, but my mind kept wandering, and my stomach growled, reminding me that it had been a long time since dinner.

It was much too late to disturb Winnelda, and I didn't fancy the idea of creeping down to the kitchen in the darkness. Instead, I moved to the water jug that sat on a little table in the corner and poured myself a glass.

As I drank, I recalled the cool glass of water and the conversation with Mr. Brown at Mr. Alden's warehouse. Why had Grant Palmer and Jemma Petrie gone to the warehouse together? What had been their aim? I realized that if I was to get an answer I was going to have to ask Miss Petrie directly. So far subtle inquiries had gotten me nowhere. The American way was direct and straightforward, after all. Perhaps I would have to try it.

Jemma Petrie was coming in the morning to discuss wedding plans with Tabitha. Perhaps there would be a few moments when I could ask her.

I sighed. Setting the half-empty glass on my nightstand, I went back and retrieved my novel.

A second attempt at reading it produced the same result. I found I had no heart for mystery tonight. As much as I enjoyed a puzzle, the thrill of the chase, I desperately wished all of this hadn't happened. I wished that we had had a quiet visit to New York and that Tabitha would be able to enjoy her wedding to Tom. I wished her a long, quiet life after this, full of happiness with Tom and their children.

A thought occurred to me, and I sat up straight, the book falling from my lap onto the floor as I stared ahead, mentally calculating.

I realized suddenly the answer to something that had absolutely nothing to do with Grant Palmer's death, and felt in a rush that I should've been more careful before careening all over the city, interviewing gangsters and searching for a murderer.

Putting myself in danger had been one thing, but I was responsible for two lives now.

I was pregnant.

22

I felt a strange mixture of elation and terror, almost like a shot of adrenaline coursing through me. I went through the timing again in my head, more carefully this time, and I was quite sure I had not made a mistake. I was very definitely pregnant.

It explained so much: my constant tiredness, the vague feeling of seasickness that had followed me even after disembarking the ship, the wave of dizziness that had caught me unawares that day I had bent to pick up my lipstick. All the symptoms were there. A fine detective I was, missing the most obvious of clues.

Unable to sit still, I rose and began pacing the room, trying to make sense of the myriad thoughts and emotions that tumbled through me.

I didn't know why I should be surprised. Most of the young women with whom I had grown up already had multiple children. If there was anything unusual about my pregnancy it was that it had not happened before now.

With our marriage on better terms, we had not been expressly working to prevent a pregnancy as of late. Perhaps I had just assumed that, as I had never gotten pregnant before, I simply wouldn't. A child had always seemed like some distant possibility, something that would happen in its own time; now I was confronted with the reality.

I was thrilled that I was going to be a mother, but I knew absolutely nothing about it. I was the only child of a mother who had foisted me upon nannies and packed me off to boarding schools from a young age. What did I know of raising a child?

What was more, I was not at all sure how Milo would take the news. It wasn't that I thought he would be displeased, but he had never seemed particularly eager to have children, though we had, of course, discussed the possibility in rather abstract terms. In general, however, Milo liked children, and they liked him. I didn't suppose that fatherhood would prove too much of a challenge. And, after all, it was not as though a great deal of the burden was going to fall on him.

Besides, I was not, as my mother frequently reminded me, getting any younger, and if we were going to start a family, there was no time like the present.

There was a small part of me that wondered if Milo and I were suited to being parents. Neither of us had especially good examples to look up to. My parents, though I had never wanted for material things, had always maintained a vague detachment.

Milo's mother had died when he was born, and he and his father had been at odds for most of Milo's life. Neither of us knew what it was like to grow up in a warm and nurturing family, and, though I had always promised myself it was the environment in which I would raise my children, there was a nagging doubt that I was equal to the task.

I drew in a breath, and stopped my mental rambling. What was done was done; there was no sense worrying about it now.

I stood still for a moment and let the news fully sink in.

We were going to have a baby.

As surprised and afraid as I was, I couldn't stop the smile that spread across my face, nor the happy tears that sprang to my eyes.

When I awoke the next morning, the first

thing I remembered was that I was going to be a mother. My beaming smile was quickly wiped away by a wave of nausea so severe that I clutched at the bedspread until it passed.

I was still lying there, afraid to move a muscle, when Winnelda knocked on my door a short while later.

"Come in," I called weakly.

"Do you need help dressing, madam?" she asked, poking her head in, eyes averted, as she often did just in case she should find Milo and I behaving inappropriately again.

"No, I . . ." I clenched my teeth, too queasy to go on. It was as though, now that I had discovered its secret source, the sickness had decided it might as well reveal itself with full force.

"Madam, are you all right?" She had come into the room now and hurried worriedly to the bed. "You look dreadful."

"No, I'm all right." Mustering all my resolve, I sat up slowly, grimacing. I wouldn't tell Winnelda, not just yet. I wanted Milo to be the first to hear, wanted it to be, for just a little while, a secret that the two of us shared.

Winnelda came and arranged the pillows behind me, and I leaned against them in relief. I felt slightly less sick in this position.

"Just feeling a bit under the weather. I wonder . . . do you suppose you could bring me some toast and tea?"

"Certainly. Is there anything else?"

"No, thank you."

She left the room, and I picked up the glass of water I had left on the bedside table, sipping it and taking in slow, deep breaths through my nose.

Now that the sickness was abating, at least momentarily, I realized that Milo had not yet come in. I glanced at the clock and was shocked to find that it was after ten o'clock. Not only had I slept absurdly late, but I would've expected Milo to be back long before now. Surely he and Leon De Lora would have finished their night of revels or business dealings, whatever they were, by dawn.

Winnelda came in a few minutes later with a tray. "Here's your toast and tea, madam. You'll be feeling all right in no time."

"Thank you," I said, seizing a piece of toast and eating it dry. "Has Mr. Ames come in?"

I knew it wasn't possible that he had slipped into our room during the night without my notice, but perhaps he had come in this morning and was still downstairs.

An expression of concern flickered momentarily across Winnelda's face before she smoothed it away. "No, madam. At least, I didn't see him downstairs."

"He had a business matter to attend to last night and said he might not return until this morning."

"I see. Shall I tell you when he comes in?"

I took a sip of the tea. It was hot, strong, and very sweet. Just what I needed. I shook my head before taking a second sip.

"Run a bath for me, will you, Winnelda? And lay out something for me to wear."

Her eyes swept over me with an assessing glance. "The burgundy suit, I think. It'll give you color."

I nodded, but my mind had already begun to wander. "Winnelda, did you hear anything else from Annie about Miss Tabitha's missing gun?"

"Oh, yes. I meant to tell you. I asked her about it, and she said that Miss Tabitha's father gave it to her for protection. But Annie said Miss Tabitha was afraid of the thing and would hardly touch it. Annie said Miss Tabitha was always saying she wanted to be rid of it."

The timing was certainly suspect, but her fear of the gun seemed a point in her favor. Did that mean she wouldn't have had the nerve or skill to use it? I certainly hoped so. Perhaps she had gotten rid of it at an earlier date and no one noticed. I was not satisfied with this theory, but I put it to rest for the moment.

A short while later found me descending the stairs, feeling unutterably improved. The mirror had showed that I was still a bit pale and wan, but I also thought I detected a subtle glow that I hadn't noticed before.

There was no one in the breakfast room, and I went to the drawing room looking for any signs of life. Mr. Alden was sitting in a chair. He was holding a newspaper, but he did not appear to be reading it, his gaze trained at something in the distance.

He looked up when I came in, rising from his chair. "Oh. Good morning, Amory."

"Good morning," I said. "I'm afraid I've slept rather late."

"The change in time across the Atlantic is always difficult. Tabitha's gone out with Tom, I believe. She said she didn't want to disturb you, but she'll be back later. I think Jemma's due to arrive before lunch. Do you want some breakfast?"

"Thank you, no. I've had some tea and toast in my room."

"Will you sit down?" He motioned to one of the chairs across from him. I thought about begging off, leaving him to continue to read his newspaper in peace, but I had the impression that he wanted to talk, or at least that he wanted company, so I went and took a seat.

He looked uneasy, preoccupied.

He lit a cigarette and then settled back into his chair.

"I guess this trip hasn't really been what you imagined it would be," he said. His tone was light, but he looked tired and there was darkness under his eyes marking a lack of sleep. I noticed, too, that his hands were not quite steady as he struck the match and brought the flame to the tip of his cigarette.

"Not exactly," I admitted. That was true in more ways than one. "I'm just sorry that all of this had to happen. It was such a shame about Grant Palmer."

"Yes. I wanted everything to be perfect for Tabitha . . ." His voice trailed off and he sighed. "I've made some stupid decisions."

I didn't know how to respond to this, whether he was looking for a confidant or simply speaking to himself.

"I'm sure everything is going to turn out all right," I said by way of encouragement.

He looked up at me then, offering the sort of smile one gives to someone who had just said something very stupid indeed.

"Maybe."

"Don't worry, Calvin," I heard a voice say from the hallway. "I'll tell them I'm here."

It was Mr. Elliot.

I thought of going out into the hallway to ask Calvin if there had been any word from Milo, but I thought I would wait until I could catch him alone. Besides, I was quite sure he would've told me if Milo had sent a note.

It was not an unusual thing for Milo to disappear for several hours without notice, but I couldn't shake the uneasy feeling that had settled over me since I woke up, since we had parted ways last night, really.

"Good morning," Mr. Elliot said, coming into the room. "I'm dropping by unannounced."

"Hello, Rudy," Mr. Alden said. "Tabitha and Tom aren't here."

"It seems they always run off and forget to tell me where they're going," he said lightly. "I thought Tom and I were supposed to have lunch today."

"Oh, well, perhaps they'll be back soon then," Mr. Alden said, rising from his seat. "Jemma is coming to discuss wedding plans, from what I understand. I've got some business matters to attend to. If you'll excuse me?"

"Certainly."

Mr. Alden took his leave then, and I was left alone with Mr. Elliot.

"Tabitha ran off without you, too, eh?" he said with a smile.

"I slept rather late, I'm afraid."

"And where is Mr. Ames?"

"He's gone out, too," I said. I didn't know why, but I felt that I shouldn't volunteer information about Milo's unknown whereabouts. I still hoped that he would arrive any minute, breezing through the door after a night spent gambling and drinking, and I didn't want to create undue alarm. And if it was something more serious than that, I wanted to wait, to give myself time to decide who to trust.

"I guess I'll wait a few minutes and see if Tom shows up. Do you mind if I smoke?" Rudy Elliot asked as he took a seat.

"Not at all."

He sat down and pulled a cigarette case from the pocket of his jacket, then felt around for matches.

"I don't suppose you have a lighter?"

"No, I'm afraid not. But perhaps if we ring for Calvin . . ."

"Oh, no, let's not bother him. He gives me the creeps." He continued feeling his pockets. "I thought I had some here. I have hundreds of matchbooks. You'd think I'd have one of them . . ."

His looking for a lighter brought Milo's ever-present silver lighter to mind, and I wondered again where my husband had gone. If he was all right, I was going to be very cross with him for having disappeared.

Not too cross, of course, for I would have to tell him about the baby and I wanted the moment to be just right. I wondered again what his reaction would be, how he would feel about the news that he was going to be a father.

What kind of parents would we be? I tried to picture the two of us with a little dark-haired child. Milo would be overindulgent, naturally. I supposed I would, too, for I already felt that this child was going to be the most important thing in my world.

"Ah. Here's some on this table!" Rudy Elliot exclaimed triumphantly. He lit his cigarette then and I pulled my attention back to him. He looked down at the matches, seemed about to put them in his pocket, and then, apparently remembered they were not his and set them down on the table.

"I have to admit, I'll be glad when the wedding is over. I think I'm going to go out of town for a while. I need a chance to clear my head."

I nodded. I felt much the same way. I very much wanted Tom and Tabitha to begin their happy life together, and I wanted to be back in England. I wanted to sit in our quiet morning room at Thornecrest and stitch clothes for the baby.

"I'm glad that they caught the killer, but I find it hard to just go back to normal life. I suppose things will never be as they were," he said wistfully.

I decided to ask Mr. Elliot the question that had been weighing on my mind. "I heard somewhere that Mr. Palmer had spent time in prison. Do you know what it was for?"

He looked up at me, a frown flickering across his brow. "Oh, it was the crowd he was running with, I think. He got sucked into some scheme or another and ended up paying for it. Luckily for him, he got a light sentence."

"I see." Though I didn't really see. It was all so vague. I was fairly certain of one thing, however. If Tom had been in prison with Grant Palmer, Rudy didn't know about it.

He looked at the clock. "Well, I guess Tom and Tab aren't going to be back in time for lunch. I guess I'll be going."

He stood, grinding out the cigarette. "Will you tell Tom to call me when he gets back? Maybe he wants to meet for dinner instead."

"Yes, I'll be sure to tell him."

He took his leave and I sat alone in the sitting room, still lost in thought. Who had killed Grant Palmer? That was still the question, for, despite Detective Andrews's announcement that he had the killer in custody, I couldn't help but feel that there was more to the story than that. There was something that had only to shift to make everything come into focus. I felt as if I knew the answer; I just had to make my mind realize it.

23

In part to distract myself from my growing worries about Milo's absence, I decided to take my usual approach and go through the list of suspects one by one.

There was Leon De Lora, of course. He was, perhaps, the most obvious candidate for being the murderer of Mr. Palmer. He had been Mr. Palmer's employer before Mr. Palmer had moved to Frankie Earl's employ. I imagined there were any number of things about his business that Mr. De Lora would not want Frankie Earl to know. So perhaps he had killed Grant Palmer to silence him.

Still, there was something lacking in this theory. I had the impression that Mr. De Lora hadn't cared much, one way or the other, about Grant Palmer. There had been indifference in his tone when he had spoken of him. That did not mean, of course, that he had not killed him.

Mr. De Lora was the type of man who was

extremely good at concealing his true feelings. Despite my inclination to believe him — even to like him, in a way — I could not be sure that he was not the killer.

I still felt, however, that Mr. Palmer's being killed on the Aldens' doorstep meant that it was likely someone who was part of the wedding party. After all, it would have been a very easy thing for one of them to have asked to meet him there and shot him when he arrived.

I thought first of Mr. Alden. He and Grant Palmer had been discussing some sort of clandestine business arrangement. Mr. Alden had been angry, Mr. Palmer flippant. I thought it was entirely possible that their disagreement might have led to violence.

Mr. Alden could very easily have asked Mr. Palmer to meet him at the house, shot him on the doorstep when he arrived, and then disappeared back into the night, making a show of returning a short time later.

For Tabitha's sake, I didn't want to believe that Mr. Alden might be guilty, but I also had to admit that he was a man who might be willing to make difficult decisions to ensure his success. He had not gotten so far in business by being indecisive, and it was possible that he had decided that Grant Palmer was too much of a liability.

I thought next of Tom Smith. He and Grant Palmer had apparently been good friends, but they had quarreled about money. There was something mysterious about Tom Smith's past, and I couldn't help but wonder if there was something he would kill to keep people from knowing.

What about Tabitha? I couldn't rule her out completely, though I very much wanted to. She was such a sweet, good-tempered girl. I found it very difficult to believe that she could kill anyone. However, I knew that even the nicest people were capable of violence when they felt there was no alternative.

I knew how much Tabitha loved her father, how fiercely loyal she was to him. If she thought that Mr. Palmer was going to harm her father in some way, do something detrimental to his business, then she might have been compelled to act. There was also the matter of her missing pistol.

I sighed. I wanted to ask her about it, but a part of me was afraid of the answer.

I pushed on with my list of suspects, unwilling to think of Tabitha's possible guilt any longer for the moment.

Next was Rudy Elliot. Both Grant Palmer and Rudy Elliot had told me that their friendship went back to childhood. There had been rumors of their arguing over a woman, and I wondered what had become of that. Jealousy was often a strong motive, and I had seen for myself how Rudy was often cast into the shadow of Grant Palmer's handsome bravado. Had it finally been enough to push him over the edge?

Perhaps they had met in the street on the way to the Aldens' home and an argument had ensued. Perhaps it had been done in the heat of the moment. Or perhaps Rudy Elliot had coldly followed his friend there and shot him. I didn't like to think it was true, but I couldn't rule it out.

And then there was Jemma Petrie. She and Mr. Palmer had apparently been engaged in some sort of secret liaison. Despite Miss Petrie's protestations that she disliked Mr. Palmer in the extreme, she had been spotted by Tom coming out of Mr. Palmer's house quite late one evening. They had been seen together at Mr. Alden's warehouse.

It seemed likely to me that they had been having an affair at some point and that things had gone awry. I couldn't, of course, know the particulars, but Mr. Palmer was a known ladies' man, and I thought it very likely he had moved on from Miss Petrie. Had she killed him in revenge? Had they had a lover's quarrel of some sort and she had killed him in a passionate rage? It was all possible, I suppose, but there was no proof of any of it.

Proof. That was always the most difficult part. It was going to be especially difficult in this case because I didn't have my friend Detective Inspector Jones here to listen to my theories or to give advice.

I thought of Detective Andrews and his perpetually sardonic demeanor and was not at all encouraged. Detective Bailey seemed more sympathetic, kinder, but I didn't think he would be inclined to listen to me either, not unless I had something definitive to show him.

Granted, I supposed there was no reason why they should listen to me, even if I chose to approach them. I was a society woman on foreign soil. What was I likely to know about the crime that had been committed?

I sighed. Whatever my qualifications, it seemed there was very little chance that I would be able to involve myself with the police in any way. They had a man in custody, and I didn't think anything was going to change their mind. No, if I wanted to be of help in this situation, I was going to have to find the answers and then bring them to the police.

I couldn't help but think I would enjoy

seeing the look on Detective Andrews's face when I presented him with the identity of the killer.

I heard the distant sound of the telephone just then, and a moment later Calvin came into the drawing room.

"Miss Petrie is on the phone, madam. She wishes to inform you and Miss Tabitha that she is unwell and may not be able to meet today as planned."

"Oh, I do hope it's nothing serious?"

"I don't believe so. She merely says she is under the weather."

"All right, thank you." Though I was sorry Jemma was unwell, it was just as well she didn't intend to meet us, since Tabitha hadn't returned.

"She also wants to know if she left her compact here. She seems to have misplaced it."

"I haven't seen it," I said, glancing around. It was then I spotted it, lying on the table near the place Rudy Elliot had just vacated.

"Yes, there it is."

"Thank you. I shall tell her."

He left then, and I returned to my contemplation of the case.

I was still lost in thought a few minutes later when I heard the front door open, and the sound of a male voice in the corridor. I had hoped, for an instant, that it might be Milo returning, but I realized at once from the raw, heated emotion in the tone it could not belong to my husband.

"I can't possibly . . . I need time. I . . . I don't know what you want me to say."

"Don't say anything. It isn't necessary. I know how you feel." The second voice belonged to Tabitha, and I realized that I was hearing a lover's quarrel.

I thought I should make my presence known, but it turned out not to be necessary.

There was the sound of the front door closing, a bit harder than necessary, and then Tabitha came into the sitting room.

She had not, I think, expected to see me there, and the raw emotion on her face clutched at my heart. She tried, for one valiant moment, to rein it in, and then her expression crumpled and she burst into tears.

I rose from my seat and moved quickly to her side, drawing her into an embrace.

"Whatever's the matter, Tabitha?"

"Tom and I had a terrible fight, and I don't know if he's going to want to marry me after this." She began to cry harder, the sobs shaking her shoulders.

Always uncomfortable with strong emotion, I nevertheless did my best to comfort her. "A fight isn't the end of everything. I'm sure he still wants to marry you, dear. Surely it can't be as bad as all that."

She looked up at me, her face red and tearstained, her eyes bright with sorrow. "But it is. You don't know. It's all my fault."

"Now, Tabitha, I'm sure there's plenty of blame to go around," I said.

"No." She turned to me and the confession came tumbling out without preamble. "I had an affair with Grant."

I could not have been more astounded if she had sprouted two heads.

"I . . . I see," I managed to answer in a calm voice. It was a scandalous admission, and it was the last thing I would've expected to hear from sweet, innocent Tabitha.

"It was before Tom and I were engaged," she said. "I mean, when we were still seeing one another, but before he asked me to marry him."

I said nothing, waiting for her to go on.

"I had too much to drink one night at a speakeasy after we had a stupid quarrel. I went to a nightclub and Grant was there. We danced and talked and . . ." She colored and buried her face in her hands. "It just happened. I . . . I don't know what I was thinking. It was only once, and I have wanted to tell Tom, but I've been so afraid . . ."

She set to crying again, and I tried to think of what I could say to comfort her.

"And how did he find out?"

"He's been acting strange lately, distant."

It was the same thing Tom had told Milo about her. I lamented again the burden that secrets placed on the hearts of those who were determined to keep them.

"At first I thought it was because of what we did," she went on.

"What do you mean?"

"We threw my gun away," she said.

So that's what had become of Tabitha's missing weapon.

"Why did you do that?" I asked cautiously.

"It was the morning after Grant was killed. I started thinking that with police and reporters everywhere someone might find out about it. I don't know. It was a stupid thing to do, but we drove to the river and threw it in."

It was all rather ridiculous, but I suppose it was a preferable reason to her having had killed someone with it.

"But he didn't seem worried about the gun. I thought maybe he knew somehow, about me and Grant. And then we got into an argument today, and it all came spilling out. I . . . he was so awfully calm about it, but I know he must hate me, and I don't know if I shall ever see him again."

She was being dramatic, of course, but she was managing to contain most of her tears now, and that was encouraging.

"What did Tom say?" I asked gently.

"He said . . . I don't know . . . that he needs to think things over."

"Well, I think that's the best thing, rather than making heated decisions, don't you?"

She sniffed, wiping her nose on an embroidered handkerchief she had pulled from her pocket. "I suppose. It's just all so horrible. But I'm glad he knows. I'm glad I don't have to keep it a secret anymore."

"Yes, secrets can be very difficult to bear."

"I just . . . I thought we were going to have a perfect marriage, like you and Milo. And now we're not even married yet and everything is going so awfully wrong."

"No marriage is perfect, Tabitha," I said. I decided not to elaborate on how close my own marriage had come to disaster. There was no sense in disillusioning her any further.

"I want to talk to him," she said. "But what if he refuses to listen to anything I have to say? I'm very much afraid that we're not going to . . . What if he doesn't want to marry me now?"

"Does he love you, Tabitha?" I asked.

"Yes. That is, I believe he does."

"And do you love him?"

"More than anything."

"Then I think the two of you should talk when your emotions have settled a bit. If you truly feel that way about each other, you'll be able to come to some sort of resolution. I'm certain of it."

It was a bit of a lie, for I was not at all certain they would work it out. But I remembered Tom's words to Milo, about the secret he wondered if he should tell Tabitha. Now, it seemed, would be the ideal time for him to do so. Perhaps if they were both honest, they could find a way to forgive each other whatever indiscretions stood between them.

"I . . . I think you're right. I suppose the only thing I can do is give him a bit of time."

She reached over and gave me a hug. "Thank you, Amory. You always know just what to say."

With that, she left the sitting room, and I drew in a breath.

Good heavens. The world was falling down around my ears, and Milo was nowhere to be found. How very typical of him, I thought irritably, to leave me pregnant and alone to deal with all of this.

The rational part of me realized this accusation was not entirely fair, given he didn't know of my pregnancy, but I still couldn't help but feel annoyed with him. I also had to admit that my annoyance was preferable to the fear that was steadily beginning to creep over me.

Milo had known I was worried when he left with Mr. De Lora last night. I did not think he would've stayed away without letting me know his whereabouts.

I sighed, moving restlessly around the sitting room. It wasn't going to do me any good to fret.

I picked up Jemma Petrie's silver compact, turning it over in my hands. Perhaps I could bring it to her. It would be something useful to do, at any rate. I slipped it into my pocket to transfer to my handbag later and then looked again at the table. Something had caught my attention, and it took me a moment to realize what it was.

I looked down at the matches that sat on the tabletop. They were from De Lora's. No. I looked closer. They were much the same as the ones I had observed that night when talking to Mr. De Lora, but these were different. They were emblazoned with the words *The Lightning Lounge,* a lightning bolt of yellow streaking across a black background. And then I remembered what Mr. De Lora had told me. They belonged to Frankie Earl's establishment, and he reportedly gave them only to his trusted associates.

Those matches could not have been left here by Grant Palmer, for I was certain they would have been noticed in the days since his death. No, they had been left here by someone else more recently. I realized what that meant. Someone else close to the Aldens was secretly linked to Frankie Earl. And if that was the case, perhaps it was Mr. Earl who was responsible for Grant Palmer's death, after all. A second realization came to me then: if these matches were here, it was very likely that Grant Palmer's killer had been in the drawing room.

24

I tried not to jump to conclusions, but I could think of no other reasons that matches from Frankie Earl's establishment, from Grant Palmer's employer, should be in this house unless another of Mr. Earl's associates had been here. It was possible, I supposed, that another person involved in the mystery was working for him in some other capacity, but the theory didn't sit well with me. I felt certain the appearance of the matches and the murder were linked.

Who else, then, had used matches in the drawing room recently? I thought back. I was fairly certain they had not been there three nights ago when I had sat here discussing the murder with Mr. Elliot. I thought I would have noticed them, for the artwork was distinctive.

Who had smoked here since then? I hadn't been in the sitting room much of the time, but there were only a few people with access to this room.

I had a sinking feeling as I realized the implications. They must belong to Mr. Alden.

I remembered Rudy searching his pockets to no avail and then his triumph when he had located some. He must have found them sitting on the table where Mr. Alden had left them.

It seemed that Mr. Alden was in league with Frankie Earl. I thought of the suspicious behavior at his warehouse. He must be involved with Frankie Earl's operations somehow, perhaps even staging the thefts to avert suspicion.

My heart began to pound, but I told myself it would do no good to panic. I needed to calm down, to think. Just because Mr. Alden might be involved in something illegal did not mean he was the killer. Did it? But I thought of his hushed conversation with Grant Palmer that day, the way Mr. Palmer had visited the warehouse. They had been connected in some way, and now it all made sense.

It seemed that Mr. Alden had gotten involved with Mr. Palmer to some extent and had been desperate to extricate himself from it.

What was I going to tell Tabitha if her

father was the killer? I didn't even want to think about it. How was she to begin her new life when the old one was about to come crashing down around her?

What was more, what was I to do about all of this? I considered my options.

It would make sense to make contact with Detectives Andrews and Bailey, but somehow I doubted very much that they would believe me. And, besides, I had no proof of anything. Not yet. With a suspected killer already in custody, they would be even less likely to listen to me.

I wished desperately that Milo was here. I needed his counsel, but, more than that, I was now terribly worried something had happened to him. Granted, I could not be entirely sure that he had not wandered off in pursuit of some amusement. He had done such things in the past. No, I didn't want to raise the alarm just yet. I needed to sort things out before I did that.

There was only one person I could think of who might be able to help me sort through this mess.

I needed to see Leon De Lora.

The day seemed interminable as I waited for evening to come so I could go to De Lora's. Leon De Lora's world was one of night and shadow, and I didn't know how to reach him in the day. I stayed in my room for most of it, listening to the ticking of the clock and hoping that Milo would arrive. He did not.

I saw nothing more of Tabitha, and I assumed that she had taken to her room as well.

Mr. Alden left word that he would be taking dinner out, and so I was able to keep to the refuge of my bedroom until darkness fell. At last it was late enough to leave.

"If Mr. Ames returns, tell him I've gone to De Lora's," I instructed Winnelda as I pulled on a wrap over a gown of emerald-green taffeta.

"Do be careful, madam," she said, wringing her hands with worry.

"Don't worry," I assured her. "I intend to."

I took a cab to De Lora's. I didn't know if Mr. De Lora would be there. Perhaps he and Milo were still together, wherever they had gone. Perhaps something awful had happened to both of them.

I tried to tell myself that if something had happened to Mr. De Lora it would have been big news and likely made the evening edition of the paper. That didn't exactly set my mind at ease about Milo's whereabouts, but I supposed I would know something soon enough.

I made my way into the basement speak-easy and directly toward the door I knew led to the corridor and Mr. De Lora's office. The place was crowded tonight, the press of bodies tighter, the smoke thicker. I felt tense and claustrophobic, dizziness and nausea barely held at bay.

The same man who had been there the evening before stood near the door to the corridor, and he moved slightly in front of it as I approached, apparently guessing my intention. His eyes swept over me in an appraising way.

"Can I help you?" he asked, though he didn't sound at all enthusiastic about offering aid.

"I'm here to see Mr. De Lora," I said, hoping that a sweet tone of voice would be all that was required to let me pass. It wasn't.

"Mr. De Lora ain't accepting visitors."

"Tell him . . . tell him it's Rose Kelly," I said. "I think he'll see me."

I had been going over in my mind how best to break the news to him that I had lied about my identity and my purpose for seeking him out. I didn't expect him to be pleased about it, but my concern for Milo was now overriding all else.

"Sorry, lady. He don't want to be disturbed."

"Couldn't you at least tell him I'm here?" I realized there was a plaintive note creeping into my voice, but I didn't care. If I wasn't able to see Mr. De Lora, I didn't know how I would proceed.

"She's all right, Bart."

The voice at my side caught me by surprise. I hadn't heard Esther Hayes approaching.

"But . . ." Bart started.

"I'll tell him I let her in."

Bart seemed to consider this for a moment, then shrugged. "Whatever you say."

Miss Hayes opened the door and we passed through. I didn't realize how tense I had been until she'd closed the door behind us and the comparative coolness and quiet of the corridor hit me like a physical relief.

"Thank you," I said. "It's urgent that I speak to Mr. De Lora."

Her dark eyes met mine incuriously. "You know the way to his office."

I nodded. "Thank you."

I began to walk away, but her voice stopped me. "Miss Kelly."

I turned.

"You can trust him," she said.

I didn't know what it was that had made her tell me this, but I hoped she was right. There was a lot depending upon it.

I tapped at the door.

"Come in."

He was alone in his office when I entered, and I felt a pang of disappointment that Milo wasn't with him. Some part of me had been hoping that their business dealings had unaccountably extended the entire day and that Milo, in his careless way, had simply forgotten to telephone me. But, somehow, I had known all along that this wasn't the case.

He glanced up at me but made no greeting or move to rise from his seat.

"Mr. De Lora, I need to talk to you," I said, moving toward him.

He motioned for me to take a seat on the chair facing his desk. Then he scraped a match across the edge of his desk, lighting the cigarette that dangled from his lips, and waited.

"I'm not really sure where to begin." I contemplated how best to go about explaining things. "You see, I haven't been exactly straightforward with you. I'm afraid I may have misled you a bit when I said . . ."

"Your accent is slipping," he interrupted.

I blinked. I had not even noticed that I

was failing to maintain the American accent I had worked so hard to cultivate.

"You're with Ames, aren't you?" he said, though I suspected it wasn't really a question.

Mr. De Lora was a smart man, but this deduction caught me by surprise. Since I had come here to learn Milo's whereabouts, there was no sense in denying it.

"He's my husband," I said at last.

He nodded, not at all surprised, and I couldn't resist asking: "How did you know?"

"I could tell the moment he came into my office there was something there."

Had he really been able to tell? I had been so certain that I had maintained my mask of indifference when Milo had so unexpectedly walked into the room, and Milo had been absolutely brilliant in his display of disregard for me.

"I thought we did a good job of hiding it. We were so careful."

"That was it," he said, pointing his cigarette at me. "Too careful. There was some kind of a wall between you, unnatural for two good-looking, unattached people of the opposite sex."

He was sharp. I hadn't thought of it from that angle, that a single woman would likely be very interested in Milo. Even not-so-single women often were. And yet I had showed very little interest in him and he'd shown none in me.

"So you're Mrs. Ames. Your name isn't even Rose, I bet."

"No," I admitted. "It isn't."

He sighed. "Like so many things in life, the truth is often disappointing."

"I do hope you'll let me explain myself."

"Oh, I'm counting on it." His expression was pleasant, but I detected a certain hardness in his eyes. Not that I could blame him. I knew how unpleasant it was to be lied to.

"But first, I need to know where Milo is."

He blew out a stream of smoke. "I haven't seen him since six o'clock this morning."

I felt my worry swell but pressed it down. Panic would do neither me nor Milo any good.

"Did he say where he was going?"

"I think it's my turn to ask a few questions," he said.

My instinct was to protest, but I knew there was really no sense in arguing. If time was of the essence, I might as well answer his questions so he would answer mine.

"First, what's your real name?" he asked.

"Amory."

"Amory Ames." He smiled. "I like that. It's got a ring to it."

"Thank you."

"Next question. What's your game?"

"There isn't any game, Mr. De Lora. Quite the opposite, in fact. You see, my husband and I came from England for Tabitha Alden's wedding. We were in the house when Grant Palmer was killed on the doorstep."

Still he said nothing, his dark eyes on my face. I had the impression he was trying to wait me out, to make me uneasy. But I had faced down Milo's impenetrable gaze for years, and I was not about to be intimidated.

"I thought that, if I came in the guise of a reporter, I might be able to discover something about his death."

Now he spoke, releasing the words with a cloud of smoke. "What made you think I know anything about that?"

"Grant Palmer once worked for you but then switched allegiance. I thought it was possible that you might have killed him or had him killed."

He grinned. "So you came here to interrogate me. You've got guts, I'll give you that."

I wasn't sure what to make of this dubious compliment, so I pressed on.

"Tonight I found this in the Alden's drawing room." I reached into my handbag and removed the matchbook. I set it on the desk.

"Someone in that house is linked to Frankie Earl, and I can only assume they were involved in the killing."

"So?"

"So I realized that it must be Mr. Alden. He was smoking in the drawing room shortly before I discovered these matches, and I think he must be involved with Frankie Earl as well. Perhaps there have been some illegal activities going on at his warehouses."

"Is your husband on the level?" This question threw me off.

"I . . . I beg your pardon?"

"Does he really plan to invest or was that all part of this" — he waved a hand — "ploy."

"Oh, he's perfectly in earnest."

He apparently took my word for this, for he reverted back to the topic of Grant Palmer's murder. I wondered if that answer had been more important than I realized. Had his decision to help me hung in the balance?

"So let me get this straight. You were invited to Tabitha Alden's wedding. When one of the groomsmen gets rubbed out, you decide to play detective. And now you're trying to prove that the police caught the wrong guy."

While I was not entirely flattered by this somewhat dismissive description of my efforts, I could not entirely deny it. "Something like that," I said at last.

"And why are you chasing down these leads on your own?"

"I feel like I need to find out who really killed Mr. Palmer."

"Again, why?"

I wasn't used to being questioned so intensely about my altruistic motives.

"Isn't the cause of justice enough?"

A smirk touched his lips. "Maybe you haven't noticed, but I'm not exactly concerned with law and order."

I could see that I was going to have to tell him the truth. "Level with him," as his vernacular would put it. "I've been . . . involved in murder investigations before. I have rather a knack for locating the truth. I wanted to do that in this case."

"What business is it of yours?"

He was using the same arguments Milo had always used when I tried to involve myself in a mystery, but there was something in his relentless dismissal of my arguments that wore me down.

I sighed. "I suppose it wasn't, not entirely. But it is now. I don't know where Milo is, and I'm very much afraid I'm staying in the home of a killer."

He looked at me for a moment, as though trying to make up his mind about something. Then he reached down and pulled open a drawer to his desk. His hand went inside, and he pulled out a gun and set it down on the surface of his desk. I wondered if this was some sort of threat, but it seemed that he was only searching for the documents beneath, for he soon pulled out a stack of papers.

Setting them on the desk, he slid them toward me.

I reached out and picked one up and studied it. After a moment, I looked up at him, surprised. "These are financial records."

"This is a business," he replied.

"Yes, but . . ."

His brows went up. "Did you think that we just collect the dough and throw it in a treasure chest somewhere?"

"Of course not. It's just that I don't understand . . ."

"Look closer at the signature at the bottom."

My gaze moved to the line at the bottom of the page, the scrawl of dark ink, and I realized that, though it was almost undecipherable, I recognized it.

I looked up at him. "This is Mr. Alden's signature."

He nodded. "Ben Alden is in on my nightclub scheme."

I stared at him. "You mean, he's an investor?"

"Not exactly. He's going to be shipping a lot of stuff for me. We've got it all worked out. That's the contract. All legal and everything."

"But . . . I don't understand," I said, looking down at the paper, then back up at Mr. De Lora. "Why hasn't he said something?"

"As you know, I'm not the most reputable person, and I don't think he cares to have his name linked to mine. Especially not with a high-profile wedding in the works. We met a couple of times, and I had to sneak into his house at night. All the money that changed hands has been in cash, too. Untraceable."

So this was the secret that Mr. Alden had been keeping, the source of the strange behavior and mysterious visitors that Tabitha had observed. He was working with Leon De Lora and didn't want Tabitha to know about it, afraid that she would worry over an unsound investment. This didn't explain everything, however.

"But what about Grant Palmer?" I asked. "I was under the impression that they were in on some sort of scheme together."

"Palmer is the one that recommended me to him initially, and he worked as my go-between for a while. Palmer even made a delivery of cash to me once. Then Palmer started trying to pull Alden into some sort of deal with Frankie Earl. Alden came here the night Palmer was murdered, in fact. Told me he'd had to throw one of Earl's guys out of his house and that he wondered if it might put his family in danger."

So that had been the cause of the angry altercation Milo and I had witnessed. And also the reason he had seemed so stricken when he had returned home the night of the murder. He had been afraid Frankie Earl's men might have harmed Tabitha in retaliation.

"Ben Alden isn't the kind of guy who would try to play both sides of the fence," he went on. "I've got a good instinct when it comes to people. Besides, I had a look at his books."

"Oh?" I was a bit surprised that Mr. Alden had turned over secure financial information to a man of Mr. De Lora's reputation. "Then you have an exceptionally close business relationship."

413

He smiled. "Not exactly. I *acquired* the books one evening and had them back by the next morning."

My eyes widened. I realized then what he'd meant. He had been behind the break-in at Mr. Alden's office.

"You . . . you got the books in a break-in," I repeated.

"I suppose I've gone and shocked you," he said.

He had, but I was too preoccupied to much care. My mind whirled. "Was there something in the warehouse you needed as well?"

"The warehouse?"

"Yes, someone tried to break into the warehouse."

He shook his head. "That wasn't me. I have enough inventory of my own to take care of."

I studied him, wondering if I should believe what he was telling me. I saw no reason not to. After all, he had admitted readily enough to breaking in for the financial records. Why would he deny breaking into the warehouse?"

"The books seem to be in order," he went on. "But my accountant can probably tell you more than I can."

I was momentarily confused. He was going to introduce me to his accountant?

He got up from his desk and went to the door.

"Esther," he called.

A moment later Miss Hayes appeared in the doorway.

"Come in here a minute and tell Mrs. Ames about Mr. Alden's books."

"Mrs. Ames?" she repeated, her eyes moving between Mr. De Lora and me.

He smiled. "It turns out Rose Kelly doesn't exist."

"I see," she said, betraying no surprise, and, indeed, very little curiosity.

She came into the room and took the other chair across from Mr. De Lora's desk, folded her hands in her lap, and looked at me. "What do you want to know?"

"You're the . . . accountant?" I asked.

"Esther's half the brains of this place," Mr. De Lora said. "My silent partner, so to speak."

"Not entirely silent," she replied.

The corner of his mouth tipped up. "No, not silent. There's the singing, of course. And the earful she gives me when I need it."

She gave him a faint smile, then turned to me. "I sing because I enjoy it. But I enjoy numbers, too."

"That's marvelous," I said. "I've never been much good at numbers."

"She's the one who's been pushing for the nightclubs," Mr. De Lora said with a smile. "I didn't exactly plan to go straight when Prohibition ended, but Esther has other ideas."

"There's no reason to go on making money illegally when it can be made without the risk," she said calmly.

"It's a very sound business decision," I agreed.

"Anyway," Mr. De Lora went on, "Esther had a good look at the books. Maybe she can answer some of your questions."

I turned to her. "Was there anything telling in Mr. Alden's books? Anything that was unaccounted for or suspicious?"

Her eyes flickered to Mr. De Lora, as though wanting to be certain that she could share this aspect of the information with me. He gave her a little nod, and she turned back to me.

"Mr. Alden's books all seem to be in order. He's been making a great deal of money. A great deal. But, so far as I could tell, everything was adding up correctly."

So Mr. Alden's sudden financial windfall had been the result of activities that were indeed aboveboard. "Nothing suspicious?

No discrepancies?" I pressed.

"I told you: he's not really cut out for a life of crime," Mr. De Lora said.

"There was one thing," Esther Hayes said suddenly.

We looked at her. "There were a series of numbers that seemed to indicate a shipment of the same type of items, but the last few shipments have been slightly heavier than the others."

The thought came to me suddenly. "Was it for tires?" I asked.

"Yes," she said. "How did you know?"

"The warehouse manager said someone had tried to break into the part of the warehouse that held the tires. And Mr. Palmer came there once, claiming to be looking for Tom Smith. He had a woman with him, Jemma Petrie. I think she was his mistress. Could it have been that they were looking for something hidden there?"

Mr. De Lora's face darkened. "If he was with Jemma Petrie, I know very well what was hidden there."

"What?"

"Jemma Petrie wasn't his girlfriend. He was selling her drugs."

I looked up at him, shocked. "Surely not."

"She's sweet, isn't she?" he said to Esther with a smile before turning back to me.

"Frankie Earl is not, shall we say, moving toward more legitimate pursuits now that the alcohol business is going down the drain. He's been moving drugs, and he's been doing it for a while. I suspect that Mr. Palmer found a way to help him out with that. Apparently, moving the drugs inside of automobile tires. I think he presented Mr. Alden with a 'legitimate' businessman who wanted his items shipped, and Mr. Alden was none the wiser. Palmer had recommended me, after all, and it turned out all right."

"But are you sure about Miss Petrie?" I was still reeling from the idea that she might be addicted to drugs. The more I thought about it, however, the more sense it seemed to make.

"Yeah," he answered. "Eddy, my bartender, said she was in here the night Palmer got rubbed out, looking for him. I suppose her supply was running low."

I suddenly remembered the compact that she had left at the house. I had put it into my handbag when I changed clothes this afternoon. I reached inside and pulled it out. Flipping the little clasp, I opened it. It was nearly empty, but there was the residue of white powder in the rim and dusted across the surface of the little mirror, far too pale in color for Jemma Petrie's complexion.

I set it carefully on the desk.

"That's not face powder," Mr. De Lora said dryly.

"What . . . what is it?"

"Cocaine."

Powdering her nose, indeed.

I had had the impression that she had despised Mr. Palmer, and yet there had always been a certain sort of awareness on her part whenever he was near. Now I knew what that was. She had been dependent upon him to supply her with drugs, and she had hated him for it.

I wondered what she had been doing since he had died. I had noticed that she hadn't been looking well. And today she had been unable to meet us due to illness. She was likely suffering from withdrawal.

That, then, was the reason she had not answered Tabitha's telephone call the night of the murder, why she had lied to the police about her whereabouts.

All of these revelations, following so closely upon one another, were enough to make my head spin. I realized that I might very well have discovered more of this earlier on if I hadn't been so caught up in my subterfuge.

"Then who killed Grant Palmer?" I asked. "Jemma wouldn't have done it, not if she was relying on him for her supply."

"You don't think it was Mr. Alden? Maybe he found out what Palmer was doing under his nose."

Something in the way he said it, in the way he watched me as he waited for my answer, let me know that he didn't believe it any more than I did.

I shook my head. "I don't think Mr. Alden knew. If he did, he could've had Grant Palmer arrested. There was no reason to resort to murder."

Mr. De Lora leaned back in his seat. "Yeah, about this murder stuff. Why don't you let the police worry about it?"

"The police aren't always concerned with justice," I said.

His eyes met mine, and I thought there was something searching in his gaze.

"I think you're right, Mrs. Ames," Miss Hayes said. "The killer should be brought to justice."

"Then I'm outvoted," Mr. De Lora said with a shrug. "I just urge you to be careful. Did you talk to your husband about any of this?"

I shook my head. "He hasn't been home since last night. That's the real reason I came to see you. I'm concerned about him."

"Not to alarm you, but I'm starting to think he may have gotten himself in a little bit of trouble."

I felt my chest clench. "Why do you say that?"

"He told me this morning when we parted ways that he was going to Mr. Alden's warehouse."

I felt a cold chill sweep through me. If that was the case, I assumed he would have been home long ago.

"I need to go there," I said, rising from my chair.

"No one is going to be there at this time of the night."

"I don't care. I need to see if anyone can tell me where he went. Perhaps one of the watchmen will have seen him."

"Rose . . . Amory, I don't think it's a good idea."

"I've got to find Milo, and it's the only place I know to start looking."

I saw Miss Hayes look at him, something passing between them, and he sighed, rising from his chair. He took the gun from the desk and slid it into a holster beneath his suit jacket.

"All right. I'll come with you."

25

The drive to the warehouse was completed mostly in silence. I was lost in my own thoughts, so many things swirling around my head, concern for Milo foremost among them.

He had been going to the warehouse to look into things this morning. Had he begun to suspect the same thing I had? Even if that was the case, there was no reason why he should have remained there for the entire day. Something had either stopped him from getting there or from arriving home.

I didn't like to think about what the possibility might be.

I was in a state of nervous tension, my hands clasped tightly in my lap. Mr. De Lora, however, was the picture of ease as he sat beside me in the shadowy backseat of his big car, the driver making his way through the streets crowded with carefree people enjoying the bright lights and pulsing life of the city.

The car moved then to quieter, darker streets as it approached the warehouse. At last we reached it. Perhaps it was only my anxiety that made them appear so, but the buildings looked to be hulking menacingly against the backdrop of the black water, the entire scene awash in sinister shadows.

Mr. De Lora got out and came around to open my door, and I stepped outside. It was so much different from the bright, cheery world full of laughing people and neon signs; it felt almost as though I had stepped into some other city.

I felt a surge of apprehension as I looked around the dark, deserted lot, but I tried to push it away. After all, it was possible that we would encounter nothing out of the usual here. Besides, it was too late to turn back now.

"Let's go," Mr. De Lora said. He took my arm and we made our way toward the main warehouse building.

Our footsteps sounded uncommonly loud as we walked along the cobblestoned ground. I considered slipping off my shoes to walk in my stocking feet, but the sight of a broken bottle and then a scurrying rat quickly relieved me of that idea.

The area appeared deserted. There was

no sign of even a watchman, and I began to wonder if we had come here on a fool's errand. Perhaps Milo was even now worriedly awaiting my arrival back at the Aldens' home.

Still, we moved forward, slowly and cautiously making our way through the towering stacks of crates and boxes, and the scattered equipment and piles of rope that lay crouched in the darkness, ready to trip us at a moment's notice.

Finally, we reached the warehouse, and I saw that the door was slightly ajar. It was then I noticed a dark shape on the ground and realized what it was.

A man lying motionless in front of the door. Milo.

My heart leapt into my throat, and before I knew what I was doing, I ran to the figure and knelt beside him.

It wasn't Milo.

I realized it almost at once and felt a sense of relief unlike anything I had ever known wash over me. The feeling was so intense that I was instantly weak with it. And then I realized that, though it was not Milo lying there, this man was dead. I stood up quickly, backing away from the body.

Mr. De Lora came up beside me and

lowered himself down for a closer look.

"The night watchman," he said after a moment. "Shot in the head."

I felt a wave of nausea pass over me, and I pressed my eyes closed, trying to steady myself.

"The killer's been here," I said at last.

"It would seem so," Mr. De Lora said, rising.

"Do you . . . do you think Milo's been harmed?" The idea was almost too horrible to voice aloud.

"This man hasn't been dead for more than a couple of hours," he said. "Your husband was supposed to come here this morning."

It was meant to be encouraging, but I was not sure that it was.

"We've got to go inside," I said.

He hesitated. "Maybe you should wait out here."

I realized then that, despite his reassurances, he wasn't at all sure that Milo was all right. I wasn't sure either. If this man had been shot here at the warehouse, who was to say that Milo had not met with the same fate? The thought made me queasy, but I also felt a sudden rush of resolve.

"I'm going in with you."

He looked at me. "Are you sure?"

"You don't understand. I . . . I need to know."

"I do understand," he said. "Because I know what it's like to love someone and then lose them."

I was surprised by this admission. To be honest, I wasn't certain that a man like Leon De Lora would feel such emotions. Oh, I knew he was human, like any other man, but there was a toughness in him that I imagined extended much deeper than just the surface, as though any volatile human emotion had been hardened like obsidian into that smooth, handsome exterior.

"I had a wife," he said at last. "She died."

"I'm sorry."

"Yeah. So am I," he replied. "So all I'm saying is that maybe you should wait here a minute. I don't expect your husband to be in there, but . . ."

He stopped and I considered. What would I do if we discovered something horrible inside that warehouse? As much as I tried to tell myself that Milo was all right, as much as I wanted to believe that I would feel it if something had happened to him, I realized that I had to prepare myself for the worst.

I thought of that awful moment when I

426

had seen the body of the murdered night watchman lying on the ground. What would I have done if it had been Milo? I felt another wave of nausea. Still, I had to face it.

"I'm coming with you," I said again.

He nodded. "All right. Let's go."

He stepped inside the warehouse and I followed behind him. Everything was dark, with the faint light from outside providing only a dim rectangle of light in the cavernous darkness. I had just turned to look for a light switch when I heard the sound of footsteps behind me.

I turned quickly and was both surprised and relieved to see Detective Andrews in his familiar rumpled trench coat, a fedora pulled low over his forehead.

"Oh, it's you, Mrs. Ames," he said. He didn't seem nearly as surprised to see me as I was to see him.

"What are you doing here?" I asked. I supposed it was a bit rude of me to blurt the question out in that way, but I hadn't expected to see him here and I didn't know why it was that he had come.

"I got a call about a disturbance," he said.

I realized suddenly that someone had likely called about a gunshot. "This man has been killed," I said, motioning to the guard who still lay, lifeless, in the doorway to the warehouse.

Detective Andrews looked down at the body without much concern.

"What happened here?" he asked.

"I don't know. We just arrived. Where did you come from? I didn't hear your car . . ."

Suddenly Mr. De Lora grabbed my arm and propelled me farther into the warehouse and behind a stack of crates just as a shot rang out.

I realized then what it was extremely stupid of me not to have realized before. Detective Andrews was trying to shoot us.

"He's the killer?" I whispered in shock.

"Just keep moving," Mr. De Lora said, his hand still on my arm, pushing me through the maze of crates and boxes. More than once I bumped my shin against something as we tried to find our way silently through the darkness.

A thousand thoughts rushed through my mind at once. Detective Andrews. I didn't know why I hadn't realized it before. The way he had tried to divert suspicion, the way he had wanted to so quickly wrap up the case. And he had been smoking that day I had discussed art with him in the drawing room; the matches from the Lightning Lounge must have been his. It was he who was in league with Frankie Earl.

I heard footsteps inside the warehouse, and suddenly the lights flickered on.

I looked at Mr. De Lora in alarm. I had not anticipated that the warehouse lights might be turned on. We were going to have to find a better place to hide. Mr. De Lora didn't look at all alarmed, however.

"You might as well come out," Detective Andrews said. "I can wait here all night."

It was then I noticed the gun in Mr. De Lora's hand. He reached behind a crate and let off a shot. I flinched at the sound of it and I heard a muttered curse from Detective Andrews.

He had probably not recognized Leon De Lora as my companion. It had been dark inside the warehouse, after all. Detective Andrews hadn't realized that his foe would also have a gun.

Mr. De Lora motioned to something behind me, and I turned to see that we had somehow found our way toward a great stack of rubber tires. Pulling a knife from his pocket, Mr. De Lora stabbed it into one, and white powder trickled out.

"The cocaine," he told me.

There was another shot just then, and I didn't have time at the moment to put all the pieces together.

Another shot rang out, but I heard it hit a crate on the far side of the warehouse, and I realized that he didn't know where we were. He was baiting us. Mr. De Lora realized it, too, and didn't fire a return shot.

If Detective Andrews was no longer sure of our location, we were safe for the moment. But as for how we would escape the warehouse, I didn't know. The doors were securely locked. I had seen as much on my earlier visit with Mr. Alden and Milo. The only way out was through the door we had just entered, and Detective Andrews was standing there with a gun.

It seemed we were likely to be at an impasse.

There was a moment of silence, and I was afraid that he would hear the sound of my heart that was drumming noisily in my ears. But it seemed he was not going to attempt to come after us, not when Mr. De Lora was armed and he couldn't be sure of our position.

"All right," said Detective Andrews at last. "Have it your way."

I was relieved. Perhaps he was going to leave. Perhaps we would get out of this alive, after all.

Then I heard a loud clang and a strange splashing sound, as though something had

430

been spilled, and caught a whiff of a strong odor. Then a scrape followed by the sound of the door to the warehouse slamming.

And then I heard the most dreadful sound of all, a low whoosh followed by a low crackling noise. The sound was unmistakable.

Mr. De Lora understood it at the same time as I did. He turned to me. "He's set the place on fire."

26

I fought down the panic that welled up in me, the mindless need to run, to escape. We had to think. I knew from my visit here that these doors were reinforced and could be unlocked from the inside only with keys. That door Detective Andrews had just locked was the last means of exit that had been available to us. Mr. De Lora and I were prisoners inside a burning warehouse.

When he had warned me that I was playing with fire and would likely get burned, I had not imagined the consequences would be so literal. But here we were. I was going to burn to death with a notorious American gangster. This was not at all how I had imagined my life ending, not when I was carrying my first child. A surge of emotion nearly choked me, and I fought down a sob.

But no. I couldn't think that way.

I glanced around. We weren't far from one of the warehouse walls, and I made my way to it. There was a door set there, and I raced to pull on the handle. It was locked, as I had known it would be.

I pounded on the door and called loudly for help, knowing even as I did so that it was a futile waste of energy. No one was here; no one was going to hear us.

I turned back to Mr. De Lora, who had followed me, though his eyes were not on my ineffectual efforts but roaming the warehouse. I was glad that Detective Andrews had not turned off the lights again, for it would have been even worse to be locked here with only the glow of the advancing fire to see by.

"We've got to get out of here," I said. I was surprised at how calm I sounded, given the circumstances. It was just as well, for hysteria would be of no use to anyone. I remembered then what Mr. Brown had told me: the windows on the upper floor weren't boarded up. Perhaps we could get out there.

"We need to get upstairs," I said. "The windows aren't boarded up."

Mr. De Lora was still looking around the warehouse when suddenly his eyes stopped on something across the room. "This way," he said.

He took my arm and led me along the outer wall of the warehouse. The fire was still crackling behind us, growing in intensity. It seemed that Detective Andrews had spilled one of the barrels of flammable fluid and it had added to the fury of the blaze. It had moved along the floor and had already overtaken the first row of crates, the dry wood igniting as easily as kindling.

Already the scent of smoke was beginning to grow heavy in the air. If the fire didn't kill us, the smoke certainly would.

I had been following Mr. De Lora blindly, lost in a series of morbid thoughts, when he stopped suddenly in front of a metal ladder that led upward to a catwalk that surrounded the second story.

I looked upward. I hoped this would work, for if not we would be more likely to roast alive as the heat and smoke rose.

"You go first," he said.

I nodded. Clasping the rungs, I began to climb.

Despite the impediment the flowing folds of my taffeta gown provided as it pooled around my legs and caught on the rungs beneath my feet, I reached the landing relatively quickly, and Mr. De Lora was soon there beside me.

The smoke was thicker here, drifting upward in quick plumes. We also had a much better view of the fire from this vantage point, and I could see it as it blazed its way through one stack of wood crates and moved on to the next. I felt another surge of alarm as the smoke seemed to grow even denser.

"We're going to suffocate if we don't get out soon," I said.

"It's a possibility," he admitted.

He didn't look in the least bit concerned about it, and I wondered if he knew something I didn't. I reminded myself that he had faced much direr situations on the battlefields of France, and perhaps even on the streets of New York. He wasn't going to let something like the possibility of perishing in a warehouse fire ruffle his calm.

I tried to affect an attitude of equal indifference. "Now what do you propose we do?"

He moved to the nearest window, looking down. "We could probably jump. Might break a leg."

"I can't. I . . . I'm expecting a baby." It was the first time I had said the words aloud, and my voice wobbled as I said them, the desperation coming to the forefront for the first time. I had to escape, not just for me, but for my child.

It was, perhaps, an indelicate topic of conversation, but I knew very well Leon De Lora was not a delicate man. Nor was there any possibility of me jumping if there was some other means of escape possible.

He glanced around, looking for some sort of rope, I supposed. One would have thought that there would be any number of such things lying around a warehouse, but the catwalk was bare, seemingly stripped of anything that might prove a hazard to those moving back and forth so high above the warehouse floor.

Mr. De Lora looked at me, seeming to consider something for a moment, his eyes sweeping over me. "Take off your dress," he said.

I stared at him, wondering at first if I had heard him correctly and then wondering just what on earth he meant.

He watched me, waiting. He was the sort of man who was accustomed to having his orders obeyed, but I was not the sort of woman accustomed to orders. "Why?"

"We'll cut your dress into strips and tie them together to make a rope. We can go out the window."

I hesitated. Though I had to admit that the plan made sense, I considered it with something like dismay. Repelling down the side of the building on a rope made of stitched-together taffeta did not sound much safer than jumping, but I supposed there was little choice. The fire was still crackling below, the glow of the flames growing brighter, and I knew we were running out of time.

My sense of modesty made me reluctant to strip off my dress in the presence of a man who was not my husband, but desperate times called for desperate measures. At least I was wearing a slip. Besides, I was certain that Leon De Lora had seen much more provocative displays.

I reached behind myself and began to unbutton my dress, wishing that I had chosen one that didn't have buttons up the entire back. The sound of the fire beneath us was a constant reminder that time was of the essence.

"Here. Let me help." Before I could say anything, he stepped behind me and, grasping the back of the neckline, gave a quick tug that sent buttons scattering as the dress ripped neatly down the back seam.

I gasped.

"Quicker than unbuttoning," he said.

I stepped out of the dress and handed it to him.

Reaching into his pocket, he pulled out his knife and began to shred the skirt. I was glad the fabric was of sturdier construction that some of my other gowns. Chiffon would not have been nearly as useful for rope making.

As he cut the dress, he handed me the strips and I began to tie the pieces end to end, creating what amounted to a rope of decent length.

It occurred to me as we were working how preposterous this whole thing was. The more I thought about it, the more ridiculous it seemed. Were we really going to lower ourselves from a window on a rope made of an evening gown? It sounded like something that would happen in a bad farce.

But the increasing heat made it clear there wasn't much of an alternative.

When we had finished, Mr. De Lora took the improvised rope and tugged on it, testing the strength. "It seems pretty strong to me. I think it will hold."

I sincerely hoped that he was right. The idea of plunging to my death was not much more appealing than succumbing to the fire.

"Stand over here," he said, motioning me to a spot away from the window. I did as he said, and then he moved to the window and shattered the panes with his elbow in one quick jab. He then pushed out the remaining pieces of glass. I could hear the faint tinkling sound of them shattering on the hard ground below.

The glass removed, he tied one end of the rope to a heavy metal pipe that moved up the length of the wall. He gave it a few tugs to test the strength, then motioned me forward. "I'll go down first in case that detective is around," he said.

I felt a momentary pang of doubt. I hoped that he would not decide to leave me here once he had reached the ground. But he had helped me this far; I decided that I would have to trust him.

I moved to the window and he took the makeshift rope, wrapping it around me loosely and then holding it together in front in a demonstration. "Tie it around you like this when you come down. It'll support you like a rope swing," he said.

I had never been on a rope swing, but I supposed I would take his word for it.

He took the rope back and moved to the ledge. Then he went over it with an agility I had not really expected of him, holding on to the sill.

He pulled on the rope with one hand, testing its strength once more. When it seemed that it would hold, he gave me a wink, and then he began to lower himself down. I looked over the ledge and watched him descend with the sound of the fire growing in intensity behind me. The warehouse was filled with any number of flammable items, so I imagined everything inside would be destroyed in a short amount of time. Just as Detective Andrews had hoped.

After what seemed to me like an extremely long time, Mr. De Lora reached the ground. He looked up and waved to me and then disappeared out of sight around the corner of the building.

I drew the rope back up and then stood there waiting, hoping he would come back. A moment later he returned and waved up at me. "All clear," he called.

There was a moment's hesitation as I realized it was my turn to climb down. Then I took another look behind me. The roar of the blaze and the crackle of the burning warehouse seemed to grow louder with each passing moment. The fire had continued to spread rapidly, consuming everything in its path with a steadily growing fury. Already it was to the place where we had stood near the tires, and I could smell the acrid stench of burning rubber and a chemical odor I thought must be the incinerated cocaine.

I turned back to the window. Breathing hard, I tied the fabric rope around me as he had instructed and went to the sill and gingerly lowered myself out of it.

For just a moment, I hovered in the air,

suspended between the heat and smoke of the warehouse and the cold night air. Then, hand over hand, I lowered myself down. At last I felt his arms around me and he lowered me the rest of the way.

I nearly wept with relief as my feet touched the ground, but now was not the time.

"No sign of Detective Andrews?" I asked.

His face darkened. "No. I wished there had been."

I was glad he had not encountered anyone, for we had had enough murder to last us quite a while.

"What do we do now?" I asked. "We . . . we can't call the police."

Whom did one contact when the police were trying to kill one?

"First, we get out of here."

We went along the side of the building quietly and cautiously through the darkness. The moon was obscured by the heavy clouds, so I could barely see Mr. De Lora in front of me, but I could sense him there. Somehow, I was able to follow him through the narrow alleyway. When we were close to the front of the building, he reached back, his hand on my arm, to stop me. We stood for a moment in the darkness, listening. It was an effort for me to control my breathing, and I was certain that, if anyone was about, he would be able to hear me dragging in lungfuls of the fresh night air.

He looked around the edge, gun at the ready, before motioning for me to follow him.

There was no sign of Detective Andrews. I supposed now that he had set the building afire he thought that there was no need for him to stay around.

I looked back into the dark alleyway we had just exited. Smoke was flowing out of the broken window where we had exited the building. All of Mr. Alden's hard-earned profits were going up in flames. I did hope that he was insured.

"Mr. De Lora . . ." I said.

"Don't you think you can call me Leon now?" he interrupted. "After all, I've seen you in your underclothes."

I was not a woman inclined to blushing, but I felt a flush creeping over my face at these words. "I think formality might be best," I replied.

He laughed. "Whatever you say, Rosie."

We began walking back toward his car when suddenly a dark figure appeared.

I felt Mr. De Lora reaching for the gun in his pocket, when I suddenly recognized the man and caught Mr. De Lora's arm.

"Hello, darling," Milo said, emerging out

of the shadows, his eyes flickering from me to Mr. De Lora. "De Lora."

"Oh, Milo," I said, and the words came out in a sob.

I threw myself into his arms and clung to him, my face pressed tight against his neck.

"What's all this?" he asked, his arms moving around me.

"I thought you might be dead," I said, my mouth still pressed against him.

"It's all right, darling. I'm all right," he said, holding me tightly.

I clung to him for a moment longer, relishing the solid warmth of him against me.

I took in everything: the fabric of his suit, the scent of his skin, the familiar fragrance of his aftershave that seemed so much more precious now after thinking I would never smell it again.

I was shaking and dizzy and half afraid to let him go. I just stood there, leaning against him, taking comfort in the reality of his arms around me. After a moment, I marshalled my composure and I pulled back from him, wiping my eyes. Now that I knew he was alive, I remembered that I should be angry with him.

"Where have you been?" I demanded.

"It's a long story. But rest assured, darling, I was in danger of my life."

I didn't know if he was joking, but now that I looked at him, I saw that he was unshaven, the dark shadow of a day's worth of whiskers on his normally smooth face, and there was an uncharacteristic glimmer of tiredness in his eyes.

He was looking me over as I studied him, and it was then I remembered that I had shed my gown in order to escape the warehouse.

He took in my state of undress with perfect equilibrium. "What's happened to your clothes, Amory?"

The night was cool, and I was standing there in my slip. I had neither the time nor the inclination to answer his silly questions.

"Give me your jacket," I said crossly.

He took it off and held it up so I could slip my arms into it. I wrapped my arms around myself, trying to soak up his warmth.

"Detective Andrews is the killer," I said. "He set the warehouse on fire."

"Yes, I know. He was here to meet another man, I believe. An employee of Frankie Earl's by the name of Tiny Davis, who is even now tied up behind the business office. We might want to move him soon in case the fire spreads."

I stared at him. Illogically, the first question that came to my mind was why all the men in Frankie Earl's employ seemed to possess strange given names.

"What . . ." I started, but I couldn't seem to find the words. Everything was a muddle at the moment, and I was still trying to make sense of it all.

"We'd better go back to my place," Mr. De Lora said. "It'll be safe there. You got a car here, Ames?"

"In a manner of speaking. Tiny Davis has a Cadillac parked near the water. I'm afraid I caught him off guard before he could leave. The keys are still in it."

Mr. De Lora gave a little nod. "All right. You take Amory in that car. I'll go get our friend and bring him with me."

"I think I should bring Amory back to the Aldens' home before we speak with Davis," Milo said.

"No," I replied, outraged at the idea that he would try to exclude me now. "I'm coming with you, so you may as well not waste time arguing about it."

Mr. De Lora looked at Milo. "You heard her, Ames. Let's get going."

27

"Now," I said, when we had settled into the strange black car and pulled out onto the street, "tell me what's been going on."

Everything had been happening so fast, I was at a loss as to how to make sense of it all. Milo, however, seemed to have a firm grasp on the big picture as he maneuvered the car out of the warehouse grounds and back onto the relative safety of the roads.

"As you know, I went with De Lora last night to look into some things for the nightclub. That was all just as I had said. But then we began talking about the attempted robberies at the warehouse, and it occurred to me that, though Mr. Alden seemed to be a legitimate businessman, it was quite possible that there was something going on there without his knowledge. With Grant Palmer involved, I figured pretty quickly that it must be drugs."

"Yes, Mr. De Lora told me as much," I

446

admitted. "But how did you know?"

"For one thing, it was fairly apparent to me that he was Miss Petrie's supplier."

"You knew she was taking drugs?"

"I thought it obvious. I think Tom knows, too, or at least suspects. He mentioned to me that he doesn't like Tabitha spending so much time with Jemma."

That was likely why Jemma was no great admirer of Tom, then.

"You didn't think to mention that to me?" I asked.

He shrugged. "Many people take drugs. I wasn't sure it was relevant until I began to put all the pieces together."

"Go on," I said, fighting down my annoyance.

"Alas, Mr. Palmer was trying to play too many hands at once, and he started to get his cards mixed up. He was working for De Lora, and that was how he had introduced Mr. Alden into the nightclub scheme. Then, somewhere along the line, he began to work for Frankie Earl. I think he knew that Mr. Alden would never agree to smuggling drugs, and so he worked it out surreptitiously. The drugs were moved in and out inside the tires, and no one knew. At least for a while.

"I think Mr. Alden was beginning to

suspect that something was amiss, however, especially after he heard that Palmer had come to the warehouse and tried to gain entry. The smugglers realized that they were going to need to try to get their drugs out of the warehouse before Mr. Alden looked too closely, hence the attempted break-ins. They were scouting to find the best way in so they could bring their own trucks and load up the drug-filled tires late at night."

"Why didn't you tell me any of this?" I asked.

"I didn't have time. I came to the warehouse early this morning to see if I could talk to Mr. Brown, the warehouse manager, or even one of the guards, but instead I encountered Tiny Davis, the gentleman who was driving this car."

"And who is he?" I asked, more confused than ever. "You said he works for Frankie Earl?"

"Yes. Apparently, there was another surveillance going on that I walked into. My being here was not at all part of the plan, so he brought me at gunpoint back to see his employer."

I felt a surge of horror go through me at this information. So Milo had been in danger, after all. I had known that something wasn't right. I had felt it.

"Unfortunately, his boss wasn't there, and they didn't want to shoot me without permission, so he and several of his colleagues were forced to keep me under guard for the remainder of the day. After a while, I think I began to grow on them and we started a friendly game of cards."

I exhaled a breath that was somewhere between aghast and exasperated. Leave it to Milo to win over a group of vicious killers.

"I told them that I was associated with Mr. De Lora but that I was not at all opposed to throwing in my lot with them in exchange for compensation."

"And so they accepted you, just like that?" I asked, still wondering how he had been able to manage it.

"They're not the wiliest of criminals," Milo said easily. "They're the muscle of the organization, after all, not the brains. Mr. Davis let me drive with him here. When we got out of the car and he wasn't looking, I managed to hit him over the head and then tie him up with some rope that was lying about. I must say, I was rather resourceful about it all."

I shook my head, trying to imagine Milo engaged in such a skirmish.

"You might have been killed in the struggle," I said, queasy at the thought.

"But I wasn't."

I sighed, still confused. "But where does Grant Palmer's murder fit into all of this? And why did Detective Andrews try to kill me tonight?"

"Frankie Earl has been paying off Andrews in order to keep the police from looking in his direction. They didn't count on Grant Palmer deciding to become a police informant, however."

I stared at him. "What on earth are you talking about?"

"I told you: Palmer was trying to play too many hands at once. He thought he could win a bit of extra favor for himself by giving the police information about what was going on inside Frankie Earl's smuggling operation."

I remembered suddenly what Mr. Elliot had told me, how Grant Palmer had told him he might want to try the side of law and order. This was the tightrope he had been walking, one between his underworld life and a life on the right side of the law.

"Unfortunately for Mr. Palmer, he didn't realize that Frankie Earl had an inside man on the police force. And when he decided to reveal that the drugs were about to be moved, Andrews had to silence him before they were all found out."

"But how did he know Mr. Palmer was going to reveal that?"

"That's something I haven't quite worked out. Tom said that Mr. Palmer wanted to tell him something the night he was killed. Perhaps he wanted Tom's advice. Whatever the case, I think Andrews must have followed him from Frankie Earl's establishment and shot him on the doorstep before Palmer could potentially give something away."

I couldn't believe it. It was all so fantastically horrible.

"And then he came back later, to investigate the crime," I said. "How diabolical."

"It is, isn't it?" Milo agreed.

"So Detective Andrews was the man Mr. Davis was supposed to meet at the warehouse tonight?"

"Yes. Andrews apparently killed the guard and was waiting for Davis to show up to move the drugs. He hadn't counted on us."

I looked at Milo's profile as he effortlessly navigated the streets crowded with cars driving on the wrong side of the road. He looked exhilarated, as though he had never had a more enjoyable time than the day he had spent playing cards with gangsters at gunpoint.

I wondered how the news of the baby

451

would add to this, but I decided that now was not the moment to tell him.

We arrived at De Lora's, and I realized that, despite the all-inclusive atmosphere of the establishment, I was going to draw attention clad only in my slip and Milo's jacket.

"I need something to wear," I said.

As if on cue, I saw Mr. De Lora approaching the car just then with something in his hand. He opened the door and tossed it in to me. It was a dress of dark orange silk.

"The best I could do on short notice," he said, and I didn't ask where it had come from.

Milo got out of the car and the two gentlemen stepped away while I pulled the dress over my head. Winnelda would be absolutely appalled if she could see me now, dressing hurriedly in the front seat of an automobile. I decided it would probably be best if she never found out.

Now nominally attired, I exited the car and Mr. De Lora led us wordlessly into the alley on the side of the building where I had witnessed the altercation on a previous visit to De Lora's. There was a door set into it, made of solid steel, I noted with interest.

He unlocked it and slid it open, and it revealed a staircase, leading down into dimness. Mr. De Lora went first and I followed, Milo behind me. At the bottom of the stairs we found ourselves in the corridor that led to Mr. De Lora's office.

He led us inside, and nodded toward one of the chairs I had occupied — was it only yesterday? — when I had interviewed him for my imaginary article.

"Wait for us here, Amory," he said.

I felt the tug of annoyance at his commanding manner, but I decided to let this pass for the moment. I knew Milo would side with Mr. De Lora, and I was much too tired for arguments.

I took a seat, and Mr. De Lora led Milo to one of the bookcases along the wall. He reached out to push something and the bookcase opened inward, revealing another corridor.

They went through without comment, and I heard a door open and close inside and then nothing.

I sat there a moment, still reeling from all the revelations that had unfolded today.

I still couldn't believe that Detective Andrews had been a part of all of this. I wondered about Detective Bailey. Was he a part of it, too?

It was all so maddening and made even worse by the fact that I was being excluded from whatever they were discussing now.

Though I knew I probably should not, I rose from my chair and moved to where the section of the bookcase still stood open.

I stepped into the little space beyond and found that it led to a door only a few feet away. That was the room into which Milo and Mr. De Lora had disappeared.

I heard voices from the other side of the door. I wondered what they were doing there.

I leaned closer, pushing my ear against the door. Unfortunately, the wood was too thick, and I couldn't make out what the voices were saying.

Eavesdropping would clearly do me no good; I would have to be more direct. I pushed the door open and stepped inside. "Milo . . ." I stopped, startled by the tableau before me.

Milo and Mr. De Lora stood over a man who was tied to a chair.

He looked vaguely familiar, and I frowned, trying to place him. Suddenly it came to me. This was the same man Mr. Alden had thrown bodily from his house. He worked for Frankie Earl and had been there trying to intimidate Mr. Alden into making a deal. No wonder Mr. Alden had been enraged. And no wonder he had looked so stricken when he'd arrived home to find the police at his doorstep. No doubt he was afraid that they had taken out their vengeance on him by harming Tabitha.

The man was doing his best to maintain a surly expression, but I was certain that there was a hint of uneasiness in his eyes. I couldn't say I blamed him. Leon De Lora was not known for being merciful, but, even being aware of his reputation, I was rather taken aback by the cold, expressionless look on his face. Even Milo looked like he'd do harm to the man without a second thought.

Milo glanced at me. "Amory, I think you'd better leave us."

I frowned. "What's going on?"

Milo didn't look at me as he answered. "Mr. Davis is being uncooperative."

"I should've killed you when I had the chance," the man spat out.

"Yes, well, that was your mistake," Milo replied.

"You're going to pay for this," he sneered. "You're all dead. The broad, too. Though we might keep her around awhile since she's a looker."

I assumed this unpleasantness was aimed at me, though the language was a bit difficult to interpret.

"Threaten the lady again," Mr. De Lora

said, "and you'll wish you hadn't."

"You think I'm scared of you, De Lora?" the man said, though I could clearly see the unease in his eyes.

"It's not De Lora you need to worry about," Milo said. "Threaten my wife again, and I'll kill you myself." There was none of his usual pleasant humor in the words.

The man scowled but said nothing further.

"Now, if you'd be so kind as to tell us the whereabouts of Detective Andrews," Milo went on.

This was a side of Milo I hadn't seen before. He was normally so blithely at ease, his effortless charm infusing everything he did. But there was a grimness about him now that I didn't recognize.

"I'm going to need you to tell us the truth. Fast," Mr. De Lora said, his voice hard. Even though the words were not directed at me, I felt the impact behind them, the threat implicit in the phrase.

The man seemed to realize it, too, for I saw his face tighten. "I don't . . . I don't know anything."

"That isn't true," Milo said calmly.

"It is true. I don't know nothing. I've got nothing to tell you."

Mr. De Lora reached casually into his jacket to pull out the gun. He held it easily in his hand, glancing down at it. "If you don't know anything, then you'll be of no use to us."

I felt suddenly as though I had wandered onto the set of a gangster film and didn't know my lines. Surely Mr. De Lora didn't mean to shoot this man. Surely Milo wouldn't let him.

"Milo . . ." I began uncertainly.

"Amory, I'm going to have to ask you to leave," he said, his eyes still on the man before him.

I hesitated. I wasn't sure if he meant it. What possible reason could there be for him to send me out?

"I . . . you can't harm him," I whispered.

"Go," he said, his eyes flickering to mine. I could read nothing in them. They were that same blank blue that I had seen there before when he hadn't wanted me to know what he was thinking.

I stood there for a moment, not knowing what to do, and then I turned and left the room, closing the door behind me. I would have to trust that Milo knew what he was doing, trust that he would not truly harm the man. They were just scaring him to get information. I had to believe that.

I went back into Mr. De Lora's study, and found that I suddenly felt very shaky.

"Are you all right, Mrs. Ames?"

I looked to see Esther Hayes standing there. Her usually unreadable face was filled with concern, and I let out a breath, glad to share this burden with someone.

"Mr. De Lora and my husband have a man in there," I said. "They're asking him questions."

"Leon will take care of things," she said.

"I . . . I'm rather afraid he means to kill that man."

If this shocked her, she gave no sign of it.

"He might not be a good man, but he will do what's best for the people he cares about." There was something in the words that made me realize something that I should have realized long ago.

"You're in love with him," I said before I could think better of it.

"I've been in love with him for a long time," she said softly. "Of course, I'm not sure anything can be done about it. For one thing, you know how society would look on a relationship between us."

Although I wanted to reassure her, I knew that it would never be easy for them.

"Mr. De Lora is not the kind of man who cares about what society thinks," I told her.

She looked at me. "I know he doesn't. He's told me that before, but . . ." Her voice broke. "He still loves his dead wife, too. He doesn't talk about her, but I know he thinks about her often. I'm not sure he will ever love anyone as he loves her."

I wasn't sure how to respond to this. I knew the power that the memory of love could have over someone, and how difficult it could be to compete with.

"He wants to take me to Paris," she said at last. "He's going to open another night-club there. He thinks that we could be happy together. There would be less talk in a city like Paris, and maybe a change of scenery would help him forget."

"If you love each other, then perhaps you should go and be happy," I said.

"Perhaps."

I wasn't sure what her future with Leon De Lora would mean. In addition to the struggles they would face as a couple of different races, there was the matter of Mr. De Lora's past. Though he was not responsible for Grant Palmer's death, I had seen first-hand the ruthlessness in him. War and the death of his wife had made him hard, and that hardness had become deep rooted. There was much that he would have to face — that they would have to face together — if they were ever to find lasting happiness.

He wasn't a good man, but perhaps a

good woman could make him a better one.

There was movement behind the bookcase then, and Mr. De Lora and Milo came out.

I looked quickly to my husband, who offered me an indulgent smile. "He's still alive."

I let out a breath. "That was a bit alarming."

"It was effective," he said, his features once again relaxed, no hint of that cold intensity that had marred his handsome features a few moments ago. He had been playing a part, I realized. It had been very convincing.

Mr. De Lora gave me an easy smile, as though he hadn't been waving a gun in a man's face five minutes before. "Your husband may look like a society snob, but he knows how to handle himself when the chips are down."

"Yes," I said, glancing at Milo. "He can be relied upon when it comes down to it."

"I think we know where we can find Andrews," Mr. De Lora said, and something about the way he said it made me uneasy.

"De Lora will have his driver take you back to the Aldens' house," Milo told me. "You should be safe there."

"No," I said.

"Amory, surely you realize you can't go

with us," Milo said with a sigh.

"I'm not going, and I don't want you to go either," I said, a bit surprised at myself. I had always tried to be the understanding wife, the wife who didn't ask too many questions or make demands upon my husband. But this was different. I didn't want Milo to go out, chasing danger and perhaps getting himself involved in another murder, however he and Mr. De Lora might couch it in terms of justice.

"Amory . . ." he began, but I shook my head, cutting him off.

"We've had this conversation again and again," I said. "You never think of the consequences for anyone but yourself." I was angry now, the pain and horror of those hours I had lived thinking he might be dead squeezing my chest until I felt breathless. "You aren't alone in the world anymore, Milo, able to do whatever strikes your fancy. There are people depending on you. I need you . . . Our child needs you."

He looked up, comprehension flashing across his eyes.

So there it was. I hadn't meant for it to come out this way, in the middle of an argument, in front of two people we didn't know well at all. I had meant to tell him in a tender moment, had imagined the way that we would look lovingly at each other. Nowhere in my imagining of this moment had I thought that I would be standing in a speakeasy as he was prepared to leave with a gangster to do heaven knows what.

"Amory?"

"Yes," I said softly. "I'm going to have a baby."

My eyes were on his face as I said the words, but I couldn't tell what he was thinking.

I let out a shaky breath, and with it some of my anger. "I've been waiting for the right time to tell you, but I suppose now is as good a time as any. Aren't you going to say anything?"

"I'm afraid you've rendered me speechless," he said.

"In a good or bad way?" I asked uncertainly.

"Good, of course." He walked to me and caught my hands in his. "I'm delighted."

"Truly?" I looked up into his eyes, and this time the answer in them was clear enough.

"Truly," he said, bringing one of my hands to his lips and kissing it.

"I guess that means you'd better take her home," Mr. De Lora said.

Milo nodded, still looking at me.

"In times of crisis, it's important to remember what really matters," Mr. De Lora said thoughtfully. I turned to look at him, but his eyes had gone to Esther Hayes.

She was looking at him, too, and I could see that some sort of unspoken communication was happening between them.

Then he turned back to Milo and me. "That's quite a woman you've got there, Ames. Take good care of her. I need you to be able to focus when we start up the nightclub."

Milo smiled. "I intend to."

We all left the office and went back into the corridor, to the set of stairs that led up to the steel door in the alleyway.

"My driver will get you home," Mr. De Lora said to Milo. "I'll send word when everything's resolved."

Milo nodded.

Mr. De Lora looked at me, that half smile tugging at his mouth. "I guess I'll see you in London, Rosie," he said.

"If you do, I think you'd better call me Mrs. Ames," I replied with a laugh.

He winked at me. Then he went over and put an arm around Miss Hayes, and the two of them walked back toward his office together.

■ ■ ■ ■

Mr. De Lora's driver took us back to the Aldens' house, so there wasn't an opportunity to discuss my pregnancy on the way. Though Milo had seemed genuinely glad to hear the news, I wondered what he was thinking. I wanted to be able to talk about it with him, to let the tensions of the past week give way to the happiness of expectancy for the future.

But there were still the unresolved elements of the case. Would Mr. De Lora find Detective Andrews? If so, what did he mean to do when he did?

I was still so uncertain as to how things might end.

It was nearly dawn when we alighted the car in front of the Aldens' house. The street was quiet, save for the chirping of the birds as they began their morning songs.

Milo took my arm and led me into the house. I had expected the silence of a sleeping household, but there were voices coming from the drawing room.

I looked at Milo, a slight frown on my face. Perhaps my absence had been noted and someone had raised the alarm.

Well, it would be best to set everyone's

mind at ease.

We moved toward the sitting room and walked inside. Tabitha, Tom, and Mr. Alden were there, as was Rudy Elliot. Only Jemma Petrie was missing.

Then I stopped, drawing back in surprise when I saw Detective Andrews standing there before the fireplace.

28

He looked as surprised to see me as I was to see him. No doubt he had thought my body lay in a heap of ashes inside Mr. Alden's warehouse.

It had never occurred to me that he might be brazen enough to return to the Alden home, but perhaps he had come here in some mock official capacity.

"Oh, Amory!" Tabitha said, leaping from her chair and rushing to me. She threw her arms around me, much as I had done when I first saw Milo. "I was afraid something terrible had happened to you. The warehouse has burned down."

"I'm so sorry," I said, looking over her shoulder at Detective Andrews. He had recovered from his surprise, and his face was now a mask. Whatever else he was, he was good at hiding his feelings.

"Never mind about the warehouse," Mr. Alden said. "Insurance will cover that. I'm just glad you're all right. Tabitha had some strange notion that you might have been there."

"I don't know why," she said. "I just kept feeling that something was wrong, and when you weren't in your room I was sure that something awful had happened to you."

"Well, I'm perfectly fine," I said.

"I called everyone to see if they'd heard from you or Milo, and Tom and Rudy came right over. We were all so concerned. I called Jemma, too, but she's still very sick. I'm going to go look in on her, now that I know you're all right." I could tell at once that she didn't suspect the true nature of Jemma's illness any more than I had, but now was certainly not the time to discuss it.

"Thank you. I'm sorry we gave you such a fright," I said, my eyes darting back to Detective Andrews.

I could feel the tension in Milo beside me. It was uncharacteristic of him, but I suspected he was having a difficult time not throttling Detective Andrews. After all, the man had attempted to murder me.

"Mrs. Ames, I wonder if I could have a word with you for a moment," Detective Andrews said suddenly.

"No, you may not," Milo replied, and there was steel beneath the words.

The two of them looked at each other, and I tensed, very much afraid there was going to be an eruption of violence. If that was the case, we would be at a disadvantage. Detective Andrews had a gun, after all.

"There's nothing to fear," he said with a smile that chilled me. "There's just a small matter I'd like to discuss with you."

"I said no," Milo told him.

But, for a moment, I considered it. Perhaps I could convince him I would not give away his secret, get him to leave so I could call for the legitimate authorities. My mind whirled as I tried to come up with some sort of plan, a way we might get out of this without any further loss of life, but then a voice in the doorway drew my attention.

"I think you'd better come outside with me, Hank."

I looked up to see that Detective Bailey stood in the doorway, hat in hand. I didn't know whether to be relieved or alarmed. Could we trust him? I didn't know if he had been part of all of this. He was Detective Andrews's partner, after all. Had the two of them been in on the smuggling — and the murder — together?

"What are you doing here, Bill?" Detective Andrews asked, and with the uncertainty in the question came my answer.

Detective Bailey was on the side of right.

"I heard there was a fire at the Alden warehouse this morning. I figured you'd be here. Come outside, will you?"

"Sure. I'll be out in a minute," he said.

"No. I think you'd better come now." Detective Bailey's tone caught all of our attention, and I realized that his manner was different. There was something official in it now. The pretense of friendship had gone out of him.

Detective Andrews seemed to realize this, too, for he frowned. "What's this about?"

"Just come outside, will you?"

Detective Andrews's dark eyes swept the room, then came back to his partner, some sort of internal struggle clearly happening in his mind. He was deciding what to do, I realized. Deciding whether it would be best to give up or fight his way out of it. At last it seemed that he made up his mind.

"No," he said, his jaw tightening, his eyes hard. "I'm not coming outside. I'm staying in here and doing my job."

Detective Bailey looked at him for just a moment, something unreadable in his clear green eyes. At last, he spoke. "In that case, you force me to do mine. Harold Andrews, I'm arresting you for the murder of Grant Palmer."

There was a moment of stunned silence, and then I heard Tabitha gasp.

Then Detective Andrews swore lustily, still keeping up pretenses, still trying to win a losing battle. "What are you talking about, Bill?"

"You know what I'm talking about."

Two uniformed officers appeared in the doorway.

The game was up now. Detective Andrews knew it, but he was not the sort of man who would take defeat easily. He was a fighter, and he would fight until the end. "You're crazy!" he said, his voice loud, his eyes bright, almost wild. "Is this some sort of joke?"

"I wish it was."

"You can't arrest me. I'm your partner. This is a betrayal!"

"Don't talk to me about betrayal, Harry," Detective Bailey said, his voice suddenly very cold. He turned to the uniformed officers. "Get him out of here."

Detective Andrews turned to bolt like a cornered animal, but the young officers were too quick for him. Grabbing him by the arms, they pulled him, shouting protests and profanities, from the room.

When he had gone, Detective Bailey turned to us. His face was grim, a terrible weariness in his eyes. I could only imagine how difficult this had been for him, how hard it was to know that the man he had trusted with his life, had worked alongside for years in the cause of justice, was a cold-blooded killer.

"I thought he was up to something the past year or so," he said at last. "He started acting strange, slipping off without me during some of our shifts. But I never had any proof of anything. Then we heard rumors that an informant was going to give information about Frankie Earl's activities, and he seemed to get uneasy. The night Grant Palmer was killed, he had left the station, saying he was going to get something to eat. When we got the call, he was eager to be the one to investigate the crime. After I learned that Palmer worked for Earl, I started to suspect that Andrews might have been behind it. It wasn't until an informant came forward this morning that we could conclusively tie Andrews to Frankie Earl."

"Another informant?" I asked.

He nodded. "A man named Tiny Davis."

I glanced at Milo, whose face revealed nothing. It was the man who had been tied up at De Lora's. I could only imagine how Mr. De Lora had convinced him to go to the police.

471

"Detective Andrews was at the warehouse this morning," I said. "He set it on fire with me inside."

I heard Tabitha gasp behind me, and Mr. Alden swore beneath his breath.

Detective Bailey nodded. "That's what Davis said. I'm sorry you had to go through that, Mrs. Ames. I'm glad you made it out."

So was I.

"What's going to happen now?" I asked.

"We might be able to tie this back to Frankie Earl, with Tiny Davis as a witness. If that happens, we can shut his drug operation down."

"And what about Detective Andrews?" Tabitha asked from behind us.

"He's going to prison, where he belongs." He shook his head, the mask of professionalism slipping for just a moment, and I saw the sorrow in his eyes at this betrayal of his partnership and friendship and the ideals he had thought they shared.

"We'll need you to make a statement," he said, pushing away whatever sadness was pressing in on him, at least for the time being. "However, I know you must be tired from your ordeal, so I'll come back tomorrow if that will suit you."

"Yes," I said, thinking longingly of my bed. "Tomorrow would be better."

■ ■ ■ ■

"I can't believe all of this," Tabitha said, when he had gone. "I would never have imagined any of it. Poor Grant."

I did feel sorry for Grant Palmer. He had made a lot of poor choices, but he had not deserved to be murdered as he had. And perhaps, in his way, he had thought that working for the police would put him on the path to redemption. At least Frankie Earl might be made to pay for his crimes as a result of Mr. Palmer's efforts.

"I wish Grant had never gotten mixed up with Frankie Earl," Mr. Elliot said. "It seems now that Mr. De Lora was the lesser of two evils."

"Yes," I agreed. He had saved my life, after all.

"I don't feel so bad that I helped him now," Rudy said contemplatively.

I looked up at him. "Helped him?"

"Yes, you see, I . . . designed the match-books for De Lora's."

My brows rose, though I didn't really know why I should be surprised. It made perfect sense. I remembered the very good ads that had hung behind his desk. Now that I thought about it, the style of the artwork had seemed vaguely familiar to me.

Rudy Elliot smiled sheepishly. "I told you Grant was always trying to throw advertising jobs my way. Well, Mr. De Lora wanted some custom designs, and I worked them up for him. I couldn't tell anyone, of course, and after Grant was killed I was so worried that I had been linked up with his killer. I'm so relieved."

"I saw them," I told him. "They were very good designs."

He smiled. "Thank you. Grant and I fought about some of them. I told him I was going to put Esther Hayes on one and he said he didn't think De Lora would like it. I did it anyway, though, and I think it ended up being Mr. De Lora's favorite matchbook."

"I'm sure it was," I agreed. I recalled the argument Jemma Petrie had overheard between Grant and Rudy. "I'm going to have her," Mr. Elliot had said. He had meant the matchbook drawing of Esther Hayes.

He looked at his watch then. "It's almost time for me to be at work. I don't suppose I'd better give up my job for a life of nightclub design just yet. I'll drop in tomorrow, maybe? When everything has settled down."

Tom nodded. "Thanks, Rudy."

"Well, this has all been a lot to digest," Mr. Alden said as Mr. Elliot left. He looked tired, but there was something like relief in his expression, too. After all, he would now be rid of the threat of Frankie Earl and could enjoy his lucrative association with Mr. De Lora's newest enterprise. "If you'll all excuse me, I have some calls to make about the insurance."

He left the room then and Tom turned to Milo. "I know now might not be the best time, but would you mind . . . could I have a word with you for just a moment?"

"Of course," Milo said. Our eyes met before he turned to follow Tom from the room, and I wondered what this was about. It was then I remembered that there had been a cloud hanging over the proceedings. Had Tom and Tabitha sorted out their differences, or were they going to tell us that the wedding had been cancelled?

I didn't have long to wait to find out. As soon as they were gone, Tabitha turned to me. "Oh, Amory. I'm so happy! Tom and I have worked it all out. He said he was in no position to hold my indiscretion against me when he has his own."

I frowned, uncomprehending at first. "You mean, he . . . there has been another woman?"

"Oh, no," she said with a shake of her head, leaning closer. "He didn't want to tell me, but he's been hiding something."

I realized then what she meant, that she had discovered what I had begun to suspect. "He was in prison with Grant Palmer," I said.

Tabitha looked shocked and then she laughed. "No, thankfully it never came to that."

"What do you mean?" I asked, surprised my supposition had been incorrect.

"Tom did something stupid when he moved to New York five years ago. He had no family left, no one to help him, and opportunities were scarce, so he took a job working for some rumrunners. He coordinated things with smugglers from Canada, which, in a funny way, gave him experience that comes in handy working for Alden Shipping. That's how he met Grant, because Grant was buying some of the stuff for De Lora's. Anyway, he made some kind of mistake and a shipment went missing. The bootleggers thought he was stealing from them, and I think they would've killed him if he hadn't been able to come up with the money. But Grant stepped in and got him a loan from Rudy's dad's bank. He was still working there at the time. I think it was a little bit underhanded the way he did it, because, of course, you can't take out a loan to pay back gangsters. But Tom paid back the money to the rumrunners and got out of the smuggling business. He learned his lesson and determined never to make the same mistake again. He's very ashamed that he was ever doing anything illegal."

It all made sense now, the secretive past, the way Tom and Mr. Palmer had both dodged the question of when and where they had met. Tom was, after all, the wholesome young man I had first taken him for, afraid his short entanglement with bootleggers would be a cause for scandal and ruin.

Then I remembered what Miss Petrie had said, about how she had overheard an argument between Tom and Grant Palmer, and that I'd heard part of it, too.

"Was Mr. Palmer demanding money to keep quiet about it? Jemma told me she overheard them quarreling."

Tabitha frowned, then her expression cleared. "Oh, no. It was Tom who was borrowing money from Grant. Tom has been trying to pay back the money to the bank. He wanted a clean slate before we were married, he said. He didn't want the past hanging over him. It's been all right working for Dad, but he needed a big sum of money for the final payment. He even tried to win it at gambling, but he ought to have known better. Grant lent it to him." Her face softened. "Grant wasn't all bad."

"No," I said. I thought of Leon De Lora. "Few people are all bad or all good."

"That must have been why Grant was coming here that night," Tabitha said suddenly.

I looked up at her. "What do you mean?"

"He said he needed to tell Tom something. I bet it was that if he was going to work for the police, that there might be the possibility his past connections would be revealed, and maybe Tom's, too."

"Yes," I said. "That makes sense."

"If only he had told me from the beginning, it would have saved him a lot of worry," she said. "But now that there are no secrets between us, I think everything is going to be all right."

I smiled. "I think so, too, Tabitha."

When the police were gone and Tabitha and Tom had gone off together, Milo and I went upstairs to rest. It had been nearly forty-eight hours since Milo had slept, and I knew he must be even more tired than I was.

For my part, I was immeasurably weary,

but also intensely relieved. I couldn't believe it was all over. The killer had been brought to justice, and now Tabitha and Tom could have their wedding and begin their life together.

In bed beside Milo at last, bathed and in fresh bedclothes, I let out a sigh of pure thankfulness.

"Wait until Inspector Jones hears about all of this," I said.

"He's going to scold you, I'm sure."

I smiled. "I'm sure you're right. But, after all, if it hadn't been for us, I don't think Detective Andrews would've ever been caught."

"Perhaps you're right."

Milo turned on his side to look down at me. "When I get you back to England, I'm taking you straight to Thornecrest and keeping you there until the baby is born."

"Are you?" I asked with a raised brow. Milo had never been the sort of husband to dictate my behavior, and I found this new protectiveness endearing.

"I can't keep you out of trouble anywhere else, but I dare say I will be able to do so at Thornecrest. Nothing ever happens there."

"We shall see," I told him.

"I've been drafted into service," Milo said, changing the subject. "Tom's asked me to stand up in his wedding."

I smiled. "That was nice of him. Did you accept?"

"I did. And I gave him some advice, too."

I looked up at him. "Oh?"

"I told him marriage changes things in ways one doesn't expect."

"How so?"

"It gives a man responsibilities other than his own happiness, a partnership in place of a solo endeavor. I haven't always been good at remembering that, but I shall try to follow my own advice in the future."

His hand moved to rest on my stomach, and I felt tears prickle my eyes.

"I'm very much looking forward to fatherhood," he said.

"I'm glad," I whispered. I knew that his father had not been the kind of man to lend support to his son, so I could only suppose that Milo would do what he could to rectify this with his own child. I was glad to hear that he was looking forward to it rather than fearing it. Then again, Milo had never been the sort of man to doubt his own abilities.

"It's going to be great fun to have a child around," he said. "I hope she has gray eyes like you."

"She?"

"Oh, yes. It's certainly going to be a girl."

I smiled at his confidence. "Well, whatever it is, it's going to be wonderful."

We lay for a few moments in a comfortable silence.

"Do you think we'll do a good job of it?" I asked at last.

He didn't ask what I meant.

"Of course we will," he answered.

"What if we don't?" I wasn't used to sharing my vulnerabilities with Milo. We did not have a history of open and easy conversations. Indeed, we had stumbled through the majority of our marriage either miscommunicating or not communicating at all. It was really only in the past year that I had begun to look at him as a confidant. Our marriage had started as a whirlwind and it was only lately that he was becoming the calm in my storm. But, as he had said, this was a partnership. We were in this together.

"You're going to be a marvelous mother," he said. "You'll more than make up for any of my inadequacies as a father."

He said this lightly, but I wondered if he was having the same doubts I was. We had lived a charmed life, if I was honest. Aside from the bumpiness of our marriage, everything had come easily to us. Would it be the same with this child? Would we take to parenthood? I supposed only time would tell.

"We've got a bit of time to figure things out," I said. "Six months or so, I think."

"We'll be all right. If we can solve murders, we can surely work our way through raising a child."

I laughed. "I suppose you're right."

"We're going to be a very happy family," he said, looking down at me.

"Yes," I agreed. "Very happy."

He dropped a kiss on my forehead and it was only a few moments later that he was asleep. I settled against him and followed his lead.

29

The church was beautiful, a stunning granite building in the Gothic style, with stone arches reaching high into the ceiling. Sunlight gleamed through the stained-glass windows and the electric lights were on, but their light was put to shame by the candles that glowed brightly all throughout the church. The gleaming wooden seats were full of people dressed in their finest clothes, and there was a sense of joyous anticipation in the room. After everything that had happened, I had expected there to be whispers and speculation, but it seemed to me that happiness and goodwill were the foremost emotions here today.

I drew in a breath and was met with the scent of roses drifting through the cool air. Beautiful bouquets of flowers were set at strategic points and silk bows bedecked the ends of each of the pews. Everything was just how Tabitha had imagined it, the perfect fairy-tale setting in which to begin her life with the man of her dreams.

I stood at the front of the church, dressed in my lilac-colored gown, a beautiful bouquet of calla lilies, delphinium, and freesia in my hands. It had been a long time coming to this moment, and I was glad that Tabitha would be able to have her happy wedding day. That, despite everything, she would be able to stand with Tom and make her vows. They would be able to begin their life together, an event made even more fortunate by the crises that had been averted.

Jemma Petrie stood beside me in her matching gown. She was mending and, though it had not been easy for her, I had confidence that the worst days were behind her. I was not so naïve as to think there would be no struggles ahead, but Tabitha had told me she meant to do whatever it took to ensure that her friend made a full recovery. And I knew very well how Tabitha went about accomplishing what she set her mind to.

Jemma was still pale today and her dress was a bit looser than it had been at our final fitting, but there was a cheerfulness in her expression and genuine warmth in her eyes as she watched the back of the church for

Tabitha's entrance. She was glad to stand here and support her friend, glad, as we all were, to put the troubles of the past few weeks behind us.

The organ began to play and the door at the back of the church opened. I saw a flicker of white and then Tabitha stepped into the aisle. I had never had the opportunity to see her in her wedding dress, and I drew in a breath when I saw her. She looked absolutely magnificent, her tall, slim figure draped in a well-fitted gown of gleaming white satin with a long train. She wore the pearls her father had given her and a pearl bracelet I had lent her for her "something borrowed." A fitted cap of Spanish lace sat atop her golden curls, a long veil flowing behind her, and even from this distance I could see the gleam in her eyes, the excitement that made her look impossibly young and pretty.

Mr. Alden looked younger, too, as though a great weight had been lifted off his shoulders. His pride in his daughter shone brightly in his eyes as they began to make their way down the aisle, the notes of the "Wedding March" swelling around us. I knew how relieved he must be that everything had gone off well, that the danger that had been hanging over his head for so long was no longer there. He could give his daughter away and know that the future held blessings for all of them as Tabitha and Tom's family grew.

I glanced at Tom. His eyes were on Tabitha, and they were bright. He was clearly mesmerized by his beautiful bride, and I felt confident that he was going to make an excellent husband for Tabitha. I knew that his heart was in the right place and that he truly loved her. I trusted they would be very happy indeed.

I looked back at the bride. With every step, the joy in Tabitha's face seemed to grow brighter. She was about to marry the man she loved. I remembered the feeling well, felt that surge of nostalgic emotion as I remembered seeing Milo standing at the altar waiting for me. I had been so certain that it meant a life of bliss.

It had not all been bliss, but it had indeed led us to a wonderful place. Milo, for all the times he had made me stunningly angry, was proving himself more with every day. Now that we had a child on the way, I was even more confident that he intended to be a committed husband and father.

I glanced to where he was standing on the other side of the aisle. He looked handsome in his dark suit, standing beside Rudy Elliot. It occurred to me how ironic it was that Milo had come to New York dreading this wedding and he had now been roped into taking part in the ceremony. He had been exceptionally good-natured about it all.

Tabitha met Tom at the altar, transferring from her father's arm to her husband-to-be's. Then they moved to stand before the minister.

I felt the sting of tears in my eyes at the swell of emotions that suddenly coursed through me. I was delighted to be standing here with Tabitha, to have Milo standing across from me, knowing that we had created a life together that would change our lives forever.

I looked over at him, expecting him to be watching the ceremony. However, his eyes met mine and held as Tabitha and Tom echoed their vows, and I felt caught in the depth of his gaze. The words echoed around us. *For better or for worse. In sickness or in health. Forsaking all others. 'Til death do us part.* Somehow, I felt as though the words were meant for us. Oh, we had said them before, but this felt like a renewal of sorts. As though we were standing on the threshold of a new era in our lives.

"I now pronounce you man and wife," the

minister said.

Tabitha and Tom embraced, and my eyes met Milo's once again. He smiled at me, and my heart swelled as the soaring organ music filled the church with the promise of happiness to come.

ACKNOWLEDGMENTS

Once again, I find myself reflecting on everyone who has contributed so much to my writing and my life, making them both richer. I would like to offer my profound appreciation:

To Ann Collette, a fantastic agent, an excellent conversationalist, and a gracious hostess.

To Catherine Richards, who is not only a top-notch editor but also an absolute pleasure to work with.

To Nettie Finn, for all she does and for her cheerful willingness to answer all my questions.

To the team at Minotaur, for their hard work in turning my words into this beautiful book.

To Stephanie Shultz, my friend and fellow night owl, for all the "Triumphant Bigs" over the years.

To my amazing family, who offer love,

encouragement, and lots of laughs on a daily basis.

To my wonderful friends, who drink coffee, read, and travel with me.

And to the Allen Parish Libraries, for all their support.

Thank you all, from the bottom of my heart!

ABOUT THE AUTHOR

Ashley Weaver is the technical services co-ordinator at the Allen Parish Libraries in Oberlin, Louisiana. Weaver has worked in libraries since she was fourteen; she was a page and then a clerk before obtaining her MLIS from Louisiana State University. She is the author of five previous Amory Ames mysteries: *Murder at the Brightwell, Death Wears a Mask, A Most Novel Revenge, The Essence of Malice,* and *An Act of Villainy.*

The employees of Thorndike Press hope you have enjoyed this Large Print book. All our Thorndike, Wheeler, and Kennebec Large Print titles are designed for easy reading, and all our books are made to last. Other Thorndike Press Large Print books are available at your library, through selected bookstores, or directly from us.

For information about titles, please call:
  (800) 223-1244

or visit our website at:
  gale.com/thorndike

To share your comments, please write:
  Publisher
  Thorndike Press
  10 Water St., Suite 310
  Waterville, ME 04901